BATTLEGROUND

BATTLEGROUND

Ten Conflicts that Explain
the New Middle East

CHRISTOPHER PHILLIPS

YALE UNIVERSITY PRESS
NEW HAVEN AND LONDON

For information about this and other Yale University Press publications, please contact:
U.S. Office: sales.press@yale.edu   yalebooks.com
Europe Office: sales@yaleup.co.uk   yalebooks.co.uk

Set in Minion Pro by IDSUK (DataConnection) Ltd
Printed in Great Britain by TJ Books, Padstow, Cornwall

Library of Congress Control Number: 2023949838

ISBN 978-0-300-26342-8

A catalogue record for this book is available from the British Library.

10 9 8 7 6 5 4 3 2 1

Contents

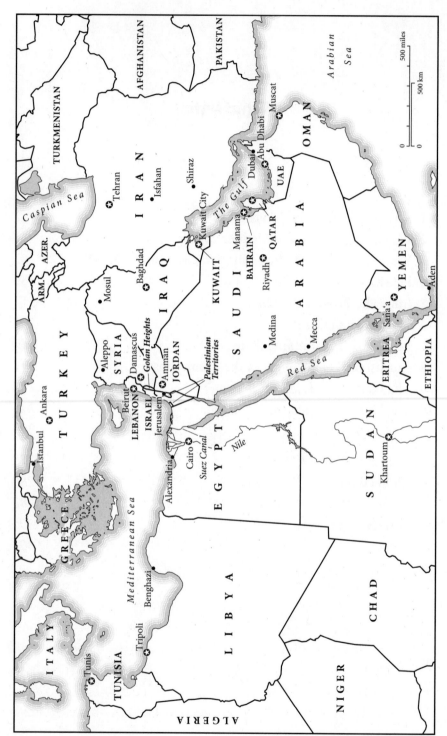

The Middle East

Introduction

The international relations of the Middle East are complicated. That should go without saying. Depending on what we define as the 'Middle East', the region consists of at least fourteen different independent states, plus the Palestinian territories, that have variously fought, meddled, traded, allied, blockaded, invaded, condemned, and forgiven one another – and that's just in the last decade. The region has also attracted particular interest from the outside world. The US has been a constant presence since the 1970s, as was the USSR during the Cold War. Before then Britain and France dominated as colonial powers, while today Russia, and especially China, are increasing their involvement. Add into this the unique domestic politics of each state, informed by rich histories and modern traumas, and 'complicated' seems like an understatement.

And yet, far too often, Western media outlets, commentators, and politicians play down this complexity. Instead, they fall back on simplified explanations for the Middle East's geopolitics.[1] Religion is one such simplification. Supposed 'ancient hatreds' between Sunni and Shia Muslims are used to explain civil wars in Iraq or Syria, or the regional rivalry between Saudi Arabia and Iran. Israel's conflict with the Palestinians and some of its other neighbours is similarly blamed on perennial differences between Jews and Muslims. Oil is another easy-to-reach-for explanation. The vast quantity of fossil fuels in the Middle East is used to explain the frequent involvement of outside powers. Another popular option is to focus on Western imperialism. This might mean blaming European empires for constructing the modern Middle East's states in a way that fostered internal and external divisions, or condemning the United States for its recent domination. Such off-the-shelf explanations might sell newspapers or help to justify certain policies, but they're of little help to those trying to understand the real dynamics behind Middle Eastern geopolitics and have frequently led to poor decisions and even poorer outcomes. These factors have all played a role at times in determining events in the modern Middle East, but there is no one, easy-to-understand explanation. The reality is, well, complicated.

This book is aimed at readers who are interested in understanding that complexity and looking for a place to start. It introduces the geopolitics of the Middle East by focusing on one key aspect: conflict. Here 'conflict' is broadly defined, meaning not just wars, like those in Syria or Yemen, but also fraught politics, like those found in Iraq and Lebanon, or region-wide disputes, as in the Gulf or Kurdistan. I am not for a moment suggesting that the Middle East should be defined only by its conflicts. Yet another cliché about the region is that it has been unusually conflict-ridden compared to the rest of the world, when in reality most of its modern history has seen it conform to global trends on the frequency and form of war. That said, in the twenty-first century the magnitude of Middle Eastern violent conflicts has grown sharply, seeing it account for a greater proportion of global war-related deaths than in the previous century.[2] The region is diverse and sophisticated, and understanding its international politics could be achieved via numerous other routes. However, in my view, examining the Middle East's conflicts, whether violent or political, offers a good entry point. They offer a window into the region's geopolitics. They show how a state or area's local politics, informed by its history and the decisions of the ruling elite of the day, interact with outside forces, whether neighbouring governments or meddling superpowers. Religion, oil, imperialism, and the other popular explanations all do play a role, but none is ever the sole, underlying cause of conflict and division. Instead, these clashes are multi-faceted events, brought about by an interaction between internal and external forces.

This book explores ten conflicts in turn: Syria, Libya, Yemen, Palestine, Iraq, Egypt, Lebanon, Kurdistan, the Gulf, and the Horn of Africa. They are all deeply interconnected. Turkey's behaviour in Libya, for example, is hard to understand without reference to its experience in Syria. The US approach to both conflicts cannot be explained without understanding the legacy of its role in Iraq. While Saudi Arabia and the United Arab Emirates' hostile attitude to their Gulf neighbour Qatar cannot be understood without considering all three states' involvements in Egypt, Yemen, Syria, and Libya. The reader is therefore invited to explore the conflicts either in isolation or as a whole. Each chapter is self-contained but can also be read as part of a ten-part narrative of international relations in today's Middle East. In addition to the ten conflicts in question, each chapter contains a discussion of one of the ten key regional and international players involved in these cases: the United States, Russia, China, the European Union (EU), Turkey, Iran, Saudi Arabia, Israel, Qatar, and the United Arab Emirates (UAE). While other governments are also often involved, the actions of these ten are by far the most consequential.

As well as acting as an introduction to the Middle East's geopolitics, this book aims to make several arguments. First, as mentioned, conflicts, whether military or political, are complex. This is true of any conflict in the world. Though the Middle East has certain unique features compared to other regions, notably its geographical location at a crossroads of three continents, its particular religious heritage, and its vast reserves of oil, reducing explanations for its fractures to these features is simplistic and inaccurate.[3] It is far more helpful to

explore how these characteristics have impacted the complex decisions being made, rather than using them lazily as a predetermined
explanation. Second, domestic and external factors play a vital inter-
acting role in the outbreak and continuation of conflict. While
scholars and commentators often tend to give primacy to either local
or outside actors when explaining disputes, the cases that follow
will show how both frequently interact to exacerbate and amplify
tensions. Third, specific to the Middle East, the United States
has been, and continues to be, the key external actor and has contributed disproportionately to conflicts there in the twenty-first century.
By first over-reaching in the 1990s and 2000s, and then stepping
back in the 2010s, Washington helped create a vacuum in regional
security and politics. Finally, this vacuum has often been filled
by regional and international powers, such as Saudi Arabia, Iran,
and Russia, contributing further to conflict. What makes the
modern Middle East particularly susceptible to such rivalries is the
number of powers willing to intervene – a far greater number than
in the past.

This was an argument I first developed researching the Syrian
civil war. That conflict was frequently characterised in the Western
press and elsewhere as a sectarian dispute between Syria's Sunni and
Shia Muslims, into which foreign rivals such as Iran, Saudi Arabia,
Turkey, Russia, and the US had been pulled. Yet in my book, *The
Battle for Syria*, I challenged this characterisation.[4] Instead, I showed
that the causes of the conflict were complex, not simply down to
sectarian tensions. I noted how the war was not a domestic war that
sucked in foreign powers but rather one where internal and external
actors interacted from the very beginning, impacting the extent and
shape of fighting. I illustrated the key role of the United States: how
rebel forces and their regional backers expected the superpower of
the day that had dominated the region for decades to intervene deci-
sively on their side, and how that strategy fell apart when Washington
refused. Finally, I showed how the war was then exacerbated and

extended by a range of external interventions by Iran, Russia, Saudi Arabia, Qatar, and Turkey, with the United States playing a more modest, less decisive role than in earlier decades. Over the course of my research, it became clear that Syria was not unique, and that the same pattern was occurring not just in similar wars, such as those in Yemen and Libya, but also in (mostly) non-violent political conflicts, as in Egypt and Lebanon. Large parts of the Middle East in the twenty-first century had become arenas for external competition. This book aims to explain how and why.

Middle of What?

Before going further, we need to clarify what we're looking at and how we're approaching it. The 'Middle East' is an artificial construct that, a hundred years ago, few would have used. It was originally a colonial term, dreamt up by Britain to distinguish regions based on their distance from London: 'the near east', 'the far east', and the place in between, the 'Middle' East.[5] The term was later adopted by American officials too, and gradually passed into common parlance in the West. While some in the region have accepted it, many would still identify themselves more with alternative regional groupings such as the Islamic or Arab world, or more local areas such as the Levant (eastern Mediterranean), Mashriq (the Levant plus Iraq), Gulf, or Maghreb (North Africa). Few would see themselves as in the 'middle' or 'east' of anything, given that everywhere on the globe is in the middle or east relative to somewhere else.

This area of (mostly) West Asia, is economically and culturally diverse, and many would not instinctively identify with those labelled fellow 'Middle Easterners'. Most in the region speak Arabic, but Iran, Turkey, and Israel are not Arabic-speaking countries, while sizeable Kurdish and other non-Arabic-speaking minorities exist within Arab-majority states. Not all those who speak Arabic – which has a huge range of dialects – see 'Arabness' as anything more than a shared language, and not all Arabic-speakers are located in the 'Middle East'.[6] Nor is religion a unifying feature. While most are Muslims, there is one state, Israel, where Islam is not the majority religion and another, Lebanon, where it shares near-equal space with Christianity. There are sizeable Christian communities elsewhere, and a range of different Islamic sects – Shias, Druze, Ibadi, among others – distinguished from the Sunni majority. Moreover, while Islam is the majority religion and its holiest sites are in the region, the majority of the world's Muslims live outside the Middle East.

Its artificial origins and lack of obvious unifying features make pinpointing exactly where 'the Middle East' is tricky. Is Turkey part of the Middle East? Is Afghanistan? Is Sudan? And what about North Africa? For this book, I focus on a narrow Middle East that stretches from Turkey in the north to Yemen in the south, Iran in the east, and Egypt in the west. I additionally look at Libya and the Horn of Africa as part of the 'wider reach of the Middle East'. However, these boundaries are largely arbitrary. I could easily have extended my study to include Azerbaijan in the north, Morocco, Algeria, and Tunisia in the west, and Afghanistan or the Central Asian republics in the east. I believe the cases I present in the following chapters, at the 'heart' of the Middle East, illustrate the region's international relations effectively, but I am not proposing this as the final word on where the Middle East is or should be. Indeed, there is a strong case for scrapping the term 'Middle East' altogether and replacing it with the less colonial 'West Asia'.[7]

Whatever we call the region, how should we approach conflict there? In the field of international relations, many scholars adopt approaches, lenses, or theories to explain events. While these are usually more sophisticated explanations than the media narratives that focus on 'religion' or 'oil', many still elevate one approach over others, risking the same simplifications. One is an emphasis on domestic politics. Among these experts, some focus on the structure of the state where conflict occurs – how the ruling regime is configured, the

legacy of how the state was formed, or how certain groups are empowered or disempowered. Others prioritise the agency of those involved
in the conflict, whether the decision-making elite or grassroots
activists. Some look at how identity concerns, such as religion or
nationalism or ideology, might influence short-term decisions or
the long-term structure of politics. A second approach places more
emphasis on the role of international actors wading into foreign
conflicts. Some, again, look at international structure: the balance of
power between neighbours and superpowers and how that impacts
the decision making of those in the conflict. Others again look to
agency, this time of the foreign rulers who choose to interfere in
another state's politics. Again, some emphasise identity, this time
looking at how it frames and shapes a foreign government's interest in
a conflict. Other approaches are more specific, focusing on how race,
gender, the environment, or other factors might influence the worldview of those involved.[8]

All these theories have value when seeking to understand conflict
in the Middle East, but none is a sufficient overall explanation.
Instead, this book adopts a pluralist approach.[9] It draws on many of
these views throughout its investigation. As will be seen from the ten
conflicts, domestic and international factors often interact in comple-
mentary ways. How states, societies and ruling regimes were built, by
colonial authorities or domestic rulers, impacts the move towards
conflict, but this doesn't make breakdown inevitable – the agency of
governing elites and the activists challenging them also plays a vital
role. The balance of power in the Middle East, especially the stepping
back of the US, and the advance of regional powers and outsiders like
Russia and China, has shaped numerous conflicts, but it is still specific
leaders who have decided to get involved. The shape and extent of
their involvement has often been down to the individual character(s)
in charge. Identity has likewise played a key role for both domestic
and external actors, from the US believing it should support (or at
least, be seen to support) pro-democracy activists, to Iran viewing

itself as the defender of Shia communities in Iraq, Syria, and Lebanon. Similarly, questions of race, gender, and the environment have all influenced outcomes, whether historical or contemporary, which impacted the conflicts explored.

Having established what the Middle East is, and how we're exploring it, a word on who is doing the looking. I am a professor of international relations who has studied the geopolitics of the Middle East for two decades, living there for several years and frequently visiting for research. I am also a white, Western man: a privileged position that has informed my interaction with the region since my very first visit.[10] The experiences I have had, which have impacted my worldview and understanding, would likely have been different had I a different gender, race, or background. I have tried to be conscious of these influences in my scholarship, but it is impossible to remove them. Importantly, I am not from the Middle East, and though I am writing about the region, I do not intend to and cannot speak for those from it. Instead, my perspective is deliberately that of an outsider. I am writing as a Westerner for a largely outside audience that is curious and seeks to understand the region's international relations, particularly the West's (mostly negative) role in it. There are countless excellent Middle Eastern scholars and commentators, many of whom I have drawn on and listed in the Notes and Further Reading sections at the end of this book. I urge readers to engage with their work to complement this study.

The 'New' Middle East

After the where, how, and who, we turn to the 'when' and 'why'. This book is centred on the Middle East in the twenty-first century, particularly during the aftermath of the 2011 Arab Uprisings – the series of protests that toppled several Middle Eastern dictators and appeared to mark a new wave of regional conflict and instability. The late Fred Halliday, Professor of International Relations at the London School of Economics, noted how, seemingly once a decade, seismic events appear to rock the foundations of Middle Eastern geopolitics, whether it be 9/11 in 2001, the 1991 Gulf War, or the Iranian Revolution of 1979.[11] The 2011 Arab Uprisings were similarly tumultuous. However, Halliday urged caution on the commentators rushing to pronounce that such events totally transform the region's geopolitics: for all the upheaval, there is considerable continuity. This was broadly true of 2011. Some states became weaker, as they descended into violence or political chaos, some became stronger as they took advantage of their neighbours' fragility, but the basics of the region remained as they were: a collection of independent states, mostly competing and aligning with each other and external actors to further their interests. That said, a decade or so on from the uprisings, it is clear that some things did change sufficiently, in my view, to justify the 'new Middle East' subtitle of this book.

The first shift was the changing role of the United States. In the two decades after the Cold War's end, the United States was the dominant external power in the Middle East. By the early 2000s most states of the region were firm American allies, often hosting their bases and (mostly) acquiescing to Washington's policies. Those that resisted American domination were portrayed as outliers: 'rogue' states like Iraq, Iran, and Libya. However, this created an imbalance, with many of Washington's allies expecting the US to lead forever and surprised when it stepped back.[12] Several factors led to this retreat. Globally, the rise of China, the increased military activism of Russia, and the shift of the world economy eastwards after the 2008 financial crash, prompted the end of Washington's post-Cold War global dominance. It remained the most powerful state but was no longer largely unchallenged.

Domestically, war fatigue after the invasions of Iraq and Afghanistan prompted three successive presidents, Obama, Trump, and Biden, to curtail global activism and repeatedly promise 'no boots on the ground', especially in the Middle East.[13] With the shadow of the 2003

Iraq invasion hanging over it, and in a weaker global position, when the 2011 Uprisings broke out, Washington recognised the limits of its capabilities in the Middle East. It was still willing to intervene in conflicts, as will be shown in the case of Libya and that of Islamic State[14] in Iraq and Syria. Technological developments, notably the growth of drone warfare, also allowed it to intervene in a more occasional and hands-off manner. It maintained key policy priorities in the region, like limiting Iran's nuclear capabilities, defending Israel, and maintaining its Gulf bases. But its reluctance to get seriously involved in Syria, Libya (after 2012), and Yemen, its acquiescence to a return to dictatorship in Egypt, and its willingness to accept regional and global powers like Russia, Turkey, and Saudi Arabia taking the lead in arenas it once dominated, marked a change. The Middle East's short-lived 'Pax Americana' was over, and a 'post-American Middle East' began to emerge.[15]

A related second shift was the increased activism of regional powers in the vacuum that followed, with *six* in particular emerging as the most engaged. Iran had already benefited from the collapse of Saddam Hussein's regime after 2003, furthering its regional influence in Iraq and beyond. The post-2011 era provided further opportunities for Tehran to expand, deepening its physical role in Iraq and Syria, and boosting its ties to allies in Lebanon and Yemen. Iran's great rival Saudi Arabia responded by upping its direct involvement in regional affairs, abandoning an historical reserve. To ward off Iran as well as its other regional enemy, the Muslim Brotherhood, since 2011 Riyadh has intervened directly in Yemen, initiated the blockade of Qatar, sponsored a coup in Egypt, and backed rebels in Syria's civil war. Alongside these old rivals, the post-2011 era has seen new regional actors emerge while traditional powers have diminished. Syria, Iraq, and Egypt are all weaker after over a decade of violence and/or disruption. In contrast, Turkey, once peripheral and preferring to face West, has become a major actor, intervening in Syria, Iraq, and Libya, and sponsoring the Muslim Brotherhood, bringing it into conflict with Saudi Arabia and the UAE. The latter has also become a surprisingly active player for such a small state, intervening in Yemen, the Horn of Africa, Egypt, and Libya, and sponsoring the Qatar blockade. Qatar itself was also more active, especially in Libya, Syria, Egypt, and the Horn of Africa, though the effect of the blockade chastened it somewhat. Israel, meanwhile, already possessing one of the most powerful militaries and economies in the region, opted to avoid entangling itself too deeply in regional conflicts, but continued its long-standing practice of intervention in its immediate neighbours of Lebanon and Syria. It has also continued its occupation and colonisation of the Palestinian territories it captured in 1967.

Such regional activism was nothing new. The region's 'great powers' of the day, like Egypt, Iraq, and Israel, had regularly interfered in their neighbours' affairs since independence after the Second World War. However, usually just one or two states would be involved: Egypt and Saudi Arabia backing rival sides in North Yemen in the 1960s, or Syria and Israel doing likewise in Lebanon in the 1980s. But after 2011, the number of players interfering, whether from the region or outside, was considerably more than in the past. Conflicts, whether violent or political, attracted multiple external sponsors, a damaging new development. As an illustration of the change, in the period 1945–2008, the various Middle Eastern civil wars attracted on average just over two foreign interveners each. Since 2008, civil conflicts in the region have brought in an average of over six.[16] Whereas civil wars in Lebanon (1975–90) and Oman (1963–76) were exceptional due to the high number of foreign powers involved – four in Lebanon, seven in Oman – this pattern became the norm in almost all of the post-2011 conflicts, with well over seven states intervening in the wars in Syria, Libya, and Yemen.[17] This trend was replicated in political conflicts, with multiple outsiders vying for influence over the politics of Egypt, the Horn of Africa, Iraq, Kurdistan, and Lebanon, not just one or two dominant players as in the past.

A third significant shift was the growth of arenas in which these regional players could compete.[18] In the decades prior to 2011, most

Middle Eastern states were relatively 'strong', in that they had a monopoly on violence and secure borders, even if they were often auto-cratic. There were a few exceptions to this – Lebanon and, from 2003, Iraq – and those spaces became battlegrounds for competition between global and regional rivals. The disruptions of 2011 added more states to that list: Syria, Yemen, Libya and, for a while, Egypt and Bahrain. The 2010s also saw these competing powers willing to plot against and disrupt rival governments not even experiencing civil war. Saudi Arabia, for example, successfully helped overthrow an elected Egyptian government (with the UAE), was linked to failed coups plots in Jordan and Qatar, and attempted to terminate a premiership in Lebanon.[19] Iran, similarly, interfered in Iraqi politics and did likewise in Lebanon.

Linked to this has been a final shift: the growth of violent non-state actors – fighters outside the formal security forces of a govern-ment or state. Again, this is not new and non-state actors have historically emerged in arenas such as Lebanon and Iraq where the state has been weak. The growth in the number of weak states, along-side an increase in the regional and international actors willing to sponsor them, has seen a corresponding growth in non-state actors.[20] These groups vary in their relationships with governments. Some, like Islamic State, reject all governments as illegitimate. Others, like the Kurdish separatists, the PKK (Kurdistan Workers' Party) or PYD (Democratic Union Party), are independent but have accepted support from foreign governments in the past, impacting some of their decisions. Others, like Hezbollah in Lebanon or some Shia militias in Iraq, were formed with the help of a state, Iran, and though they remain independent and have their own local constituency, remain deeply indebted to and aligned with their foreign sponsor. At the extreme end of the scale are those groups formed primarily to serve a foreign agenda, like some other Shia groups in Iraq serving Iran, or some Syrian rebel groups serving Turkey. In addi-tion, there has been a rise in mercenaries being deployed by foreign governments, such as Russia's use of the Wagner Group and Syrian mercenaries, Turkey sending different Syrian groups to Libya or the UAE employing a range of foreigners in Libya and Yemen.

These four shifts combine to present a 'new' geopolitical picture in the Middle East that looks quite different today than at the beginning of the 2010s, warranting exploration. There are more unstable states and regions, more non-state actors operating within them, and more regional and international powers willing to intervene in these arenas, either through sponsoring domestic players or deploying their own militaries. The ten conflicts explored in this book will help to illustrate how and why.

How to Read This Book

This book is arranged into ten further chapters, all focusing on a different country or region in conflict, whether violent or political, followed by a conclusion. Each can be read alone or collectively to gain a comprehensive picture of how the rivalries profiled overlap and intertwine. As part of the book's pluralist approach each chapter will explore first the history of each zone of conflict, looking at how states and societies have developed, before moving on to examine the contemporary crisis. There is a consideration of the domestic and international drivers of the conflict, discussing the structural causes and the agency of the individuals involved. This is primarily a political account, so much of the focus will be on elite decision making both internally and externally. While there is a recognition of the importance of broader social and economic developments on domestic and international politics, the space for such discussion is limited here to where these dynamics directly impact politics. Each chapter also features an extended section on one of the ten major external players in the Middle East's geopolitics, often because this conflict is more important to that external player than others. By the end of the book, readers will have a fuller understanding of the ten conflicts and the ten major external players involved.

The first three chapters focus on violent conflicts: states that have been ripped apart by civil war since 2011. First, we look at Syria, with a focus on Russia's involvement. We then move to Libya in chapter 2, with a profile of Qatar, which intervened early on, before looking at Yemen in chapter 3 and Saudi Arabia, which led an intervening military coalition in 2015. Chapter 4 follows with an examination of the delicate case of Palestine, and Israel's role in the ongoing conflict there.

The next three chapters look at political conflict in three states that have seen external rivalries influence their domestic politics. This is sometimes violent – often in the case of Iraq – but hasn't seen the same existential struggle for supremacy as in the first four cases. In chapter 5, we explore Iraq, particularly the role played by neighbouring Iran in its politics. Chapter 6 then looks at Egypt, and its close ally the USA's involvement in its post-2011 traumas. Chapter 7 profiles Lebanon, with a focus on the EU's attempts to influence its byzantine elite.

The final three chapters focus on regions, rather than states. Chapter 8 looks at Kurdistan, the mostly mountainous area that straddles four Middle Eastern countries, and how Turkey in particular has sought to stifle Kurdish separatists. Chapter 9 then focuses on the Gulf, with a profile of China's increased penetration of the traditionally US-dominated region. Finally, chapter 10 takes us beyond the Middle East to the Horn of Africa, where several Middle Eastern-based rivalries have spilt over, with a focus on the ambitious UAE.

First, though, we explore Syria, where a brutal war after the 2011 uprisings transformed a once stable state into a battleground fought over by the US, Russia, Turkey, Iran, Israel, Saudi Arabia, and Qatar.

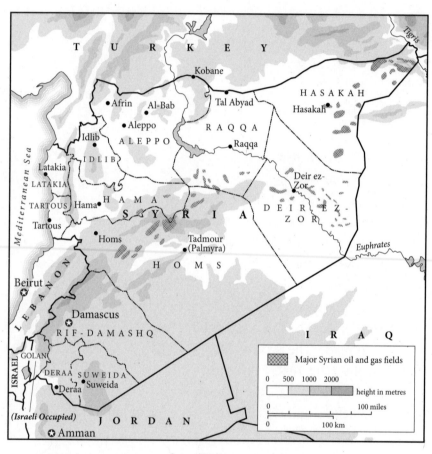

TURKEY

Kobane

Afrin   Al-Bab   Tal Abyad   HASAKAH
                                         Hasakah
Idlib   Aleppo   RAQQA
       ALEPPO   Raqqa
Latakia
IDLIB   Deir ez-
LATAKIA   Zor
TARTOUS   Hama   HAMA   DEIR EZ-
                 SYRIA   ZOR
Tartous
         Homs   Tadmour   Euphrates
                      (Palmyra)
                 HOMS

Mediterranean Sea

Tigris

Beirut

LEBANON

Damascus

RIF-DAMASHQ   IRAQ

GOLAN

ISRAEL   DERAA SUWEIDA
                Suweida
         Deraa

(Israeli Occupied)   JORDAN

Amman

	Major Syrian oil and gas fields
0 500 1000 2000	
	height in metres
0	100 miles
0	100 km

Syria

1

Syria
The Shattered Mosaic

In early 2023 an earthquake devastated southern Turkey and northern Syria. In Turkey, poorly constructed tower blocks, some without the correct protections, flattened like pancakes killing tens of thousands as they slept. Neighbouring Syria similarly suffered, but the pictures broadcast around the world were quite different. Buildings hit by the earthquake were indistinguishable from pre-existing destruction wrought by over a decade of war. While Turkish emergency services scrambled to find survivors, parts of Syria saw no aid arrive for days, leaving young boys to remove rubble with their bare hands. The Syria of 2023 was a long way from the country listed in the *New York Times'* 'places to visit' in 2010.[1] That Syria boasted Crusader castles, Roman ruins, labyrinthine bazaars, enticing cuisine, and welcoming hosts. Today, the organised tours and boutique hotels are long gone. Instead, for most observers, the country's name has become synonymous with conflict, mass murder, refugees, and terrorism. The civil war that began in 2011 fractured the country. The castles were shelled, ruins dynamited, and bazaars set ablaze. Meanwhile the Syrian people, once renowned for their hospitality and friendliness, faced destitution. Over half the population had to flee their homes and, by the end of the decade, 80 per cent lived in poverty.[2] For many, searching for relatives in destroyed buildings was not a new experience, but something they had become sadly accustomed to.

This tragedy was not wholly of Syria's own making. Yes, much was down to the president, Bashar al-Assad, who had violently clung on to power when facing peaceful protests that sparked the war. His opponents were similarly no saints, with some espousing a violent Islamist ideology. But from the very beginning this war attracted intervention from foreign governments, each of which sought to tilt the war in their favour. Money, weapons, and troops poured into Syria as the civil war morphed into a battleground for regional and international rivalries. The interaction of these domestic and foreign tensions left Syria a shattered shadow of its former self. Assad remains in charge of most of Syria, propped up by his key allies Russia and Iran, both of which now have a deep military and economic presence. But parts of the east and north remain beyond his grasp, blocked by the United States and Turkey respectively, supporting their Syrian opposition allies. In all likelihood, it will be these foreign governments, rather than Damascus or the remaining pockets of rebels, that will ultimately decide Syria's fate one way or the other for years to come.

Assad's Syria

Like many of its neighbours, modern Syria was born in the aftermath of the First World War. Before then it was part of the sprawling Ottoman empire, which at one point ruled over most of the Arab world, Turkey, and the Balkans. However, in 1920 the victorious French and British stripped the Ottomans of their remaining Arab lands, creating instead a series of Western-style nation-states where once there were none: Syria, Iraq, Lebanon, Palestine, and Jordan.[3] These artificial states with their straight-line borders were all somewhat incongruous and 'Syria' was no exception. It had two thriving major trading cities, Damascus and Aleppo, but the ports they had previously relied on for trade were now in different countries. It had a majority religion, Sunni Islam, but significant Shia Muslim and Christian minorities. Most spoke the same language, Arabic, but there was a sizeable Kurdish-speaking community in the north and east. Though many living in the cities had lost the tribal identities of the past, in the countryside and eastern desert tribalism remained strong – and many had been cut off from kin by the new colonial borders.[4]

Fostering a national identity with such building blocks was a challenge, and not helped by French rule (1920–45), as Paris deliberately encouraged divisions along religious, regional, linguistic, and tribal lines.[5] A 'Syrian' identity did emerge however, but one that meant different things to different people. Syria's 'mosaic' of different peoples included multiple identities alongside being Syrian – whether based on religion, Arabness, Kurdishness, tribe, region, or class – that could be manipulated by domestic or foreign leaders.[6] This all contributed to political instability after independence. Military coups were commonplace, bringing to power short-lived regimes of strongmen and political parties, sometimes backed by foreign governments, and often reflecting regional rivalries between the USA and USSR or local Middle Eastern powers. Stability was eventually achieved when Bashar's father, Hafez al-Assad, an air force colonel, seized power in 1970. Hafez combined populist socialist politics with harsh authoritarianism to persuade or cajole people into accepting his rule. He ruled with an iron fist and violently crushed dissent, most notably massacring at least 10,000 when Islamists seized control of the city of Hama in 1982. However, his thirty-year dictatorship did largely halt the meddling of foreigners in Syria. In fact, he transformed Damascus into a regional player itself for the first time, driven by a rivalry with neighbouring Israel, which still occupied Syria's Golan Heights, captured in 1967.

Hafez had groomed his eldest son, Bassel, to succeed him, but these plans were scuppered in 1994 when the princeling was killed, crashing his Mercedes at 150 mph into a barrier on the Damascus airport road en route to a skiing holiday. So, instead, it was the second son, Bashar, who had trained as an eye doctor in London and did not expect to rule, who eventually became president when Hafez succumbed to a heart attack in 2000.[7] Assad's election to the presidency, in an uncontested referendum where he won 99.7 per cent of the vote, raised hopes in Syria and abroad. While more bookish than his debonair deceased brother – Bashar headed the Syrian computer society while Bassel was an accomplished equestrian – at only 34 he nevertheless seemed a sharp contrast to his austere father. Assad and his propagandists built a carefully crafted image of a young, accessible moderniser. The stiff portraits of Hafez that remained hung from public buildings and in popular restaurants were now joined by images of Bashar and his glamourous British-born wife, Asma, relaxing at home with their children. The floundering socialist economy was gradually phased out. Up-market shopping malls and hotels were built in central Damascus and Aleppo. Syrians suddenly had access to satellite television, mobile phones, and the internet and Assad seemed to enjoy some genuine popularity among his people as a result.

But beneath the surface deep problems remained. The autocratic structures were only rolled back to a modest extent. A common Syrian joke was that life was better under Bashar because if you criticised the president only you disappeared, rather than your family and friends also disappearing for the same offence under his father. The economic reforms benefited only limited sections of the urban elite and middle classes, while workers and rural peasants saw the job security and subsidies they'd enjoyed under Hafez's socialism erode.[8] This was exacerbated by a brutal drought that struck during Bashar's first decade in power, prompting millions of rural Syrians to leave their villages for shantytowns on city outskirts, yet still finding little employment. In the cities these internal migrants' frustrations swelled when they saw the growing excesses of the elite. While under

Hafez's austere socialism the elite were more modest, under Bashar, the well-connected flaunted their wealth.

Religious and ethnic divisions added fuel to the fire in the widening gap between haves and have-nots. Hafez and Bashar were from the Alawi community, a mostly secular, loosely Shia branch of Islam, that made up about 10 per cent of Syria's population and was based origi-nally in the eastern Mediterranean mountains. Both Assads promoted extended family members and other Alawis in the military, govern-ment, and business. This transformed most of the Alawi community into a loyal core of support for the Assad regime, but also generated considerable resentment from some in the Sunni Muslim majority who dominated under the Ottomans and after independence, but now felt excluded.[9] Not all Sunnis were dissatisfied. Under Hafez, many urban and rural Sunnis benefited from the socialist policies, as did many among the middle classes. But when Assad's economic reforms disproportionately hit poor Sunnis in the 2000s, while many among those enjoying the new wealth were the president's relatives and other Alawis, it made some feel that an 'Alawi elite' was bene-fiting at the expense of the Sunni majority. Further pressure was added by the arrival of up to 250,000 Iraqi refugees fleeing the chaos in their own country after the US-led invasion of 2003, telling fearful stories of the communal violence the occupation had unleashed.

From Protests to War

These tensions simmered below the surface, but civil war was far from inevitable. A series of events at home and abroad coalesced to erupt into violence. The initial spark came from the outside. In early 2011 several neighbouring countries suddenly erupted into revolu-tion. Peaceful demonstrations in Tunisia forced its ruling dictator to flee in January, while the same occurred in Egypt the following month. Copycat protests demanding the end of autocracy spread across the Arab world, in what became known as the 'Arab Spring' or

'Arab Uprisings'. But at first Syria seemed immune and attempts by a handful of oppositionists to launch demonstrations fizzled out. Assad even boasted in an interview with the *Wall Street Journal* that, unlike his fellow dictators who had been toppled, his regime was stable.[10] He was wrong.

Barely a month after he said this, a group of teenage boys in the southern town of Deraa graffitied 'Your turn next doctor!' on the wall of their school, implying that Assad would go the way of the leaders of Tunisia and Egypt.[11] They were immediately arrested and, as was common in Assad's Syria, tortured. Perhaps emboldened by the protests abroad, the boys' families did something quite unusual: they took to the streets and demanded their release. Deraa's residents were typical of the group that had lost out under Assad's rule: mostly Sunni and in the rural areas suffering from the recent economic reforms, so many joined the families protesting. Assad's local security forces met them with violence, opening fire and killing four people. Again, atypically, this did not deter the crowds. The next day at the funerals of those killed, even more joined the protests, now shouting anti-Assad slogans and smashing up the symbols of his rule. The security forces opened fire again, killing more and sparking bigger and bigger protests.

In one of history's ironies, the modern technology that Assad had encouraged now facilitated moves to challenge his rule. Syrians elsewhere learned of the government crackdown via social media and satellite television and themselves took to the streets in protest. They were similarly met with force prompting the same snowballing of protests and further government violence seen in Deraa. Some still clung to the hope that the violence was being led by rogue security heads rather than Assad himself, but this myth was soon dispelled. In a series of public speeches in 2011 the president refused to condemn the violence or grant significant concessions, and instead he blamed the unrest on a foreign conspiracy, calling the protesters 'germs'.[12]

Despite the government being responsible for almost all the initial violence, from the very beginning it depicted the protest movement as led by Sunni Islamist terrorists, justifying a harsh crackdown. This ploy successfully persuaded many to stay away from the demonstrations: including Alawis and other non-Sunni groups: the 10 per cent of Syrians who were Christian or the 3 per cent who were Druze (another Shia group), who feared persecution should Islamists take over.[13] Those that had benefited from Assad's rule, such as the middle classes, many of whom were Sunni, also kept their distance. As a result, Syria became fragmented: the opposition thrived in poorer Sunni-majority towns and suburbs, while the major city centres of Damascus and Aleppo, as well as the Alawi-dominated coastal region, remained loyal. This soon led to a physical as well as an ideological division. In the face of repeated government violence, oppositionists took up arms, at first to protect the demonstrations but soon concluding that the only way to remove Assad was by force. Thousands of rebel militia were hastily formed and enjoyed success at first. They pushed government forces out of rural towns across the north, east, and south of Syria and captured parts of Aleppo, Damascus and the third city, Homs.

But the rebels couldn't stay united. Ideological and ethnic divisions made them fight each other as well as Assad. Partly justifying Assad's characterisation, violent Islamists did emerge, including many that the government had cynically released from prison with the express goal of radicalising the opposition.[14] To Assad's delight this caused friction within the rebellion, between religious and non-religious fighters, and even among Islamists over how radical they should be. The most radical left the rebel cause altogether and joined Islamic State, a Jihadist terrorist organisation originating in neighbouring Iraq. Taking advantage of the chaos in Syria, Islamic State captured large parts of the eastern Syrian desert and declared it and its territory in Iraq as a new 'Caliphate'. Meanwhile many of Syria's Kurds, who had no love of Assad after decades of discrimination, but who also distrusted both the rebels and Islamic State, formed their own militia. When Assad withdrew from the Kurdish-majority areas in north-east Syria to focus on the more populated and strategically valuable west of the country, these Kurdish militia moved in, forming an autonomous enclave.

Foreign Hands

Perhaps the long-standing tensions, coupled with the inspiration of events in Tunisia and Egypt and Assad's fateful decision to meet protests with violence would have led to civil war irrespective of outside players. However, they certainly helped. In the early stages of the war, they sent weapons and money to combatants on all sides. As the war continued, some foreign governments even sent their own troops to influence the outcome. Over the years, Syrians increasingly lost the chance to determine their own fate as foreign patrons muscled in.

The outsiders were motivated by a mixture of fear and opportunity. For Iran, the worry was that Assad's potential fall would benefit its regional enemies. Tehran had been one of Syria's closest allies since Iran's Islamic Revolution of 1979. When the rest of the world turned its back on the new revolutionary government, Hafez al-Assad saw an opportunity and forged a close alliance. Ideologically the two governments were very different. Bashar al-Assad, like his father, was a secular Arab nationalist, while Iran's government was a Shia Islamic theocracy. However, they had common enemies in Israel, the United States, and, in the past, Saddam Hussein's Iraq, which bound them together. Alongside its long-standing loyalty, Iran was worried that if Assad fell, he might be replaced by a government that was friendly to its rivals Saudi Arabia and the United States, since both were supporting the opposition. As well as turning Syria from an ally into a potential enemy, this would sever the key supply route via Damascus from Iran which Tehran has used for decades to send money and weapons to the Shia Lebanese militia, Hezbollah (see chapter 7). Cutting this route would therefore weaken Iran's position in Lebanon and its ability to use Hezbollah to harass and threaten Israel. Finally, as radical Sunni Islamists emerged among the Syrian rebels, they began to threaten Syria's Shia communities, including the Alawis. As the self-declared protector of the region's Shias, Iran felt compelled to defend them. For the Iranian government then, Assad's potential fall could have been disastrous, and it was determined to help him survive.

As a result, Iran was early to intervene. By summer 2011, while Assad was still largely facing a peaceful protest movement rather than armed militia, Tehran sent him riot gear to help counter the opposition, and social media specialists to undermine their organisation online. As the opposition began to arm itself, Iran sent officers from its elite fighting unit, the Quds Force, to help advise Assad's military. This, however, did not turn the tide, and by 2012 Assad was losing territory and thousands of soldiers were deserting. In stepped Iran again. The head of the Quds Force, Qassem Suleimani, took effective charge of Assad's war effort.[15] He reorganised Syria's military and supporting paramilitaries. Ramshackle regiments were streamlined. Marauding bands of pro-government militia were disciplined and organised. Yet even then, Suleimani was not convinced they could do the job: 'The Syrian Army is useless!' he reportedly told a colleague.[16] Instead, the man nicknamed the 'Shadow Commander' called on those he did trust, bringing in Hezbollah from Lebanon to fight on Assad's side. He likewise brought in some of the Iraqi Shia militia he had trained to fight the Americans during the 2000s (see chapter 5), and built new militias made up of Afghan and Pakistani Shias recruited from refugee communities in Iran. Eventually, this reaped rewards. By 2014 the reorganised Syrian military and its pro-Iranian allies had seemingly turned the tide, going on the offensive to take back key neighbourhoods and towns.

The opposition also looked to regional governments for external help, but when it came it was as much a curse as a blessing. Turkey, Qatar, and Saudi Arabia all had reasons to oppose Assad and back his enemies. Turkey had actually enjoyed a close friendship with Syria before the war. Trade had grown, tourism between the two states flourished and the countries' leaders, Assad and Turkish leader Recep

Tayyip Erdoğan, even holidayed together. But Erdoğan felt betrayed when the Syrian president had promised to end his violent crackdown on protesters in 2011 but then reneged. Ideologically Erdoğan was already sympathetic to the moderate Islamists in the opposition, so when Assad betrayed him, it followed that he would back them.[17] Ankara worried that a prolonged conflict would inevitably spill over its 800 km border with Syria and, wrongly concluding that Assad would soon go the way of the presidents of Tunisia and Egypt, backed the rebels in the hope of nudging history along more quickly. From summer 2011 Erdoğan allowed the rebels to use Turkey as a base, giving them a platform to capture large parts of northern Syria.

Qatar was a close ally of Turkey and fellow sympathiser with Islamists but was more gung-ho in its initial backing of the rebels. Having enthusiastically supported the revolutions in Egypt and Libya, Doha sought to amplify its regional importance by positioning itself as the lead sponsor of the popular uprisings sweeping the region. At first in Syria this meant backing the peaceful protesters and giving them significant coverage on the Qatari-owned regional satellite television station, Al Jazeera. But when the protests did not dislodge Assad, Qatar was the first government to openly urge the opposition to take up arms. By late 2011 it was sending money and weapons into Syria for the rebels via Turkey, and a year later was sponsoring an array of different militias.[18]

Saudi Arabia viewed the conflict differently. Riyadh was no friend of Assad, and the two states had clashed repeatedly for several decades. Syria's alliance with Saudi Arabia's regional enemy Iran was a particular sore point. That said, Saudi Arabia also feared both democracy and Islamism, particularly the Muslim Brotherhood that had followers across the Middle East, including in Saudi Arabia. It worried that Assad's fall would usher in an elected Brotherhood government, emboldening Saudi Islamists to demand the same. Ultimately Riyadh realised the chance to topple a key Iranian ally was too good an opportunity to miss but was selective in which rebels it sponsored. While

Qatar mostly sent money and weapons to rebels aligned with the Syrian Muslim Brotherhood, Saudi sponsored alternatives: initially secular former Syrian army officers and later Salafists, conservative Islamists who opposed the Brotherhood.[19] The role of the Brotherhood became a source of tension between Turkey, Qatar, Saudi Arabia, and the UAE across the Middle East after 2011, and this rivalry influenced all bar the latter's involvement in Syria. This weakened the rebels, ensuring they remained a disparate collection of militias with different ideologies and foreign sponsors, who at times were reluctant to help each other when under attack, to Assad's advantage.

State governments were the most significant foreign hands intervening in Syria, but other outside forces played a role too. Foreign fighters flocked to the eastern Mediterranean. Some were part of organised non-state groups, like Hezbollah and the other pro-Iranian Iraqi Shia militia. Similarly, the Turkish Kurdish militia, the Kurdistan Workers' Party, known by its Kurdish acronym 'PKK', sent weapons and fighters into north-east Syria to help the Syrian Kurdish militias (see chapter 8). Likewise, Islamic State, which conquered large parts of eastern Syria, was originally an Iraqi, not a Syrian organisation, even if some radicalised Syrian rebels later joined. Alongside these organised groups were foreign individuals. Most were Sunni Muslims, from Europe or elsewhere in the Middle East, inspired to fight either for the Islamists among the rebels or for Islamic State. By late 2015 it was estimated that up to 30,000 people from 70 foreign countries were fighting in Syria.[20]

No less significant was the money sent into the war by private individuals. Framing the conflict as a religious struggle against Assad and Iran's Shia fighters, Sunni religious figures in the Gulf urged private citizens to donate money to help the rebels. They were quite open about this and faced only limited opposition from their governments in the first few years of the war, taking to social media to ask for $800 donations to buy rocket-propelled grenades, for example.[21] Of course, controlling where these donations went proved difficult and much ended up in the hands of radicals, including Islamic State, whether by accident or design. Eventually Gulf governments, led by Saudi Arabia, cracked down on this, but only after millions of dollars' worth of funds had been transferred to Syria, helping to fuel the fighting.

American Ambivalence

The United States was ambivalent towards the Syria conflict, a position that itself significantly impacted the war. Being the only global superpower and, theoretically, a defender of human rights and freedom, many inside and outside Syria expected Washington to intervene in the crisis. After invading Iraq in 2003 to topple Saddam Hussein's dictatorship and bombing Colonel Gadhafi in 2011 to help Libyan rebels (see chapter 2), this did not seem an unreasonable expectation. Moreover, US President Barack Obama made encouraging noises. After Assad's repeated violence against his own population, Obama and other Western leaders called for the Syrian leader to 'step aside'. Soon afterwards they began openly supporting the opposition and eventually sent them money and weapons, helping to coordinate distribution in both Turkey and Jordan.[22] This convinced the rebels and their patrons, Saudi Arabia, Turkey, and Qatar, that it was only a matter of time before Obama joined the war and bombed Assad into capitulation, as had occurred in Libya.

But they were wrong. Obama was deeply sceptical of intervening in any Middle Eastern conflicts, as were the American public, scarred after the gruelling war in Iraq. The US economy had been hit by the global economic crash of 2008 and Obama wanted to move away from the gung-ho interventions of George W. Bush to focus on his domestic agenda. While he had joined the NATO campaign in Libya, he had to be persuaded, only to later regret it. Syria was a far more complex picture than Libya, with a bigger population and more foreign powers involved, and Obama wanted to keep the war at arm's length. He misjudged how much he could do that though. He and his advisers mistakenly believed Assad would fall quickly and so called for him to step down in order to appear to be on the 'right side of history', rather than as the first step in a concerted anti-Assad campaign.[23] When the Syrian dictator clung on, Obama came under pressure to do more, hence his arming of the rebels. But, even then, he had long arguments with staffers, complaining that such covert warfare rarely worked. Moreover, the White House was seriously alarmed by the rise of Islamists among the rebels and worried that American weapons would end up in the hands of radicals. This was made worse when Islamic State appeared in eastern Syria and was joined by some former rebels, taking their foreign-supplied weapons with them. As a result, Washington was willing to back only a very narrow group of moderate rebels who were ineffective compared to the powerful Islamists.

Obama's unwillingness to get dragged into the Syrian morass became clear in late summer 2013. As the war had dragged on, an increasingly desperate Assad had been more and more willing to use his full arsenal against the rebellion. In 2011, his soldiers relied mostly on machine guns, by 2012 they used attack helicopters, and by 2013 bombers and ballistic missiles were being deployed. This raised fears that he would have no qualms about utilising the extensive stock of chemical weapons Hafez had accumulated as a deterrent to Israel in the 1980s. Obama had warned Assad publicly that any use or move-ment of these chemical weapons represented a 'red line' for him, but the Syrian leader seemingly ignored the threat and the rebels claimed they had suffered chemical attacks several times. Then, in late August 2013, just a few miles from where United Nations (UN) inspectors sent to investigate these allegations were stationed, 1,400 civilians were killed in a rebel-held suburb of Damascus by a chemical attack. Blaming Assad, who protested his innocence, Obama sent gunboats to the Mediterranean, gearing up for a missile strike. But no attack came. UK parliamentarians, scarred by their support for the invasion of Iraq in 2003 on tenuous grounds, voted against joining the strike, prompting an unsure Obama to seek approval from Congress before attacking.

Obama was also conscious that an assault on Syria might stymie his then-secret nuclear programme negotiations with Assad's ally, Iran (see chapter 5). With cracks beginning to show, Russia offered the US president a way out, brokering a deal that saw Assad peacefully give up his chemical weapons in exchange for Washington calling off the strike.

In a sign of Obama's priorities, a year later he did order bombing in Syria, but of Islamic State, not Assad. When the so-called Caliphate captured Iraq's second city, Mosul, and then released highly polished but gruesome videos of them decapitating captured American prisoners, the US acted. Obama saw Assad as monstrous dictator, but not one who threatened US interests. In contrast, he feared that Islamic State could spread across the Middle East, toppling US allies and creating a base for terrorist attacks on the West. In October 2014 he therefore initiated 'Operation Inherent Resolve', a military operation supported by other Western and Middle Eastern governments to degrade and ultimately destroy Islamic State and its 'Caliphate'.

But despite seeing Islamic State as a threat worth acting on, Obama still didn't want to get stuck in another Middle Eastern quagmire, and so was reluctant to deploy American troops. Instead, his strategy was to use American air power and a handful of special forces, but for the ground fighting to be done by local allies. In the Iraqi parts of Islamic State's territory, the US had allies in the Iraqi army and Iraqi Kurdish forces to do this, but what about Syria? Assad was too unpalatable to enlist, despite sharing a common enemy, while the moderate rebels were too weak. Washington attempted to train a new force of moderate Syrian rebels specifically to take on Islamic State, but the group was too small to be effective. Despite having fought Islamic State before, most rebels, now dominated by Islamists, saw Assad as their main enemy and had no interest in fighting the US's 'war on terror' when Washington hadn't really helped them fight the Syrian dictatorship. So instead, Obama looked to Kurds. Kurdish fighters, led by Syrian allies of the PKK (known as the PYD – the Democratic Union Party), had been locked in combat with Islamic State as it attacked the

Kurdish-majority regions of north and eastern Syria. After the PYD had miraculously repulsed an onslaught on the Kurdish-majority town of Kobane, Washington saw this group as the ideal ally.[24] Unlike the rebels, most Kurds were secular and not interested in Islamism, and they had little problem fighting just Islamic State, which threatened their homes, rather than Assad, who was far away in Damascus.

Russia's War

Yet for all Washington's activity in Syria's underpopulated desert east against Islamic State, this had limited impact on the primary conflict between Assad and the rebels. Instead, it was America's rival, Russia, that stepped forward and turned the tide. In September 2015 the Russian air force was dispatched to a new base on Syria's west coast, initiating a major military offensive. Within a few years Moscow would emerge as the key external player in Syria: using military might and diplomatic heft to defeat the rebels. Significantly, Russian President Vladimir Putin was able to use his position in Syria to amplify Russia's presence in the Middle East region, returning as a major player for the first time since the collapse of the Soviet Union.[25]

Before the war, Russia's role in Syria was relatively marginal. Russia and Syria had been allies since the 1960s, when the Soviet Union had provided money and weapons to fellow anti-Western socialists, but the relationship had drifted after the USSR's 1991 collapse. Moscow retained the Tartous naval base on the Syrian coast, its only military installation in the Mediterranean, but it was tiny, hosting barely 50 Russian sailors. Syria was a modest trade partner, purchasing most of its arms from Russia, but far less than Assad's enemies in Turkey and Israel. Moreover, Putin disliked Bashar al-Assad, viewing him as incompetent and once disdainfully commenting that he preferred to spend time in Paris rather than in Moscow.[26]

However, once the rebellion began, Putin concluded that Assad's survival was vital to Russian geopolitical and domestic interests.

Geopolitically, Assad's defeat might benefit the US at Russia's expense. As a former KGB officer who once remarked that the collapse of the USSR was the greatest geopolitical catastrophe of the twentieth century, Putin was committed to reviving Russia's fortunes and deeply suspicious of the US. As an autocrat who derailed Russia's fragile post-communist democracy once he became president in 2000, he was unnerved by Washington's toppling of fellow dictators in Iraq and Libya. So even though the US was reluctant to get involved in the Syrian war, Putin was convinced the rebellion was led by Washington. Obama's call for Assad to stand aside and his support for the rebels only seemed to confirm this.

Putin had domestic motivations too. Though he was an autocrat, he was also a populist and valued public opinion, which was hostile to the US and approved his standing up to Washington. Many Russian Orthodox Christians, who tended to support Putin, were worried about the fate of fellow Orthodox Syrians, who largely backed Assad and were threatened by Islamists among the rebels and by Islamic State. Putin also worried about the Islamist presence in Syria impacting domestic security: 14 per cent of Russians were Muslim and the foreign fighters in Syria among the rebels or Islamic State included a sizeable Russian contingent. Having experienced several Islamist terrorist killings over the years, Moscow had no desire for these forces to win the war and provide a platform for future attacks.[27]

After Syria's war broke out, at first Russian support for Assad was mostly diplomatic and economic. Putin vetoed a series of resolutions aimed at punishing Assad for his violence at the UN Security Council, while also providing new weapons on generous credit and other financial support to help Damascus withstand Western sanctions. But by summer 2015 it was clear things were going badly. Though Iranian support had stabilised Assad's lines, the rise of Islamic State in 2014 prompted many of the vital Iraqi Shia militia to head back to Iraq to defend their homes, leaving Assad depleted. At the same time, rebels in both the north and south became better organised, aided by

Saudi Arabia, Qatar and Turkey agreeing on a strategy for once. In 2014–15 they advanced on Assad's floundering forces, making significant inroads, especially in the north where they captured the regional capital of Idlib, and were edging towards Assad's Alawi-dominated coastal mountain heartland.[28] On top of this, Islamic State, fresh from their victories in Iraq, headed westward. They captured the desert city of Tadmour, brutally dynamiting parts of the ancient Roman ruins of Palmyra soon afterwards, and looked to be advancing on Homs and other major Syrian cities.

Fearing Assad was on the verge of collapse, Suleimani was sent by the Iranian government to Moscow to talk to Putin. Though Tehran and Moscow were not in a formal alliance, many of their interests overlapped, both being anti-Western and, importantly, wanting Assad to survive. In Moscow the Russian president and Iranian general hashed out a plan: Putin would send air power and special forces while Suleimani would bring in extra Shia fighters to push back the advancing rebels, even if officially Putin claimed he was helping Assad to fight Islamic State. The operation took longer than expected, and Russia had to get more involved than was first hoped, including having to retrain divisions of Assad's army. Eventually, though, the investment paid off. In late 2016 Assad, Iran, and Russia's forces pushed the last rebels from the second city Aleppo. In 2017 they advanced eastwards, pushing Islamic State out of Palmyra/ Tadmour. By the end of 2018 the last rebel strongholds in the centre and south of Syria had fallen, including the birthplace of the uprising, Deraa. In western Syria, only Idlib remained in rebel hands.

The military campaign was brutal. Moscow, Tehran, and Damascus were condemned by Western leaders for their seeming deliberate targeting of civilian areas, including hospitals, to demoralise the rebels. But in a sign of how Syria had fallen down the list of Western priorities, actions rarely followed words of condemnation. The US and others tried to push Assad into a UN-led peace process to halt the violence, but he repeatedly violated ceasefires and ignored attempts at dialogue, with Russian acquiescence. For the EU, priorities had shifted to containing the flow of refugees flooding out of Syria after a million headed to Europe in 2015. For the US, the priority was fighting Islamic State, not stopping Assad's bloody reconquest. This, at least, was successful. Assad's recapture of Tadmour and other parts of the east was down to Islamic State being distracted by fighting the US-backed Kurdish forces, and being decimated by sustained American bombing. Obama's successor as president, Donald Trump, intensified the campaign, and by 2019 the so-called 'Caliphate' had been destroyed in both Syria and Iraq. This left the US's Kurdish allies controlling a large swathe of its former lands in north and eastern Syria.

By the time of Russia's intervention, one of the major regional powers involved earlier, Qatar, had already stepped back, distracted by failures elsewhere in Egypt and Libya and a change of leader at home (see chapter 8). The other main Gulf player, Saudi Arabia, concluded that Moscow's dramatic escalation, coupled with Washington's evident lack of interest in toppling Assad, meant the game was up. Also distracted, by a war in Yemen it launched in 2015 (see chapter 3), Riyadh quietly stepped back from the Syria conflict. Ankara, however, could not do so given the war was on its doorstep and was spilling over into Turkey. Turkey hosted the largest number of Syrian refugees in the world, up to 4 million in total. It had also seen an increase in domestic terrorist attacks linked to Syria, from both Islamic State and the PKK. Of these, the PKK was by far the biggest problem. Ankara had been at war with the Kurdish separatists since the 1980s and was horrified that its close ally, the US, was now giving money, weapons, and training to the PKK's Syrian affiliate in the war against Islamic State. Russia's military involvement therefore prompted Erdoğan to re-evaluate his priorities in Syria. While he still wanted Assad gone, he privately recognised that with the US not willing to match Moscow's escalation, this was unlikely to happen. Instead, he shifted focus to two more modest goals: keeping the PKK and Islamic State away from his border and preventing Assad's conquest of the last remaining rebel holdout, Idlib, to avoid yet more refugees flooding into Turkey.

So Turkey cut a deal with Russia. Erdoğan agreed to be a co-guarantor, alongside Iran and Russia, of the new Russian-led 'Astana peace process', named after Kazakhstan's capital where the talks were first held. This process effectively green-lighted Assad's reconquest of most of Syria. Erdoğan scaled down his support for rebels everywhere but Idlib and did little beyond condemning Putin and Assad's recapture of Aleppo, the east, and south.[29] In exchange, Moscow allowed Turkey to invade and capture two pockets of northern Syria along its border, and expel any Islamic State and militant Kurdish forces. Erdoğan likewise persuaded Donald Trump to evacuate a third pocket of former Islamic State territory, which Turkey moved into in 2019 forcing out Washington's Kurdish allies. To administer these new pockets, Erdoğan created a new pro-Turkish militia made up of many former Syrian rebels. Eventually the Turkish leader would use these rebel militias as mercenaries, sending them to other combat theatres like Libya and Azerbaijan to fight on Ankara's behalf.[30] These rebels, who once took up arms to fight Assad for a better Syria, were reduced to being an arm of the Turkish military.

The New Syria

Over a decade of civil war and outside intervention left Syria divided and heavily influenced by foreign governments. Yet while the primary cause of the conflict seemed to be resolved – the rebels were defeated, and Assad remains in power – Syria is far from at peace and its people suffer in different ways. Most of Syria is now back in Assad's control, but conditions are much worse than before the war. Dissent remains outlawed and the notorious security services loom large for anyone who steps out of line. The war is now more distant for most, but its legacy remains. The economy is in dire straits, suffering from the Western sanctions designed to punish Assad, political and economic

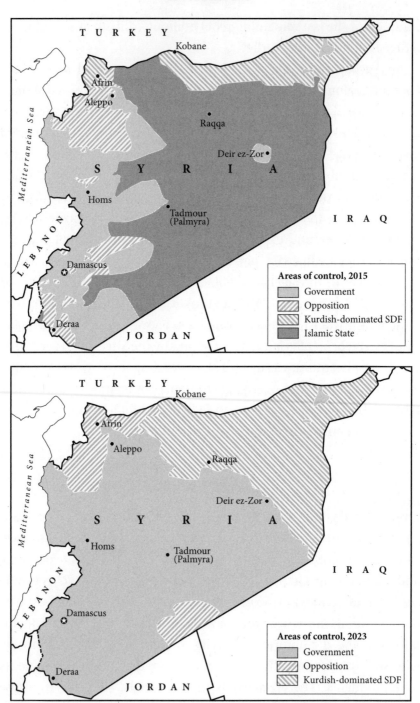

Political map of Syria in 2015 and in 2023

chaos in neighbouring Lebanon, and the endemic corruption that sees Assad's cronies profit while ordinary people struggle. Violence is not completely absent, however. Some reconquered areas have sporadically rebelled, particularly in the south around Deraa, prompting government crackdowns. Meanwhile Islamic State cells still operate and launch occasional terrorist attacks. Foreign enemies, notably the US and, especially, Israel, have launched frequent air strikes.

Iran and Russia now both have a sizeable presence in Syria they lacked before the war. While Assad is no puppet, he regularly plays the two off against each other to get his way, but both constrain his and Syria's freedom of action. Russia has benefited the most. It now has two major military bases on the Mediterranean and its companies have been rewarded by Assad with sizeable chunks of Syria's economy, including the modest oil and gas sector. Beyond material gain, Putin used his intervention to become a significant external power in the Middle East. He has acted as mediator for the states involved in Syria: Turkey, Iran, Jordan, and Israel, permitting the latter to regularly strike Iranian positions, much to Tehran's chagrin.[31] He has also used the intervention to get closer to some of Washington's regional autocratic allies, especially Egypt and Saudi Arabia, claiming he is someone who stands by his friends, unlike the US, which abandoned Egypt's and Tunisia's dictators in 2011. The benefits of this were seen after Russia invaded Ukraine in 2022. The US and European states urged Middle Eastern allies to join anti-Russian sanctions but all, including Israel, Turkey, and the Gulf states, refused, remaining neutral. The quagmire Putin encountered in Ukraine proved a major distraction, limiting Russia's ability to engage as actively in the Middle East as it had before the 2022 invasion, but this did not appear to have seriously impacted Moscow's power in Syria. That might change, however, should the war eventually lead to Putin's removal, given how much the intervention in Syria was his decision.

Iran's successes were more mixed. Tehran kept Assad in power and, like Russia, now has several military bases and access to the economy in Syria that it lacked before the war. But it has come at a far greater cost than for Moscow. Tens of thousands of its fighters have been killed and billions spent that the struggling Iranian economy couldn't really afford. It has maintained the supply line to Hezbollah to continue to pressure Israel, but Russia gives Israel permission to strike back regularly. Defending Assad has cost Iran credibility in the wider Middle East, especially among some Sunnis, who no longer see Iran as the anti-Western role model Tehran hoped it could be, but rather as a Shia imperialist thug.

Beyond Assad's control are the Kurdish-led east and the Turkish-dominated north. In the relatively pacified east, the US's Kurdish allies administer elected local councils in many of the areas once ruled by Islamic State. Their admirers see these committees as the only democratic governance in all of Syria, but their critics argue these are simply window-dressing, disguising the PYD's (and by extension the PKK's) dominance. Criticism especially comes from some Arabs in the east now ruled over by Kurds, reversing their historical role, which is resented by some. For the meantime, the situation is stabilised by the US, which retains a skeleton force on the ground and a sizeable presence in the air to protect Kurdish-led rule. However, with the US having betrayed Kurdish allies in Iraq in the past, and as recently as 2019 Donald Trump handing over Kurdish territory to Turkey, many worry the US will not stay for long. Fearing Turkey more than Assad, many Kurds favour reconciling with Assad and Russia to protect them from Ankara, while others hope the US's fear of an Islamic State revival will keep them in eastern Syria indefinitely. Washington, which lost a lot of international credibility in the Syrian war but still managed to defeat Islamic State, holds the fate of Syria's Kurds in its hands.

Much of the north remains under Turkish influence. Three 'pockets', around the towns of Afrin, Al-Bab, and Tal Abyad, are closely aligned with Turkey. They use Turkish, not Syrian currency, are connected to Turkey's electricity grid and postal system, and schools follow a version of the Turkish curriculum. Erdoğan relocated some Syrian refugees from Syria and Turkey into these areas and they are administered by a mixture of Turkish and pro-Turkish Syrian rebel forces, transforming them into loyal buffer statelets.[32] These being his personal project, few expect them to be evacuated while Erdoğan remains in power, but the Turkish president has shifted on Syria several times before. If he opted to reconcile with Assad, as hinted at during his successful re-election campaign in 2023, giving up some or all the buffer zones might be on the agenda. Erdoğan misjudged the Syria conflict, a costly error that left Turkey impacted by spillover along its longest border. His buffer pockets have slightly eased this strain, but they were correcting an error of his own making.

Idlib, meanwhile, remains under Islamist rebel rule, albeit heavily influenced by Turkey. With Assad having arranged to dump surrendering rebel forces from elsewhere in Syria into Idlib, the population swelled to over 2.6 million and many live in crowded refugee camps. Assad and Russia have repeatedly tried to conquer the province, fighting several mini-wars that Turkey eventually was able to stop, and there is no guarantee there won't be more to come. It is also possible that Erdoğan could offer up Idlib in exchange for normalisation with Damascus. In 2023, in a major step towards his regional reintegration, Assad was readmitted to the Arab League, having been suspended when the war erupted. Though Turkey is not a member, Erdoğan adopted a more conciliatory tone towards past rivals like Saudi Arabia, the UAE, and Egypt after 2021, partly in order to access much-needed investment from the Gulf for his ailing economy. With the UAE in particular keen to see Syria reintegrated into the Middle East's economic and geopolitical life, not least to minimise some of Iran's influence there and to reduce the quantities of illegal drugs being smuggled to the Gulf by Assad's cronies, Abu Dhabi and others might seek to pressure Turkey into a deal. In such circumstances, the fate of this last rebel holdout, like so much of the Syrian war, will likely be determined more by outsiders than by any Syrians.

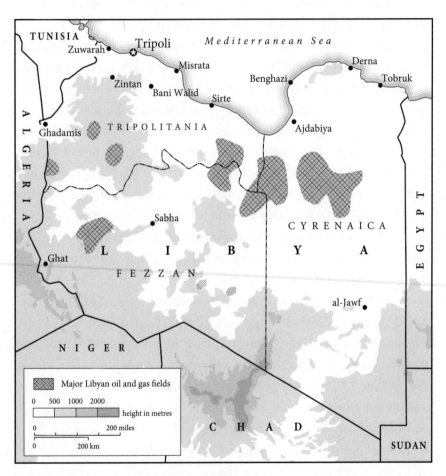

Libya

2

Libya
Anarchy on the Mediterranean

Libya is vast and empty. The mostly desert state nestled on the southern shores of the Mediterranean is three times the size of France and seven times that of the UK, yet with only 10 per cent of the population, at 6.5 million. It is also resource rich. Alongside sizeable gas fields, Libya has the largest proven oil reserves in Africa and by the late 2000s was extracting somewhere between half and two-thirds of the oil produced by more well-known exporters like Kuwait and the UAE.[1] This combination of oil and a small population might have seen Libyans enjoying the kind of prosperity seen in Gulf, but their experience has sadly been quite different.

They were dominated for decades by the eccentric dictator, Muammar Gadhafi, who closed the country off from the world, including banning English, and diverted much of Libya's wealth from its people towards foreign adventures or his own family's pockets. Yet when he was eventually toppled in a 2011 popular uprising, hopes of a new democratic dawn were scuppered as the various militants who overthrew Gadhafi turned on one another. Gadhafi's regime had deliberately fostered an environment of mistrust and division among Libyans, and this greatly impacted how politics played out after his fall. Within a few years Libya had fragmented. Ideological, tribal, and regional differences all played a part, but the fighting was primarily over access to the state's wealth, and different warlords clashed over who got what. Foreign governments, of course, were deeply involved and partly responsible for Libya's collapse. The international community, led by NATO and endorsed by the UN, backed the anti-Gadhafi movement to help topple the dictator. What little unity they had, however, deserted them almost immediately as different governments sponsored different factions, all trying to further their interests, with seemingly little concern for ordinary Libyans. The US, France, Italy, UK, Turkey, Russia, the UAE, Egypt, and Qatar have all had military forces in Libya at some point since 2011, each playing their own role in making things worse in the failed state.

Failed State

Libya's collapse was not inevitable. Domestic and foreign leaders made choices after 2011 that greatly contributed to the divisions that followed. That said, Libya does not have much stability or unity in its recent history. For centuries the cities along what is now the Libyan coast, and some of the desert interior, were ruled loosely by the Ottoman empire from distant Istanbul. This ended in 1911 when Italy invaded, initiating a brutal colonial occupation. Hundreds of thousands were killed, either resisting militarily or dying from disease or starvation in Italian concentration camps.[2] Rome was eventually ejected by the Allies during the Second World War, after which the victorious Western governments granted Libya independence. The new state was comprised of three historic regions: Tripolitania on the western coast, around Tripoli; Cyrenaica on the eastern coast, based on Benghazi; and the sparsely inhabited Fezzan in the desert south. But differences between the regions were pronounced and tensions arose over distribution of wealth and power, especially after oil was discovered in 1959. King Idris, the ageing Cyrenaican religious resistance leader enthroned by the Allies, proved unable to manage the growing problems and was toppled by Gadhafi in a military coup in 1969.

While Idris struggled to build a united state, Gadhafi took a sledgehammer to it. As part of a self-declared 'popular revolution' he dissolved the constitution and all laws, replacing them with General People's Committees. In theory these would lead to direct local democracy, but in practice Gadhafi's Libya was a mess, with few national institutions and without the rule of law. Everything was centred on its eccentric ruler and his homemade ideology that would frequently shift in often contradictory ways. To stay in power Gadhafi encouraged Libyans to distrust the state and each other, with multiple security agencies keeping people in line. He aggravated existing divisions: empowering the rural tribes rather than those living in the coastal cities and favouring his native Tripolitania at the expense of Cyrenaica and Fezzan.[3]

Luckily for Gadhafi, he had oil money to finance his 'revolution'. Libya's oil is of particularly high quality, and the country is geographically much closer to European markets than the distant Gulf. The consequent wealth allowed Gadhafi to build an expansive welfare state, ensuring that Libyans had a higher quality of life than their North African neighbours. It also prompted a massive increase in public sector jobs. As in many oil-dominated economies, Libya's autocratic government used its wealth to create unnecessary jobs that tied people to supporting the regime: 75 per cent of the working population was on the public payroll by 1987 – one of the largest public sectors in the world. Gadhafi simultaneously banned most private businesses – partly due to his revolutionary ideology, partly to prevent the growth of powerful companies that might challenge his power.[4] The result was a grossly under-developed economy, entirely dependent on oil and everyone looking to the state for jobs. There was very little agriculture or industry, with basics like dairy and meat imported from abroad.

Yet despite the oil money, Libya was no Abu Dhabi on the Mediterranean. Benghazi and the east were neglected by Gadhafi, with Second World War damage left unrepaired for decades, and Tripoli far shabbier than you'd expect for a petro-state capital. Gadhafi did invest in large-scale infrastructure projects like 'the Great Man-Made River', the world's largest irrigation project that pumps fresh water across Libya, but highways were potholed, and the hospitals and schools built in the 1970s were dilapidated. Instead, money was sent abroad. In the 1970s and 1980s Gadhafi sponsored an array of foreign Arab and African militants, some of whom launched terror attacks on Western targets, including the notorious 1988 Lockerbie bombing. This provoked Western sanctions, hampering the economy and Gadhafi's regional ambitions. After being ostracised by other Middle Eastern leaders for his disruptive activities, in his later years Gadhafi instead looked south. This included, bizarrely, having himself crowned 'King of African Kings' by various traditional African tribal leaders, and setting up a $5 billion African investment fund.[5] Libya's wealth also found its way into the Gadhafi family's pockets, with several of his seven children gaining notoriety for their fast and lavish lifestyles, prompting resentment.

Ironically, as domestic outrage grew against the ruling dictator, the foreign governments that had longed for his overthrow for decades warmed to him. After Gadhafi handed over the chief suspect for the Lockerbie bombing in 1999, and then renounced weapons of mass destruction in 2003, Western states dropped all sanctions on Libya and headed to Tripoli in search of contracts and investment. Gadhafi hosted various leaders, including UK Prime Minister Tony Blair, in his elaborate tent outside Tripoli. Meanwhile, his son Saif al-Islam led efforts to rehabilitate the regime's international image, presenting himself at home and abroad as a youthful moderniser. This included a controversial collaboration with the London School of Economics that saw the university accept several millions of pounds from the Gadhafis and award Saif al-Islam a PhD.[6] France similarly took Gadhafi money, with significant sums allegedly donated to President Nicolas Sarkozy's 2007 election campaign.[7]

This whitewashing of past crimes and continued autocracy succeeded in attracting foreign commerce, with European, Turkish and Gulf companies lining up to invest. However, once again, ordinary Libyans felt few benefits. Opening up to the world solved none of the deep problems caused by Gadhafi's rule.

When their neighbours erupted in protest in early 2011 it was therefore unsurprising that Libyans followed. Like Tunisia and Egypt, which toppled their dictators in January and February, Libya had been ruled by the same corrupt autocratic family for decades. Yet unlike its poorer neighbours, Libya was resource rich, fuelling even more frustration that the wealth was not filtering down to ordinary people. Libya's protests began in the east. Cyrenaica, despite holding at least 60 per cent of Libya's oil, had seen few of its benefits. After eagerly following the Tunisian and Egyptian protests on Al Jazeera, copycat demonstrations sprouted up, most significantly in Benghazi, where several hundred marched on the central police station. But unlike in Tunisia and Egypt (see chapter 6), where the revolutions were mostly peaceful, events in Libya quickly turned violent. Gadhafi's security forces killed several protesters, sending more onto the streets and with some taking up arms. A significant number of soldiers and regime officials defected, building momentum for an uncoordinated and diverse rebellion, evolving differently in different parts of the country. Within days Gadhafi's forces had been driven out of Benghazi and all of eastern Libya, as well as the western cities of Zintan and Misrata, where rebel militias formed.

Gadhafi met the rebellion with defiance, making televised speeches where he labelled the protesters 'rats' and 'cockroaches' and bizarrely claimed they were both linked to Al-Qaeda and had been influenced to protest by hallucinogens in their Nescafé. Saif al-Islam, meanwhile, appeared on Western television describing the Benghazi rebels as terrorists and murderers.[8] Foreign governments were not convinced. Embarrassed that they had been slow to back protesters in Tunisia and Egypt, the British and French governments were quick to abandon their new-found friendship with Gadhafi and pressed the UN to mandate military intervention to help the rebels. With the government launching a counter-attack, many feared Gadhafi would massacre the inhabitants of Benghazi and other rebel centres should he conquer them. Such fears prompted the usually conservative Arab League, with activist Qatar holding the rotating presidency, to back NATO-led military action, which was authorised by the UN on 17 March.

What began as a no-fly zone to stop Gadhafi using his air force to crush the rebels soon expanded into a full intervention in the civil war. Government military targets were bombed and special forces, notably from the US, France, UK, Qatar, and the UAE, were deployed to aid the rebels. Eventually this tipped the balance. By late August Tripoli had fallen. By the end of October Gadhafi himself was murdered by rebels as they advanced on his hometown of Sirte. A month later Saif al-Islam was captured as he tried to flee. Forty-two years of Gadhafi's rule was over. Unfortunately for Libya, the foreign and domestic forces that ended it struggled to agree on what should follow.

Post-Gadhafi Chaos

In the early days of the rebellion a National Transition Council (NTC) was formed by opposition members to try to coordinate the anti-Gadhafi movement. Days after his death this council declared Libya officially liberated and formed an interim government. While the NTC presented itself to its international allies as the unified leader of the rebels, it had limited authority. The rebellion had drawn in an array of different Libyan oppositionists: exiles returning from abroad; local militias that had formed to defend particular cities or regions; rural tribes; Islamists; Jihadists; and defecting regime officials. While most deferred to the NTC while the war was under way, with the dictator gone differences emerged.

One major issue was the fate of the armed militias. Gadhafi had hollowed out most national institutions and there was no national army or police force to fold them into, so the interim government tried to create new national structures to control them. But few fighters were interested in giving up either their arms or autonomy. Instead, armed men registered for the government schemes, pocketed the monthly salary but continued to operate as before.[9] This was made worse by politicians within the government who prioritised their own local interests over any national agenda. They pushed schemes and contracts that benefited militias from their home regions, empowering the armed men further while weakening the new government. As a result, the militias never laid down their weapons, and towns, cities, and neighbourhoods remained controlled by armed groups. Not only did this balloon Libya's already high wage bill – with 75 per cent of the annual budget in 2018 spent on salaries and subsidies – it also laid the groundwork for further fighting.[10]

Another tension emerged over the role of former regime officials. During the war some rebels had launched revenge attacks on loyalist regions, such as Sirte and Bani Walid. After Gadhafi's fall, revolutionary hardliners were unhappy at the prominent role former officials played in the NTC and interim government. The Islamists, who had been persecuted under Gadhafi, especially pushed to find ways to dilute the former officials' role. They first pressed, successfully, for swift democratic elections to replace the unelected interim government. Yet these, held in July 2012, saw the party of former official and NTC leader, Mahmoud Jibril, outperform the Islamists. While a compromise government was formed under a new prime minister, Ali Zeidan, which included both groups, the hardliners persisted. They proposed a Political Isolation Law that would bar Gadhafi-era officials from public service, including Jibril. In a sign that the gun now ruled, as the bill was debated between January and May 2013, armed militias besieged parliament and other ministries to intimidate the deputies. They succeeded and the bill was passed, but at great cost.

A whole swathe of former officials was excluded, providing eager recruits for anti-government forces in the second civil war that would soon erupt. Meanwhile the new parliament's authority was already shot, with the militias showing it could be violently intimidated.

With the militias empowered and few politicians daring to face them down, violence grew. Low-level clashes between militias were commonplace, while there was a notable increase in thefts and murders. Prime Minister Zeidan was even briefly kidnapped by one militia, though he was released soon afterwards. The militias disrupted the vital oil economy that paid their salaries, when one leader, Ibrahim Jathran, seized several oil ports in August 2013 and tried to sell the crude privately. His actions cut oil production by half and lost the government $3 billion a month for eight months.[11] In a sign of the post-Gadhafi government's weakness, however, when he eventually agreed to give up the ports after his plan to sell oil failed, Tripoli put him and his militia back on the state payroll. Zeidan, in contrast, was forced to resign.

The foreign governments that sponsored Gadhafi's ouster similarly diverged once the dictator was gone, backing rival Libyan factions and exacerbating the domestic divisions. Though they wanted the Tripoli government to assert its control and develop into a functioning democracy, Western governments deliberately stepped back once the military campaign was over. This was partly at the rebels' request. The NTC rejected the idea of foreign troops stabilising the country, fearful that its authority would be undermined and conscious that many Libyans, especially the Islamists, distrusted Western governments. It was also due to reluctance on the part of the United States. US President Barack Obama had taken some persuading to back the NATO campaign, keen to avoid another Middle Eastern war after the scars of Iraq (see chapter 5). He had hoped to 'lead from behind' Britain and France but had to step in when these allies proved ill-equipped, furthering fears of a Libyan quagmire. Obama was therefore happy to avoid a long-term presence when the NTC asked for this. NATO did attempt to train 20,000 or so of the new government's security forces, but with these institutions struggling as the militias flourished, little progress was made.[12]

The Western presence retreated further after Jihadists attacked the US consulate in Benghazi in September 2012, killing four Americans, including the ambassador. Domestic criticism for this security failure, and continued turbulence across Libya, prompted the US to cut its diplomatic presence to a skeleton staff in Tripoli. They in turn would be evacuated, along with the staff of other Western embassies, when renewed fighting reached the capital in 2014. A few years later Obama would blame his French and British allies for their lack of interest after Gadhafi's death and the internal divisions of Libyan politics for what he called the 'shit show', that followed the revolution.[13] While this might be true, he was arguably too quick walk away. After helping create instability by defeating Gadhafi, turning away following the death of four US citizens, however tragic, was premature.

With Western powers losing interest, the importance of regional governments became more pronounced. Many of these, notably the UAE and Qatar, had been involved in the anti-Gadhafi campaign from the beginning, sending special forces to aid the rebels (see chapter 9). These two ambitious Gulf governments were genuinely fearful of regime massacres, but once Gadhafi had fallen, both sought to nudge events in their favour. The UAE was vehemently opposed to the Muslim Brotherhood wherever it appeared in the Middle East and had backed anti-Islamist forces in Libya since 2011. Abu Dhabi was alarmed when Libya's branch of the Brotherhood came second in the 2012 election, built on support from several key militias. The UAE's de facto leader, Crown Prince Mohammed Bin Zayed, therefore welcomed the success of Jibril's more secular party and backed armed groups opposed to the Islamists.

Libya became part of a wider battle over the Muslim Brotherhood's role in the region. In July 2013 the Egyptian military launched a coup against the elected Muslim Brotherhood government in Cairo, encouraged by the UAE and Saudi Arabia. This fed paranoia among Libyan Islamists and hard-line revolutionaries that the UAE would sponsor a similar plot in Tripoli, prompting them to be even more uncompromising. In turn, the Egyptian coup helped solidify their opponents, including many of the excluded former regime officials, who labelled all their rivals 'Islamists' whether or not this was an accurate description. Reinforcing their prejudices were media outlets from the UAE, Saudi Arabia, and now Egypt that characterised all their Libyan opponents as Muslim Brotherhood radicals.[14]

Qatar's Failed Adventure

On the other side of the divide was Qatar, which, along with the UAE, was the most active regional player in Libya in the early years after Gadhafi's fall. With revolutions erupting across the Arab world in early 2011, Doha saw an opportunity. Its ruler, Emir Hamad Bin Khalifa, had come to power in the mid-1990s determined to use Qatar's vast gas wealth to raise the principality's profile and influence. At first this involved 'soft' power ventures like brokering deals between factions in Lebanon and Palestine, buying British department stores, sponsoring Barcelona Football Club and, most famously, financing and hosting Al Jazeera, which became the world's most watched Arab news station.[15] When the governments of Tunisia and Egypt were toppled and rebellions broke out in Libya and Syria, however, Hamad and his ruling circle changed their strategy. While fellow Gulf rulers in Saudi Arabia and the UAE were worried that the Muslim Brotherhood would come to power, Qatar had no such concerns, having long been close to the Brotherhood. Rather than fearing the revolutions, Doha embraced them, believing it could boost its regional influence if friendly governments were elected.

In Libya, this led to a counter-productive dual strategy. Doha enthusiastically backed the NTC in its war with Gadhafi and the interim government afterwards. The Qatari government and Al Jazeera frequently called for Libyan unity and respect for the new democratic order. But at the same time Doha funded a diverse range of fighters, frequently bypassing the NTC and establishing direct links with militias, a practice it shared with its regional rival, the UAE.[16] Doha utilised Muslim Brotherhood exiles and other Libyans living in Qatar alongside newly forged relationships that emerged out of the civil war, such as links to Misrata merchants. Consequently, many of Libya's militias developed their own sources of external funding and arms, further disincentivising them from accepting subordination to government control.

As the interim government struggled, Qatar exacerbated the situation by continuing to support its militia allies, despite paying lip service to respecting Tripoli's authority.[17] Its continued backing for Brotherhood-aligned groups also put it on a collision course with the UAE and Saudi Arabia. Ultimately, events outside of Libya forced Doha to retreat. The coup in Egypt was a major blow, with Qatar's Muslim Brotherhood allies imprisoned and Al Jazeera banned. Meanwhile, in Qatar itself, Hamad handed over power to his eldest son, Tamim, who was not as internationally experienced or ambitious. In Libya the UAE's allies were in the ascendancy while Qatar's allies were divided and not producing the stable friendly government Doha had, perhaps naively, hoped would emerge in 2011. With Tamim focused on consolidating power at home, Doha quietly dropped its involvement in Libya in 2014, having greatly contributed to the divisions that would spark a second civil war.

Second Civil War

Though violence was never absent from post-revolution Libya, it erupted into a second civil war in 2014, fuelled by the domestic and international tensions of the previous three years. In February protests broke out in Tripoli after parliament voted to delay elections.

In support of the protests, a retired general, Khalifa Haftar, announced that he was suspending parliament and the constitution. This was met with derision as Haftar lacked the military force to do this.[18] However, he tapped into growing frustration at parliament, and the dominance of Islamist and hard-line revolutionary militia. Haftar was a former Gadhafi official who had fallen out with the regime in the 1980s, spending two decades in exile in Virginia, before returning during the uprising. Now barred from office by the Political Isolation Law, Haftar drew support from fellow former regime officials and military officers, including Jibril's supporters, helping to build his own militia in the months after his announcement.[19] Cleverly, Haftar named his organisation the Libyan Arab Armed Forces (LAAF), giving the impression at home and abroad that his was a nationwide force that could bring order to Libya's post-revolutionary chaos. In reality he was just another warlord.

Haftar was of mixed Cyrenaican-Tripolitan heritage, but it was in the east that he found support among those angered once again by the neglect of the Tripoli government. Tensions and violence had been developing in the east since 2012, but Haftar severely escalated matters and ignited what became known as the second civil war by launching a major military assault on Benghazi. Echoing the anti-Islamist narrative encouraged by the UAE and others, Haftar declared his assault would 'cleanse Benghazi of extremists and outlaws', targeting pro-parliament Islamist and revolutionary militia. It took three years for Haftar to win the battle, reducing much of the city to rubble, but that didn't stop the LAAF from expanding elsewhere, capturing most of Cyrenaica, including the oil ports, by September 2014.

Abdullah al-Thinni, the prime minister who succeeded Zeidan in March 2014, expressed support for Haftar and fled Tripoli for Cyrenaica, along with many parliamentarians. This followed the results of the delayed elections that eventually took place that June. With a low turnout of barely 40 per cent (compared to 60 per cent in

2012) the Islamists and revolutionaries did worse than expected, prompting a coalition of hard-line militias to march on Tripoli.[20] Calling themselves 'Libya Dawn', this group of mostly Tripoli and Misrata fighters were fearful that Haftar might use the election results to advance on the capital and so took it themselves. They purged parliament, ejecting al-Thinni and other MPs, restoring allies from the previous session in a new rump body. They also forced out militia from Zintan who had been in Tripoli since 2011, transforming the western town into a pro-Haftar outpost by default.

Within months Libya was witnessing its worst fighting since 2011. Over 300,000 were displaced, the country was divided and the last hopes of a transition to democracy seemed extinguished.[21] Haftar controlled most of the east and was establishing a shabby despotism that brooked little dissent and saw his picture displayed on roadsides. Though al-Thinni and his parliamentarians set up the constitution-ally mandated 'House of Representatives' in the eastern city of Tobruk, it became increasingly toothless, and authority ultimately lay with Haftar. Similarly, in the west, although the rump parliament theoretically governed, the Libya Dawn militias commanded Tripoli and its environs. Though the physical division between east and west appeared neat, the forces fighting one another were complex coali-tions that blurred Libya's varying dividing lines. Haftar had more support in Cyrenaica from former regime officials and rural tribes, while Libya Dawn mostly had support in Tripolitania from urban dwellers and Islamists. Yet Haftar had Islamist Salafists within his LAAF and support from the western Zintanis. Similarly, Libya Dawn included many Western-minded businessmen alongside the Islamists and was backed by Berber tribes. Some divisions were long-standing, going back to before the Gadhafi era, others were new, following the particular politics of the revolution, and some were exacerbated by foreign patrons.

The anarchy of the second civil war provided opportunities for Islamic State to expand its newly declared global 'Caliphate' into

Libya (see chapter 1). Many Libyan Jihadists had travelled to Syria to fight in its civil war, particularly from the eastern town of Derna, and now they returned to wage Jihad at home. Linking up with domestic radicals, several hundred armed fighters took control of Derna in October 2014 and pledged loyalty to Islamic State. The following month Islamic State's leader in Syria declared that Libya's three provinces were now statelets within his 'Caliphate'. Islamic State in Libya drew in foreign Jihadists from neighbouring Tunisia and elsewhere in North Africa, and expanded into neighbourhoods of Benghazi, Tripoli, and remote parts of the eastern mountains and southern desert. Significantly, they captured all of Gadhafi's hometown of Sirte in early 2015, initiating a brutal two-year reign.

But Islamic State struggled for support and resources and never threatened to be a major force. Unlike in Syria and Iraq, the Libya branch did not capture oil fields or large caches of weapons, leaving it to rely on donations and kidnappings for income.[22] It was also far less popular. Resentment at the ruling Shia-led governments mobilised some Sunnis in Iraq and Syria to join Islamic State, but almost all Libyans were moderate Sufi Sunnis, and identity politics gained little traction. Moreover, Islamic State had not taken part in the anti-Gadhafi rebellion, which reduced its credibility compared to other militias. As a result, it never grew beyond a few isolated pockets, and was eventually expelled from these. Haftar's forces pushed Islamic State out of Benghazi and Derna. Misratan militias, acting on behalf of a new UN-brokered government in Tripoli recaptured Sirte in December 2016. The remaining handful of Islamic State fighters withdrew to the desert, from which they launched terrorist attacks but never again threatened to take territory.

International Battleground

Like the first civil war, the second was highly internationalised. Yet while the anti-Gadhafi campaign drew in a united foreign coalition, now the outsiders backed different sides. A key actor was the UAE, which became Haftar's most important supporter. Believing him to be the Libyan equivalent of Abdel Fattah El-Sisi, the anti-Muslim Brotherhood military dictator it had backed in Egypt, Abu Dhabi sent a variety of financial and diplomatic support. The UAE sent its own forces too, its fighter jets and drones attacking Libya Dawn, Islamic State, and others, while it built an air base in Haftar's eastern fiefdom to deliver supplies.[23] Sisi also lent Haftar considerable support, with the Egyptian air force launching regular sorties, including bombing Islamic State in Derna after the Jihadists released a video showing the beheading of twenty-one captured Egyptian Christians.[24]

The UAE's role went beyond military assistance; it also deployed its extensive wealth and influence with international allies. It funded and trained Sudanese mercenaries to fight with the LAAF. It worked to improve ties between the United States and the Libyan general. Donald Trump, Obama's successor as US president, softened his attitude to Haftar, possibly as the result of UAE lobbying.[25] Similarly, the UAE's close economic and military relationship with France may have helped oil Paris's closer ties to the LAAF, especially through French foreign minister Jean-Yves Le Drian. Abu Dhabi further bankrolled Russian mercenaries to fight for Haftar, which played a role in bringing Moscow into the war. While Haftar was never a puppet of Abu Dhabi, or any other foreign backer, his military campaigns and rule in eastern Libya were heavily dependent on external support, giving the UAE considerable leverage over his role in the civil war.

In contrast Haftar's rivals in Tripoli received little foreign support and the Libya Dawn-backed leaders were soon replaced by a UN-endorsed unity government. Haftar's early military victories prompted alarm at the UN, leading it to sponsor a peace process that led to a reconciliation agreement signed in Morocco in late 2015. With foreign governments worried by the 2015 migrant crisis in Europe and the dramatic rise of Islamic State in Syria, there was renewed momentum to try to stabilise Libya. The agreement saw the two rival parliaments in Tobruk and Tripoli agree to a Government of National Accord (GNA) under a new prime minister, Fayez al-Sarraj. Significantly, however, Haftar was excluded. Sarraj arrived in Tripoli with his new cabinet in March 2016, and received support from an array of militias, who persuaded most of the Libya Dawn fighters to dissolve their coalition. Within months, though, fissures emerged between east and west and the Tobruk parliament declared the agreement void, reigniting the fighting. However, Tripoli was now ruled by a government officially recognised by the UN and nominally endorsed by Western governments, including the US and European states.

Yet Western support was tepid. The Obama administration, in its final year, helped Mistratan militias affiliated with the GNA defeat Islamic State. The US launched over 500 air strikes against Sirte in support of fighters who eventually retook it in December 2016.[26] Yet Trump was more ambivalent. Though it was official US policy to only recognise the Tripoli government, when Haftar launched a military assault on the capital in 2019, Trump telephoned the general to praise his 'counter terrorism efforts'. Meanwhile, his national security adviser, John Bolton, was reported to have green-lighted the attack.[27]

European governments were similarly mixed in their support for Tripoli. The EU was keen to ensure stability as Libya's anarchy had resulted in it becoming a major source of illegal immigration into the bloc: 600,000 crossed the Mediterranean on dangerous sea craft from 2014 to 2017.[28] Consequently the EU poured millions of euros into efforts to halt the flotillas, including through improving the coastguard, judiciary, and police. Yet with the GNA still dominated by militias, most of this money ended up in the pockets of militiamen who were often linked to the human trafficking that was a significant part of the migrant flows. The EU's efforts had some limited success, and there was a decrease in the crossings made, but this further empowered militias in Tripoli rather than the GNA and saw tens of thousands of migrants rounded up to be held in miserable makeshift prisons.

Complicating European strategy was a rivalry between Italy and France. Italy, the most impacted by the migrant flows and the former colonial ruler, had several interests, not least extensive oil and gas contracts dating back to the Gadhafi era. These had made it reluctant to endorse the NATO campaign in 2011. By 2016 Rome was vocally backing the GNA and the UN process, despite flirtations with Haftar. Italy therefore grew frustrated with its ally France, which seemed to be backing the Libyan general.[29] France had long wanted to be the leading foreign power in the Sahel region in which Libya's southern desert sits and was alarmed when the post-revolutionary instability started to spill over into the neighbouring states of the Sahara. Though it officially backed the various Tripoli governments, successive French leaders were attracted to the idea of a 'strongman' in Libya and aided Haftar. This included supplying arms and special forces, which undermined European unity on both Libya and the GNA. In one example, just as Western diplomats and the UN were trying to prevent Haftar's 2019 Tripoli assault, Le Drian told him, 'We were waiting for your victories.'[30]

Russia and Turkey were relative newcomers to the conflict, having not been involved in the 2011 intervention, yet a decade later they were among the most important foreign players. Russia reluctantly endorsed the NATO campaign, but soon regretted it. To Moscow, the humanitarian mission it thought it was approving at the UN quickly transformed into Western-led regime change, something it firmly opposed. Russian leader Vladimir Putin was further alarmed when the new NTC government cancelled several infrastructure contracts Gadhafi had agreed with Moscow. There is no evidence that Russia encouraged Haftar to launch the second civil war, but once it began Putin was happy with some instability in Libya. In Putin's mind, post-revolutionary chaos would serve as a warning to future Western leaders against orchestrating regime change. Once war broke out, Moscow weighed in behind Haftar, who had trained in the Soviet Union during his time as a Gadhafi regime officer and spoke Russian.

Putin shared the view that only a strong man could stabilise Libya and saw Haftar as equivalent to Bashar al-Assad, whom he had backed to do likewise in Syria. A Haftar victory might also provide Russia's military with new bases and its companies with new contracts. Backing Haftar had a regional dimension too. It helped foster a growing UAE–Russia friendship, which frustrated the Emirates' principal ally and Russia's enemy, the US. Similarly, Turkey's increasing support for the Tripoli government gave Russia more incentive to work with Haftar, as Ankara was becoming a rival for regional influence.

Russian mercenary companies linked to the Kremlin began training the LAAF. The most notorious of these, the Wagner Group, eventually played a combat role. Though Russia insisted the Wagner Group was a private business, and was at least partly funded by the UAE, the US Department of Defense described them as a surrogate of Moscow.[31] The group's closeness to the Kremlin would be seen a few years later, when Wagner took a leading role in the invasion of Ukraine, before its leader Yevgeny Prigozhin launched an abortive coup against Putin in 2023, leading to Prigozhin's exile and death. Syrian mercenaries who had fought in the war there were also recruited by Russia and hundreds were sent to Libya.[32] Soon after this increase in support, Haftar's LAAF took over Libya's sparsely populated third province, Fezzan, in 2019. Such efforts greatly enhanced Russia's role in the conflict and made it a significant player in the east alongside the UAE. Yet, while the UAE was a staunch Haftar supporter, Moscow was more ambivalent: indicating it might be willing to jettison the general if necessary.[33]

On the other side, Haftar's attempts to capture the capital were thwarted partly due to a surge in support for the GNA from Turkey. Like Russia, Turkey had commercial ties with the Gadhafi regime that were lost when his regime fell. Yet unlike Moscow, Ankara was supportive of the various Tripoli governments that followed, particularly the Islamists, as part of a wider regional policy of backing the Muslim Brotherhood. Yet, as discussed above, it was its ally, Qatar, that led support for these factions immediately after the revolution, Ankara's attention being elsewhere, notably Syria and Egypt. Turkey supported the UN-backed GNA, which included some of its Islamist allies, when it formed in 2016, but it wasn't until 2019 that Ankara became a major player.

Haftar's main foreign backers were Turkey's leading rivals in the Middle East at the time. The UAE had helped dislodge the Muslim Brotherhood from power in Egypt and initiated a blockade of Qatar, while the new government in Cairo was supporting anti-Islamists across the region. Yet it was Russia's intervention that proved most significant. Though they cooperated in Syria at times, they had also violently clashed there and in general Turkey saw Russia's greater involvement in the Middle East as a threat to its regional ambitions. While Turkey had accepted UAE and Egyptian involvement in Libya for years, it was Moscow's entry that prompted a reaction – from both the GNA who were increasingly desperate for Turkish help, and from Ankara, which was now receptive to the pleas. Turkish president Recep Tayyip Erdoğan had further motives to get involved. He was alarmed at the insistence by Turkey's historic rival, Greece, that it had the exclusive right to explore parts of the eastern Mediterranean for gas. With Libya bordering the south-western corner of the disputed area, Ankara therefore signed a maritime agreement with the GNA that recognised Turkey's claims. In exchange, Erdoğan agreed to significant military aid.[34]

Turkey's intervention illustrated how much the Libya conflict was now being determined by outsiders. Haftar's advance on Tripoli had stalled in the capital's suburbs but by early 2020 his forces still held all eastern Libya and most of the underpopulated parts of the west – though the major coastal cities of Tripoli, Misrata and their environs were firmly in GNA hands. On Erdoğan's request, Turkey's parliament granted a mandate to send troops and Ankara subsequently dispatched special forces, drones, air defences, naval vessels, and intelligence officers. In a neat symmetry with Russia, it also sent several thousand Syrian mercenaries that it had recruited from the opposition-held parts of that country. These forces combined to help the GNA launch a successful counter-offensive, retaking much of western Libya. The counter-attack culminated in a showdown over Sirte. Gadhafi's former hometown was held by Haftar but GNA forces advanced in summer 2020. Not only did this provoke Russia to send fighter jets against Turkish troops, but Egypt even threatened to invade on the side of Haftar, raising the possibility of a direct clash between Turkey, Russia, and Egypt. Eventually all agreed to a ceasefire that saw Sirte stay in Haftar's hands, but the showdown indicated just how internationalised and perilous Libya's war had become.

Divided Libya

The 2020 Sirte showdown and subsequent ceasefire jolted the international community into reviving the flagging UN peace process – though it helped that the major foreign belligerents were distracted by the global Coronavirus pandemic. After several rounds of talks a new government of national unity was formed, theoretically unifying the rival eastern and western governments of Tobruk and Tripoli. Yet while the ceasefire held and positions in the cabinet were spread across the rival administrations, little changed on the ground. Haftar refused to submit to the new government and his LAAF continued to control most of eastern Libya, including the oilfields. Moreover, though the new Tripoli regime tried to build bridges with Haftar's foreign backers, the UAE, Egypt, and Russia continued to support Haftar, while Turkey refused to withdraw its forces. Many suspected the various domestic and foreign players were just biding their time till the next round of fighting. Hopes were raised when presidential elections were scheduled for December 2021, but they ended up indefinitely postponed after failure to reach an agreement on candidacy, leaving the conflict frozen once more.

The domestic and international response to the latest unity initiative in many ways typified Libya's post-revolutionary politics. All paid lip service to calls for unity, while ultimately still pursuing their own interests. Western governments promoted the UN process but were not willing to put in the attention or resources to help it succeed, giving them less leverage than those regional powers that were willing to do so. Having led the charge to topple Gadhafi in 2011, Western leaders, especially the United States, were quick to disengage, contributing to the subsequent chaos. Some Western governments, like France, and the US under the Trump administration, further weakened the UN process by working with Haftar. Trump's successor, Joe Biden, took more interest immediately after being elected, but was then distracted by the 2022 invasion of Ukraine, and seeking a long-term solution to Libya slipped down his priority list. As a result, Libya represents a failure for Western leaders. Though it may have prevented mass slaughter by defeating Gadhafi, its subsequent lack of interest combined with some states' mendacity contributed to the violence that followed.

Another state that failed in its goals in Libya was Qatar. While it helped topple Gadhafi, its diplomatic inexperience meant that the friendly stable Islamist government it hoped would come to power in his wake did not materialise, and its policies contributed to division. Other regional powers were less ambitious and arguably did achieve their goals, as most sought only to boost their regional profiles by gaining leverage in Libya's conflict, rather than resolving it. Indeed, one of the challenges facing Libya moving forward is that four of the main foreign players – Russia, Turkey, the UAE, and Egypt – benefit from the status quo of unresolved conflict and so have little incentive to encourage resolution. In different ways they have all outsourced their involvement in the war, using mercenaries and air power to minimise any losses to their own troops that might prove unpopular at home. Moreover, with the possible exception of Egypt, which fears spillover on its western border, none really sees Libya as their primary area of concern. Instead, they view it as a place where pressure can be exerted on regional rivals when other battlegrounds are looking less favourable. Turkey's late entry, after losses to Russia in Syria and maritime threats from Greece, is a perfect example of this. Yet with involvement carrying little cost, and none of the parties having an incentive to end the war, their involvement and meddling could continue for years.

All of which gives little comfort to ordinary Libyans, who have witnessed a dramatic drop in their standard of living after over a decade of war and instability. Sadly, Libya's leaders have mirrored their international patrons' unwillingness to place common interest over individual benefits. This was seen right after the 2011 revolution, when militias refused to disarm and politicians proved unwilling or unable to force them to, ensuring the permanent militia-fication of Libya. Similarly, the revolutionaries' insistence on excluding former Gadhafi officials from power, despite many having joined the revolution, fuelled division and civil war. Like the outside powers, too many Libyan leaders now benefit from the status quo to make real concessions to their rivals. Post-revolutionary Libya certainly didn't start with a good hand, having suffered for decades under colonial brutality and Gadhafi's autocratic misrule, but its collapse and fragmentation were not inevitable. Decisions were made after 2011, by leaders inside and out, that have turned what was potentially one of the Mediterranean's richest states into its most anarchic.

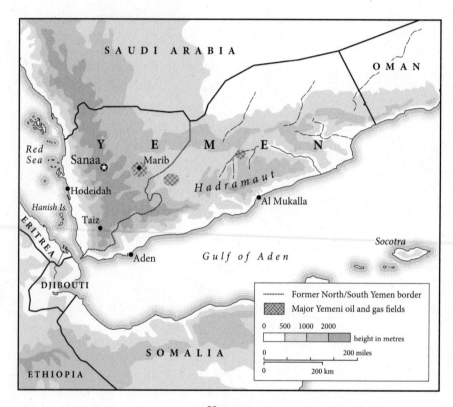

Yemen

3

Yemen
'The Worst Humanitarian Crisis in the World'

Recent history has not been kind to Yemen. The modern, unified republic is barely thirty years old, but in that time it has experienced dictatorship, drought, poverty, bombardment, and a horrendous civil war that UN Secretary-General António Gutteres called 'the worst humanitarian crisis in the world'. In 2020 three-quarters of the population of 27 million needed humanitarian assistance and just under a third did not know where their next meal was coming from. Millions were suffering from cholera while starvation and famine were widespread.[1] With little hope of a permanent resolution to the conflict, despite several ceasefires, Yemen's future looks as grim a prospect as its recent past.

It was not supposed to be this way. North and South Yemen united in 1990 with an air of optimism, but hopes were soon dashed as the North's ruler, Ali Abdullah Saleh, asserted control over the whole country. His domestic and foreign policies hamstrung the economy, his divide-and-rule tactics prompted years of internal fighting, and his disastrous ecological practices added further water shortages in one of the countries of the world where water is most scarce. Yemen was already the poorest country in the Middle East long before its civil war, so when a wave of protests shook the Arab world in 2011, it was understandable that Yemenis took to the streets to demand Saleh's departure. But disagreements over what a post-Saleh Yemen would look like bred disunity, while the dictator's reluctance to go stalled the uprising and led to an eruption of violence.

While Saleh and Yemen's other leaders shoulder much of the blame for the collapse, outsiders are also culpable. Past imperial over-lords, the British and Ottomans, ruled in a detrimental way, while Saudi Arabia, Egypt, and other regional players meddled after inde-pendence. The 2000s saw Saudi Arabia and the United States facili-tate Saleh's disastrous rule, while international institutions like the International Monetary Fund (IMF) pursued policies that caused economic and environmental damage. Since 2015, however, this outside meddling has gone into overdrive, with Saudi Arabia and the UAE spearheading a regional intervention force, while Iran and its allies have backed their enemies. Meanwhile, the US and other Western states have aided Riyadh and Abu Dhabi's war. The conflict may well be the world's greatest humanitarian disaster, but it is one that is man-made, and as much by foreigners as Yemenis.

Two Yemens Become One

Historically, Yemen's location has been both a blessing and a curse. Wrapped around the south-western corner of the Arabian Peninsula, where the Red Sea meets the Indian Ocean across the Bab al-Mandab Strait, Yemen has long been a regional trading hub. Its capital, Sanaa, shows the signs of this past wealth with stunning ancient clay tower buildings that create labyrinths through the old city, a UNESCO World Heritage site. Yet this strategic location has also attracted foreign interference. It prompted the Ottomans to capture the north, including Sanaa, and Britain, which coveted the port of Aden to protect the route to India, to conquer the south. This colonial parti-tion ultimately led to the development of two Yemens. North Yemen gained independence when the Ottoman empire collapsed in 1918, ruled over by the Zaydi Shia religious leaders who variously collabo-rated with and resisted Turkish rule. But the religious monarchy they fashioned ended in 1962 when idealistic military officers launched a coup and declared North Yemen a republic. Meanwhile, in the south, the British took longer to leave. London made various attempts to extend its overlordship, even after India had gained independence, and then planned a gradual withdrawal, but a sustained guerrilla campaign and mounting costs expedited a departure in 1967. Leftists among the insurgents claimed power and created the Middle East's first ever Communist state.[2]

Superficially, the two Yemen's looked similar. Both were tribal societies, overwhelmingly rural, and with mostly agrarian econo-mies. Yet the two governments were very different. North Yemen was ruled by Arab nationalist military officers who, despite their initial secular idealism, increasingly relied on conservative tribal leaders. South Yemen's socialist leaders, in contrast, sought to radically remake society. They set up programmes to lessen the importance of tribalism and religion and to improve women's rights, and developed one of the most progressive constitutions in the Arab world.[3] Yet the government's poverty and relatively short lifespan meant that these changes had only limited reach, especially beyond the capital Aden. Moreover, South Yemen was an autocracy like its northern counter-part, with power held by the ruling socialist party. Both states also suffered regular violence. Each was born in war, the North having had a civil war between republicans and monarchists from 1962 to 1970, and the South its four-year insurrection against Britain. Border disputes also saw the North fight the South twice in the 1970s. The south then endured its own brief but bloody civil war in 1986, caused by tensions within the ruling party.

The 1986 civil war, which resulted in up to 10,000 deaths and created 60,000 refugees, shocked the South Yemenis and helped pave the way to unification.[4] Despite their occasional hostility, both Yemeni governments had long expressed a desire to unify. The crisis of legitimacy after 1986, as well as the discovery of oil in the borderlands between North and South and the withdrawal of Soviet aid as the Cold War wound down, prompted Aden to negotiate with Sanaa. The result was a unification agreement in 1990 that saw North Yemen's president, Saleh, become head of the new unified state, while South Yemen's leader became vice president and head of the government. A democratic system was agreed, and free parliamentary elections held, ushering in an era of relative political freedom. But it didn't last.

Saleh gradually extended his power over all of united Yemen, applying the same divide-and-rule tactics he had employed in the North since coming to power in 1978. While the parliamentary system nominally remained in place, Saleh concentrated power in his own hands and engineered allies into key positions. Rivals were assassinated, political freedoms rolled back, the military packed with loyalists, and companies forced to accept Saleh cronies onto their boards.[5] Many in the south soon learned that unification meant absorption into Saleh's fiefdom. North Yemen's laws were extended across the country, reasserting tribalism and ending the gains made by women. In 1994 some southern leaders tried to secede and re-establish independence, only to face a military assault from Saleh's army that saw Aden sacked and occupied. Such violence became a regular feature of Saleh's rule. In 2004 his government launched the first of several conflicts with the Houthis, a Shia Islamist movement. There was also a low-level campaign against Al-Qaeda, which started to operate in Yemen in the 2000s.

This violence came amid a severe drop in living standards, brought about by a combination of Saleh's policies and external forces. While the 1970s and 1980s had seen both Yemens boom, benefiting especially from remittances sent home from the Gulf, this trend was reversed in the 1990s and 2000s. Saleh's unwise decision at the UN to vote against authorising the US-led coalition to liberate Kuwait from Saddam Hussein in 1990 prompted fury on the part of the US and the Gulf states. The former cut aid to Yemen while the latter expelled up to 800,000 Yemeni workers.[6] The newly discovered oil helped mitigate this, though it strengthened Saleh's power, as more people became dependent on state-distributed wealth rather than income they'd earned themselves abroad. Yet Saleh and his inner circle hoarded much of the oil money themselves, and mismanaged what wealth was distributed, buying off tribal supporters rather than investing in education, health, or transport. Moreover, Yemen's oil reserves were limited and nowhere near the quantities found in the Gulf, and few plans were made for what would happen after they ran out. The same was true of Yemen's limited water reserves, estimated in 2010 to be depleted within thirty years.[7] Saleh's government focused on mechanisms to extract more water, not increase sustainability, leaving multiple villages abandoned due to drought and desertification.

Saleh also entrenched his rule via his foreign relations. Learning from his error at the UN in 1990, when the US was attacked by Al-Qaeda in 2001 he was quick to offer his support to Washington. Al-Qaeda had a limited presence in Yemen, famously launching a suicide attack on the USS *Cole* in Aden in 2000. This allowed Saleh to present himself as a partner in America's 'war on terror', leading to a massive increase in US military aid from $14 million to $170 million between 2006 and 2010.[8] Saudi Arabia similarly aided Saleh, sending a steady stream of financial support and joining the military campaign against the Houthis. Western financial institutions like the World Bank and IMF were also welcomed, providing funds for the regime while urging structural adjustment policies that ultimately impoverished ordinary Yemenis. High-value export crops were recommended at the expense of local food security, subsidies were cut, and state industries privatised, placing more strain on the populace.[9] Though many Yemenis had longed for unification for decades, the reality had ushered in only disappointment, oppression, and increased poverty.

The Road to War

Saleh's determination to hold on to power at all costs ultimately helped drive Yemen into civil war, but he was greatly aided and abetted by domestic and foreign players that placed their own interests above all else. Like other parts of the Arab world, Yemen was shaken by protests inspired by the revolutions in Tunisia and Egypt in early 2011. The immediate trigger was Saleh's proposal in January to amend the constitution to allow him to serve a third term as president – the latest of many manoeuvres he'd made over his thirty-three years in office to stay in power. Mimicking events in Egypt, these mostly young demonstrators staged long-running sit-ins in central Sanaa and other cities, demanding Saleh's departure. As momentum grew, the traditional opposition parties joined in, with Islamists, southern separatists and members of the Houthi movement attending sit-ins and forming committees to debate what a post-Saleh Yemen might look like. Numbers swelled further when Saleh ordered his forces to violently supress the movement, massacring dozens in Sanaa in March, prompting defections from Saleh's own party to the opposition.

Saleh's external backers, notably Saudi Arabia, quickly concluded that this was one hurdle too many for the long-standing dictator. Led by Riyadh, the Gulf Cooperation Council (GCC) offered in April to mediate between the Yemeni factions and proposed a deal that would see Saleh resign in exchange for immunity, with his deputy, Abdu Rabbu Mansur Hadi, taking over. But Saleh refused to sign. His demurral sparked a violent response. While the peaceful sit-ins remained in place, and would ultimately stay there for several years, other opponents resorted to violence. This culminated in an assassination attempt on Saleh in June that saw him seriously wounded and evacuated to Saudi Arabia. But Saleh's loyalist troops continued to fight both the armed and the unarmed opposition, escalating tensions. The president returned to Yemen in September, still initially refusing to sign the GCC deal, but when the UN Security Council ordered its implementation and threatened him with sanctions and travel bans, he reluctantly did so in November. However, though he agreed to hand over power to Hadi, Saleh was far from done, and the immunity granted allowed him to remain at liberty and plot a return.

In February 2012, Hadi was elected as president of a national unity government, as agreed by the GCC deal. Though all elements of the opposition were theoretically represented, many were soon disappointed with the new regime and Hadi proved unable to manage the transition to a new inclusive Yemen. The Saleh loyalists who dominated parts of the military and other security positions never truly accepted Hadi, and frequently refused to follow government orders.[10] This forced the new president to rely on others for his government to function, and he ended up leaning heavily on the Islamist party, Islah, which had become a prominent voice within the opposition in 2011. But Islah was unpopular among other oppositionists, and their rise to prominence caused resentment among those who felt left out. It didn't help that Hadi's government soon proved itself as corrupt as Saleh's, putting cronies, often linked to Islah or loyal tribes, into leading positions.

Among the most dissatisfied were southern separatists. Many in the south blamed the decline in living standards and increased corruption of the previous two decades not just on the Saleh regime but on unification in general. While an official independence movement was launched in 2006, they were far from united and by 2011 there were almost a hundred different separatist groups. In addition, there were regional differences among southerners: urban Adenis were disparaging of the rural hinterland; oil-rich Hadramaut wasn't keen to share its wealth; and some in the easterly provinces wondered if they might do better to join neighbouring Oman rather than an independent south.[11] Moreover, there were many southerners who opposed independence altogether. The question of southern separatism nevertheless remained a prominent one in the national unity government and the 'National Dialogue Conference' that was set up as part of the GCC deal for the various factions to work out how post-Saleh Yemen would be governed. The southern representatives were ultimately dissatisfied with the proposals of the National Dialogue Conference when it reported in 2014: the south was to be partitioned into two federal zones, alongside four other regions, instead of the single southern federal region they hoped for.[12] However, before the southern secessionists could respond, another of the parties unhappy at this proposed solution, the Houthis, invaded Sanaa.

The Houthis, or Ansar Allah, were formed in the late 1990s and early 2000s as a radical offshoot of a political-religious Zaydi party and youth movement. They protested, among other things, the marginalisation of the Zaydi Shia, the Saleh regime's corruption, and its closeness to the US. The Zaydis form 30–35 per cent of Yemen's population and are mostly located in the far north, near the Saudi Arabian border, although their religious practices are very close to those of the Sunni majority, unlike Shias elsewhere.[13] Historically, Zaydis, whose leaders are descendants of the prophet Mohammad, were the rulers of northern Yemen until the monarchy ended in 1962, after which their influence waned. At times Saleh favoured the Houthis as a counterbalance to Islah, which was also based in the north, but he increasingly saw them as a threat, hence his military campaigns from 2004 to 2010. Yet these military assaults, which were often indiscriminate and caused considerable civilian suffering, only boosted the Houthis, swelling their popular support and prompting them to improve their military capabilities. By the time Saudi Arabia joined Saleh in fighting the Houthis in the late 2000s, the insurgents proved more than capable of matching their enemies – even crossing into Saudi Arabia in a humiliation for Riyadh. On the eve of the 2011 uprising, then, the Houthis had become a powerful militia and an increasingly popular revolutionary anti-Saleh force, attracting support from beyond their original Zaydi base.

Given their hostility to Saleh, it was predictable that the Houthis would join the opposition in 2011, but they remained notably separate from others, setting up their own tents in the various sit-ins. Once Saleh fell, their leadership engaged with the national unity government and the National Dialogue Conference. However, there remained hard-line elements in the Houthis opposed to any dialogue, and they were empowered when some of their more dove-ish leaders were assassinated. They also grew frustrated by the prominence of their rivals Islah in Hadi's government and the National Dialogue Conference's recommendations that did not grant the far north the autonomy it craved. While the various discussions over Yemen's future were taking place, the Houthis had been gradually expanding, solidifying their control of the north, including militarily defeating Islah there, and moving south. Moreover, to much surprise, they formed an illicit alliance with their old enemy Saleh.

The Houthis launched an assault on the government in summer 2014. Though these would ultimately prove to be the first shots of the civil war, the fighting was initially subdued. Houthi forces swiftly defeated government units loyal to Islah, and then marched unopposed into the capital. Their capture of Sanaa was helped by several factors. The public offered little resistance to the Houthi takeover, having lost faith in the Hadi government, which had not brought about the rapid changes the population expected after Saleh's ouster and had recently raised fuel prices. The Houthis' claim that they were the true voice of the people carried increasing appeal. In addition, the parts of the military still loyal to Saleh were deliberately standoffish, with their master secretly seeing the Houthis' defeat of Hadi as a route back to power. Hadi also miscalculated. Having seen Islah dominate his government since 2012, he saw advantage in the Islamists' military forces being chastened by a Houthi defeat, in the hope of making them more pliable and less domineering. He expected the Houthis to remain in the background, allowing his government to proceed unencumbered, but the Zaydi militia had other ideas.[14] After a few months, in January 2015, the Houthi leaders demanded Hadi accept their nominees for vice president and key government ministries and officials. To accept would have made Hadi's government Houthi puppets and so the president and his ministers all resigned. The Houthis then dissolved parliament and set up a 'Revolutionary Committee' to rule, but Hadi, who had been placed under house arrest, escaped, and fled to Aden.

At this point Hadi appeared on television to rescind his resignation, declaring himself the true president of Yemen and denouncing what he called a Houthi coup. This prompted an eruption in fighting and the beginning of the civil war. The Houthis now controlled almost all of the old North Yemen, alongside Saleh, who soon denounced Hadi and made the secret alliance public. Most of the old South Yemen, meanwhile, was nominally loyal to Hadi, though in practice his government in Aden had little reach and local groups and rulers often dominated.[15] Moreover, Houthi ambitions were not yet satisfied, and they and Saleh loyalists launched an immediate military drive south, reaching all the way into Aden in March. Hadi begged the GCC for help, fleeing Aden for Saudi Arabia. Ultimately this saved his government, when Saudi Arabia led an international coalition of Arab governments in support of Hadi. But this decision would transform the conflict and, ultimately, prolong and amplify Yemen's misery.

Saudi Arabia's Vietnam

Saudi Arabia has historically been Yemen's most important and most intrusive neighbour. With the two states sharing their longest land border, Saudi has long wanted a stable and friendly Yemen. This prompted it to intervene in North Yemen's civil war in the 1960s, backing the ousted monarch against the military, who were sponsored by Riyadh's then-rival, Egypt. While the pro-Egyptian forces won, Saudi quickly reconciled with Sanaa, allowing it to influence the new regime through direct funding, backing tribal groups, and ensuring the education system was dominated by pro-Saudi clerics.[16] It opposed the unification of the two Yemens in 1990, possibly fearing a united, more populous state to its south would be harder to control, but soon adapted and poured money into Saleh's pockets. The Riyadh leadership disliked Saleh, believing him untrustworthy and insufficiently deferential to the Saudi monarchs. Even so, they were reluctant to back his departure in 2011, partly because they couldn't see an alternative that could hold Yemen together, and partly because they wanted to limit the success of the popular protests sweeping the Arab world for fear they might soon appear at home. Eventually though, they accepted Saleh needed to go and helped engineer the GCC plan.

The decision to intervene in 2015, however, was not simply to uphold the GCC plan, which had been looking moribund for years. A combination of domestic and international factors drove Riyadh into action. A few months earlier the Saudi king, Abdullah, had died, and was succeeded by his brother, Salman. Salman, though, was 79 and frail, and his eldest son, Mohammed Bin Salman (known widely as MBS), immediately became the active face of the new leadership. Appointed deputy crown prince on his father's succession, MBS was not yet 30 and highly ambitious. With the Saudi throne traditionally passed down from brother to brother rather than father to son, the young royal was determined to disrupt this order and plot a route to his own succession, bypassing the many princes ahead of him.[17] In time this would work, and he used a mixture of charm and intimidation to be named crown prince and heir in 2017. In March 2015, however, his position was less assured, and he viewed the Yemen conflict as a means to bolster his domestic standing. The intervention came alongside a PR campaign at home to paint the young prince as a military leader. However, MBS had little knowledge of his southern neighbour. Indeed, the Saudi royal family had traditionally given the Yemen brief to one prince at a time and, after the holder died in 2011, no one had taken charge, leaving MBS and his government under-informed of the changing dynamics on the ground.[18]

This was not simply an ambitious prince's folly though: Riyadh had serious concerns over developments in Yemen. First and foremost, they worried about Iran and the Houthis. In the 2000s, when Saleh was seeking support from Saudi Arabia for his wars on the Houthis, he persuaded Riyadh that the Zaydi militia were receiving money and weapons from Iran. Saudi leaders were convinced and ever since feared that any Houthi victory in Yemen would benefit their arch-rivals. Even before the civil war, they worried the Houthis would become a Yemeni equivalent of Hezbollah, the Iranian-sponsored Lebanese Shia militia that fires rockets into Israel. With the Houthis' march into first Sanaa and then Aden, Riyadh now worried that the whole of Yemen would be transformed into a pro-Iranian satellite. Indeed, some of the first Saudi aerial assaults in 2015 were on Houthi military installations believed to house ballistic missiles that could reach Saudi soil. These fears were certainly fuelled by sectarian considerations: Saudi Arabia is a staunch defender of Sunni Islam. However, in the past, Riyadh backed Yemen's Shia monarchs in the North Yemeni civil war, while Saleh himself was of Zaydi origin, so their concern was more motivated by the Houthis' perceived pro-Iran ideology rather than an automated anti-Shia agenda.[19] The recent context mattered too. Since 2003, when Iran had benefited from the US invasion of Iraq to turn that country from an enemy into an ally, Saudi Arabia feared that its rival was in the ascendancy. From Iraq to Syria to Lebanon, Riyadh already felt its regional influence squeezed, and now it believed Iran was getting a foothold on its doorstep.

Beyond the threat from the Houthis and Iran, and a general fear of instability in Yemen, Saudi Arabia was also worried about the Jihadist presence to its south. Al-Qaeda in the Arabian Peninsula (AQAP) had stepped up their activities in recent years, including targeting Saudi officials. Many in Riyadh rightly feared that prolonged anarchy in Yemen would provide space for Jihadists to thrive. This fear was particularly acute given that the recent wars in Syria and Iraq had led to the emergence of Islamic State in 2014. A further factor was

Riyadh's relationship with the United States. Despite the US being historically Saudi Arabia's most important international ally, ties were strained under Barack Obama, whom Riyadh felt had been too quick to abandon their ally, the president of Egypt, when he faced public protests in 2011. They were also strongly opposed to Obama's negotiations with Iran over its nuclear programme, with Saudi urging a more hard-line approach. Fears about the United States' reliability, particularly in the face of the Iranian threat, had prompted Saudi Arabia to invest heavily in its armed forces. Military spending jumped from 7 per cent to 13 per cent of GDP from 2011 to 2015, for a while making Saudi the fourth highest global spender on arms after the US, China, and Russia.[20] MBS therefore felt he had to get involved directly to sort out Yemen, given the US was unlikely to help, but also that he had a vastly superior military to the Houthi–Saleh coalition. Indeed, MBS believed the whole campaign would be over within six weeks.[21]

Instead, it became a quagmire that some have labelled 'Saudi Arabia's Vietnam', after the South-East Asian conflict that drained the US in the 1960s and 1970s.[22] Even though Riyadh suffered far fewer casualties than the US did in South-East Asia due to a reliance on air power rather than ground troops, Yemen became a war in which it struggled to achieve its goals or exit without a huge loss of face. Moreover, Saudi intervention had the opposite effect to that desired regarding the Houthis and Iran: the invasion prompted the Houthis to deepen their ties with Tehran as they sought help to repel the Arab coalition. While the war may have boosted MBS's domestic position, this might have happened anyway given his other moves against his rivals, and it increased criticism of him, especially when the Houthis launched drone and missile attacks on Saudi soil. The war also damaged Saudi's international image, as it seemed to be bombing Yemen recklessly, causing untold civilian casualties, while its navy blockaded ports and so worsened the humanitarian crisis. It further dented their military prestige as years of intervention still didn't defeat the Houthis, despite their vastly inferior forces.

A Bloody Stalemate

The coalition that intervened in Yemen in March 2015 was genuinely international. All the GCC states bar Oman were represented, as well as Egypt, Jordan, Morocco, Sudan, and Senegal, and mercenaries from as far away as Colombia and Australia, who were employed by the UAE. It further received support from the United States and other Western governments, though not in combat roles. However, this was a Saudi-led operation, with Riyadh paying for most of the military costs and financing various sweeteners to persuade countries to join. The only other real player of note was the UAE, which had its own agenda in Yemen. The other states took a back seat, leading critics to claim they were there to offer Saudi Arabia's actions an air of international credibility rather than having any true commitment to the cause.

The assault began with weeks of air strikes against Houthi positions, followed by the deployment of a limited number of ground troops. At first this saw rapid success. The Yemeni air force was destroyed, giving the coalition air supremacy, and by July this helped a Hadi counter-attack drive the Houthis from Aden. But progress soon stalled. The coalition was reluctant to commit large numbers of troops, fearing high casualties, and the anti-Houthi forces were too disunited. The result was a gruelling stalemate whereby the Houthis remained firmly lodged in their 2015 positions, roughly covering the old North Yemen, while an array of forces loosely loyal to Hadi remained in the south, backed by the coalition. Fighting continued along the border zones and over hotly contested cities like Taiz, but with only limited movement. At times one side sought to break the impasse, like the coalition attack on Hodeidah in 2018, or the Houthi assault on Marib in 2021, but these were few and far between, and rarely shifted the conflict. Without a war of movement, partly due to his reluctance to commit troops, MBS and his commanders concluded that the best strategy was to rely on air power and a naval blockade to force submission. But this didn't work, leading instead to the Houthis consolidating their position, while ordinary Yemenis suffered under the blockade and bombardment.

Nor did the coalition bolster Hadi, quite the opposite. Riyadh supported Hadi's claim to the presidency, but much of its support was channelled to Islah elements in the government. Despite their general hostility to the Muslim Brotherhood, with whom Islah is aligned, Saudi Arabia had historically financed the Yemeni Islamists and saw them as the best way of beating the Houthis, especially along the Yemen/Saudi border in the north. In contrast, the UAE could not ignore Islah's affiliation with the Muslim Brotherhood, whom Abu Dhabi deeply opposed. Saudi Arabia and the UAE also had different goals in Yemen. While Riyadh was focused on removing the Houthi threat in the north, Abu Dhabi hoped to strengthen its position in the south as part of a wider desire to boost its situation in the Gulf of Aden. It used the conflict to build new positions in Eritrea and Somaliland (see chapter 10). Early on it established Aden as an operations base, built airstrips on Yemen's Red Sea islands and a military base on the Yemeni Indian Ocean island of Socotra. To help facilitate this ambition the UAE largely shunned Riyadh's traditional Yemeni allies and cultivated its own clients in the south.[23]

The UAE financed and trained their own Yemeni militias, with names like the 'Security Belt' and 'Elite Forces', who were independent of Hadi's government. Ironically, many were drawn from southern Salafists, more religiously conservative than Islah, with some even linked to AQAP. However, for the UAE, they constituted a loyal, non-Islah force in south Yemen. But their ties to the government were fraught and, when Hadi sought to reassert his position by sacking the governor of Aden in 2017, tensions erupted. The sacked governor, with the backing of the UAE and Security Belt militia, quickly formed a 'Southern Transitional Council' (STC), declaring the south independent of Yemen and Hadi. In early 2018, STC forces seized control of Aden, ejecting the government. A year later Hadi began a counter-offensive, prompting the UAE to launch air strikes that forced them back. This open warfare between Saudi and UAE-backed Yemeni factions was a sign of how chaotic and unsuccessful the coalition's intervention had become. Eventually Saudi Arabia brokered a loose power-sharing agreement between the STC and the government. But it left the south effectively partitioned. The UAE-aligned STC and its militia controlled Aden, a few other coastal cities and the island of Socotra. Hadi, who had now lost two capitals, both Sanaa and Aden, nominally ruled over the southern interior, though in reality it was local militias, including Islah-aligned forces and, in some places, Jihadists, that governed. After years of war the internationally recognised president of Yemen had little left of Yemen to rule over.

In contrast, the Houthis' hold in the north was strengthened. Partly this was due to increased support from Iran, the very thing Saudi Arabia had wanted to avoid. Despite Iran's increased regional activism after the 1979 Islamic Revolution, Yemen was not considered important for Tehran. Though they shared the Shia faith, Zaydis were theologically very different from the Twelver Shias in Iran and elsewhere in the region, like Hezbollah in Lebanon. A handful of Zaydi leaders (who would go on to become prominent Houthis) studied theology in Iran but beyond that relations were limited.[24] While Saleh claimed there were deep ties between the Houthis and Iran in the 2000s, the US among others believed this to have been a story concocted by the Yemeni dictator, and that the Zaydi rebellion emerged organically not at the behest of, or with much help from, Tehran.

This changed in 2009 when the Houthis began to attack Saudi Arabia directly, prompting Iran's leaders to recognise they could prove a useful asset to harass Riyadh. Contact between the two sides increased and, while little material support was actually sent, Tehran mischievously played up its closeness to the Houthis, correctly assuming that Saudi would expend energy focusing on Yemen that it might alternatively deploy trying to block Iran's ambitions elsewhere in the region.[25] MBS's intervention of 2015 might be seen as Riyadh 'taking Tehran's bait', given that it led to a draining war for Saudi Arabia fighting what it saw as an Iranian proxy, when the Islamic Republic had committed few resources. With Riyadh opting in 2015 to reduce its role in the Syrian civil war, where it had been financing rebels fighting Iran's allies, in order to focus on Yemen, this proved a huge return on a very limited investment for Tehran.

After the 2015 invasion, however, Iran did step up its support. Sophisticated weaponry was smuggled into Sanaa, allowing the Houthis to fire long-range missiles deep into Saudi Arabia. Money and training were provided, including the dispatch of Hezbollah and Iranian officers to share methods and tactics.[26] Yet while this constituted a significant increase from Iran and certainly aided the Houthis' survival against the coalition's assault, Iran's support was never even close to that provided to Hadi's government by Saudi Arabia and its allies.

More significant in explaining the Houthis' survival were their domestic policies. Though the war led to widespread suffering, it was not difficult for the Houthis to (correctly) point to the Saudi-led coalition, rather than themselves, being the primary source of people's misery. For those who were inclined to criticise, the Houthis developed their own security and intelligence networks, akin to those of the Saleh era, to keep people in line. They also ruled differently in different places: seeking consensus in the Zaydi-dominated northern highlands, while ruling more like occupiers in the Sunni-dominated port of Hodeidah.[27] Moreover, given the levels of starvation and suffering, few were in a position to make much of a challenge. The one group that did pose a threat, Saleh and his loyalists, were dispatched in 2017. Houthi operatives in the intelligence service had intercepted messages between Saleh and the UAE, in which the former president appeared to be readying to switch sides once more. This led to armed clashes between Houthis and Saleh supporters, prompting Saleh to formally renounce the alliance. Yet this proved a trick too far for Saleh. The enraged Houthis attacked his home in

Sanaa and killed him. This prompted a purge of pro-Saleh forces from Sanaa and northern Yemen, leaving the Houthis in sole charge.[28] Their confidence grew, prompting them to reorganise the government structure, set a new education curriculum, enforce strict conservative laws, and send ambassadors to Iran and Syria. Though they remained under bombardment and siege, the rebellious militia now had an ever-tighter grip on the state in the north.

The longer the war dragged on, the more it attracted international attention. The United States and other Western powers had been involved indirectly from the beginning, and long before. US counter-terror funding had facilitated Saleh's divisive rule in the 2000s and the US had been reluctant for him to depart in 2011. Seeing Yemen primarily through an anti-terror lens though, Washington accepted Hadi, as he also proved subservient to the US in the war against Al-Qaeda. The White House was given free rein in its pursuit of terror-ists, leading to over 100 US drone strikes on Yemen's citizens in Hadi's first five years in office.[29] Washington was wary about military inter-vention in Yemen and chose not to join the Saudi-led coalition, despite Riyadh's lobbying. President Obama had pledged to reduce American involvement in the Middle East and had just started a new military campaign against ISIS after it rampaged across Iraq and Syria, so wasn't keen to send troops to Yemen as well. He did not see the Houthis as a major threat to American interests and believed that Saudi Arabia, with its arsenal of Western weapons, would be able to contain the threat without him. That said, he still endorsed the invasion, which was announced by Riyadh in Washington, and offered significant material support, such as sharing intelligence, arms resupply, and vital in-air refuelling.[30] Obama's endorsement was partly aimed at recom-pensing Saudi Arabia for the US nuclear talks with Iran, about which Riyadh was furious. The UK and France similarly offered the coalition support, continuing to sell weapons and share intelligence.

Western publics, however, increasingly challenged their govern-ments' support for the coalition as horrific images of bombing and famine appeared in the media. More pressure was added in 2018 when dissident Saudi journalist Jamal Khashoggi was murdered in Istanbul – on the orders of MBS, it was widely believed – making the prince and his Yemeni war even more unpopular abroad. There was a particular focus on arms sales, with Western editorials and lawmakers asking why their leaders continued to sell weapons to a leader who was bombing and starving children in Yemen. Yet most Western governments were not deterred. In his final days in office, Obama symbolically withheld £350 million of military aid over concerns the Saudis were breaching humanitarian law, but this was a drop in the ocean compared to the $115 billion worth of arms sold to Saudi over the course of his eight-year presidency.[31] Moreover, Obama's successor, Donald Trump, immediately reversed this decision and then agreed the biggest single Saudi–US arms deal in history, worth $110 billion. Trump was far closer to Saudi Arabia and MBS than his predecessor, being more comfortable cosying up to authoritarians, and sharing Riyadh's strong opposition to Iran. This provided the Saudi-led coalition with some shielding from international criticism during his four-year presidency. Even the UK, which had no such affinity with MBS, continued its arms sales. In 2019 its High Court temporarily forced London to halt arms sales due to concerns this would be a breach of humanitarian law, but when a government report concluded there was 'no clear risk' of this, shipments resumed the following year.[32]

There were attempts by the UN and others, notably Yemen's neighbour Oman, to end the conflict, or at least ease the suffering, but with little success. Before the war, the UN passed resolutions in support of the GCC process and mediated the National Dialogue Conference, although critics argued they were unhelpful. With the UN recognising Hadi as the legitimate ruler of Yemen it is unsurprising that it blamed the Houthis and Saleh for the outbreak of war, sanctioning both. With Western powers backing the Saudi-led coalition and Russia and China showing little interest in the conflict, the UN was slow to make serious attempts at peace-making. But with so many states supporting the conflict, as well as most of the Yemeni protagonists, the UN proved impotent when efforts were eventually made. Proposals for a Ramadan ceasefire in 2017 went nowhere. It was only in 2018, three years after the war began, that any kind of serious negotiations took place.

This process, known as the Stockholm Agreement, came after major advances by UAE-backed forces along the Red Sea coast, leaving the Houthi-held port of Hodeidah under siege. This prompted the first face-to-face negotiations of the war between Hadi's government and the Houthis, in Sweden. A deal was struck that prevented a major military confrontation over Hodeidah, which many feared would be a humanitarian catastrophe, given it was the main port for vital food imports for northern Yemen. The agreement included provisions for a prisoner swap, humanitarian corridors, and a withdrawal of forces by both sides from Hodeidah, and some hoped it might be the first step in further negotiations to end the war. However, critics charge that the UN rushed the process, leaving the language ambiguous and open to interpretation, which the Houthis exploited. Indeed, once UAE-backed forces had withdrawn and their hold on Hodeidah was secured, Sanaa transferred troops eastward and launched a massive military attack on the Islah stronghold of Marib. This battle saw the Houthis come incredibly close to capturing the heart of Yemen's oil- and gas-producing territory, prompting a fierce government rearguard action. Yet there were few consequences for the Houthis for reneging on the Stockholm Agreement and the international community showed little interest in renewing peace efforts.

The global Coronavirus pandemic, followed by a change of leadership in Washington, put Yemen on the international backburner. Trump's successor, Joe Biden, had initially placed Yemen high on his foreign policy agenda, but events shifted his focus elsewhere: on reviving the nuclear Iran deal, global competition with China, and, from 2022, the war in Ukraine. While he rolled back some of Trump's pro-Saudi measures, including removing the Houthis from the designated 'terrorist' list and ending support for 'offensive' Saudi military operations, there was little indication that he or other leaders in the UN Security Council would make a renewed effort to help bring the conflict to an end.[33] The arrival of a new administration prompted some rethinking in Riyadh and Abu Dhabi (see chapter 9). Already the UAE had recognised the war couldn't be 'won' and pulled back its forces in 2019–20. Saudi Arabia, conscious of the failure of its campaign and the negative press its bombing was receiving, especially from the Biden administration, also changed tack. It pressured Hadi, who had lost all authority, to resign in April 2022, transferring power to a newly formed Presidential Leadership Council (PLC), set up to seek a solution to the conflict. A few days before Saudi Arabia had announced a unilateral ceasefire in all military operations to allow for dialogue. This then led to a UN-brokered truce from April 2022. Though it theoretically lasted only six months, when the October deadline passed, hostilities did not resume. Instead, the Houthis and Saudis engaged in talks brokered by Oman, with the former pushing for recognition of its control at the expense of the PLC. While Riyadh was tired of war it was reluctant to make such a concession given the loss of face that would come with it

An Arabian Somalia

Of all the states facing instability after the 2011 Arab Uprisings, Yemen's situation seems the most bleak. Already the poorest Middle Eastern country after decades of poor governance and economic mismanagement, aided by foreign governments and international financial institutions, Yemen was the state least able to absorb the shocks of prolonged conflict. Given the decades of divide and rule by Abdullah Ali Saleh, perhaps some kind of conflict after his fall was inevitable. Hadi's Government of National Unity always faced an uphill task to reconcile Yemen's various factions, whether Houthis, southern separatists, Islamists, or former Saleh loyalists, and it was not helped by the decision to allow Saleh to remain in Yemen after leaving office, where he plotted his return. However, the scale and extent of the conflict was not necessary and foreign actors hold a lot of the responsibility for escalating the situation.

Saudi Arabia is especially culpable, given its decision to launch a major intervention in 2015. Without it, it is possible that Hadi could have been defeated, the war could have been concluded far sooner and the humanitarian crisis been avoided. Yet Riyadh instead transformed a local civil war into a major international conflict, bringing in billions of dollars' worth of firepower to rain down on the Yemeni people. Moreover, an aversion to using ground troops meant Saudi was not able to land the decisive blow it had hoped for, ensuring a long-running quagmire. Yet other powers also contributed greatly. Iran played a less prominent but equally unhelpful role. Though the Houthis are no Iranian puppets, Tehran played up their relationship in the 2000s to provoke Saudi Arabia, and then sent considerable military aid and assistance after 2015, seemingly with little thought for the violent consequences for Yemen's population. The UAE, meanwhile, pursued its own agenda in the south, helping to fragment Hadi's weak government further and lessening its already slim chances of success. Finally, Western governments, especially the United States, have been deeply hypocritical. They helped Saleh rule for decades, contributing to the emergence of the initial crisis, and then refused either to end their lucrative arms contracts or exert real leverage on the belligerents to help the UN resolve the conflict once it began.

The result is that, thirty years after an optimistic unification, a formal or informal partition looks likely. Yemen increasingly resembles the long-running disorder of Somalia on the other side of the Gulf of Aden. Some hope was raised in 2023, after China brokered a regional détente between Saudi Arabia and Iran, potentially paving the way for serious negotiations on Yemen to follow up the existing ceasefire. But whatever the outcome of any peace negations, Riyadh's original war goal of removing the Houthis from Sanaa looks unachievable. At home, MBS's priorities had shifted towards economic diversification, including promoting Saudi Arabia as a global sport and entertainment destination, an agenda damaged by the ongoing conflict and the prospect of missiles being hurled over the southern border. MBS might therefore cut his losses in Yemen, either by negotiation or unilateral withdrawal – something likely to be welcomed by ordinary Yemenis who by now have little love for Riyadh. Such a move would likely see the Houthis in charge of the north but leave the south in a precarious situation. Like Hadi before it, the PLC has little authority and, without the Gulf states' financial and military backing, the various militias could turn on one another as they compete for southern Yemen's limited resources. A second Yemen civil war, in the south only, could easily break out. Combined with ongoing water shortages and climate change, such a scenario would bring with it refugee flows as well as providing a safe haven for the AQAP Jihadists and others already present. None of this is desirable for Western or regional actors, but they have played a considerable role in bringing it about.

LEBANON

SYRIA

Tyre

Golan
Heights

Acre

*Occupied by Israel
since 1967*

Haifa

Sea of Galilee

Nazareth

*Mediterranean
Sea*

Jenin

Netanya

Nablus

Jordan

W E S T

Tel Aviv

B A N K

Lod

Ramallah

Jericho

J O R D A N

Jerusalem

Ashdod

Bethlehem

Ashkelon

Dead Sea

Erez

Gaza City

Hebron

GAZA

Rahat

Khan Younis

Rafah

Beersheba

E G Y P T

*N e g e v
D e s e r t*

| Palestinian Authority areas |
| 0 .... 40 miles |
| 0 .... 40 km |

Palestine

4

Palestine
The Vanishing Land

Palestine. Israel. The Holy Land. Names that arouse passions far beyond the Middle East. The conflict over this thin strip of land in the eastern Mediterranean remains a global *cause célèbre*, with people who have never set foot there arguing vehemently over rights, wrongs, and responsibilities. Yet despite its high profile, the dispute today looks more and more irresolvable. This has been made worse by an apparent growing disinterest by global leaders. Where once US presidents would put resolving the conflict at the heart of their international agenda, recent inhabitants of the White House have treated it like an afterthought. While Middle Eastern leaders were once compelled to publicly back the Palestinians, a new generation of Arab autocrats have explored peace with Israel. This declining salience reflects changing global, regional, and local trends. Western governments have been less concerned with the Middle East and have de-prioritised resolving a conflict at its heart. The Arab solidarity that once drove neighbouring states has weakened, at least at a governmental if not a popular level. Locally, Israel's governments have successfully normalised their preferred option of conflict management over conflict resolution, containing international criticism of its behaviour sufficiently to maintain the status quo. But such neglect is unsustainable and, left to fester, the unresolved conflict retains the threat of suddenly exploding, as occurred in October 2023. Palestinian Islamists, Hamas, launched an unprecedented attack, in turn prompting a massive reprisal that saw Israeli forces decimate Gaza.

The conflict is often incorrectly viewed as primarily a religious one between Jews and Muslims.[1] Sadly, from this false starting point, supporters of one side or the other use the dispute to justify an ugly anti-Semitism or Islamophobia towards Jews or Muslims respectively. But religious difference did not cause the problems. For centuries, Jews lived among the Palestinians, who themselves are a mixture of Muslims and Christians, without their religious differences provoking war.[2] Instead, it was the development of nationalism in the late nineteenth century: European Jews moving to Palestine to form their own safe haven from persecution, and the Palestinian reaction against them. Religion has played a role. Judaism was the uniting characteristic of the Zionists and the holy Jewish sites located in Palestine made it their preferred homeland. Meanwhile the importance of holy Islamic sites in East Jerusalem form an important component of Palestinian nationalism.[3] Moreover, in recent decades extremists on both sides have used religion to justify their violence. These religious differences may have been exacerbated by the conflict rather than causing it, but the Israeli and Palestinian extremists who emphasise them today make bridging the divide even harder.

Such extremists might also be viewed as a symptom rather than a cause of the continuing impasse. More moderate leaders on both sides have had opportunities to resolve the dispute but either not taken them or have done so and then failed. Their actions have been supported and facilitated by outside players, especially the United States, which has at times been almost blindly indulgent of Israeli intransigence. But regional players have not helped, with Egypt, Syria, Iran, and others making their own negative contributions.

A Century of Dispossession

Where to begin? Even the starting point is hotly contested. For many Israelis, their claim to Palestine dates to biblical times, when Jews were led to the promised land by Moses. Jews lived there for centuries, until the first and second century AD, when a series of expulsions by the ruling Romans, alongside later emigrations, saw the Jews scattered around the Middle East and Europe. For nearly two millennia Jews lived in Christian Europe but experienced regular persecution. In the nineteenth century, a group of European Jewish intellectuals concluded that the only way to be safe was to build their own state. This nationalist ideology, known as Zionism, quickly adopted the goal of returning Jews to their ancestral home in Palestine. This is where the story begins for the Palestinians, with the arrival of European outsiders. The people who became known as Palestinians were the Arabic-speakers who had settled in the area in the intervening millennia. By the nineteenth century this was a mostly Muslim population, with a sizeable Christian minority. Jews, Arabic-speakers with little connection to the European Zionists, made up only 4 per cent of the population.[4] However, Palestinian nationalism was in its infancy, and most would have identified themselves by their religion, Arab ethnicity or as citizens of the ruling Ottoman empire rather than as Palestinians. This prompted some Zionists to argue these Arabs could move elsewhere in the Middle East, having less attachment to the land than the Jews. However, the advent of Zionism sparked a fierce reaction by the native population.

Settlers started to arrive from the 1870s, mostly buying land from absent landlords who lived elsewhere in the Ottoman empire. This was a time of mass migration of Jews fleeing European persecution, and the tens of thousands who headed to Palestine formed only a fraction of the millions who headed elsewhere, to New York for example. At first there was little objection from the native Arab population. After all, this was a tiny Jewish enclave in the vast

Ottoman state.[5] This changed during the First World War. Zionist lobbyists persuaded Britain that a Jewish state in Palestine, close to the Suez Canal and safeguarding the route to India, was in its interests. The British government was also motivated by its own anti-Semitism: a desire to reduce the number of Jewish immigrants coming to the UK. London also, conspiratorially, believed Jews had such influence over both Washington and the new revolutionary government in Moscow that supporting this enterprise might persuade the US to join the war and keep Russia in it.[6] In 1917, then, the British cabinet issued the Balfour Declaration that stated it would 'view with favour the establishment in Palestine of a national home for the Jewish people'. Once the war ended, an entity called 'Palestine' was carved out of former Ottoman lands and created as a League of Nations mandate to be administered by London with the explicit task of helping to create a national home for Jews. Both the Balfour Declaration and the articles of the Mandate insisted that 'nothing shall be done which may prejudice the civil and religious rights of existing non-Jewish communities in Palestine'.[7] Yet this was contradictory. How could a Jewish majority state be created without impacting the civil rights of the existing population? And why should they accept being displaced by outsiders?

It soon became clear that Britain had sown disruptive seeds. Jewish immigration increased during the mandate period, prompting increased resentment from the Palestinians. The rise of the Nazis in Germany led even more Jews to flee Europe, increasing the Jewish population of Palestine from 18 per cent in 1932 to 31 per cent seven years later. They brought considerable wealth and expertise, allowing the Jewish part of the economy, which excluded Arabs, to become larger than the Palestinian sector.[8] Meanwhile, Jewish settlers were building shadow institutions, whether educational, military, or economic, creating a de facto state in the background. While the British administrators quietly supported this, they obstructed Palestinian efforts to do likewise. Palestine's elite, the leading families from the Ottoman era, struggled to effectively confront the challenge. With the elites failing, popular opposition to both Britain and the Zionists erupted in a major revolt in 1936–39. This had three significant consequences. First, it was violently crushed by Britain, leaving the Palestinian leadership weakened, making it harder for them to resist a bigger crisis a decade later. Second, Britain armed and trained Jewish groups to help defeat the revolt, improving their capabilities for the wars to come. Finally, exasperated, London considered partitioning Palestine. Their proposal, to create a small Jewish state and a large Arab state, was rejected by both sides, but the idea of partition was born.

The Second World War proved as transformative as the First. For the Zionists, the horrific murder of 6 million Jews in the Holocaust underlined their urgent need for the safety of their own state, and boosted global sympathy. After the war, Britain was exhausted and broke. When the Zionists turned on their former ally in a violent campaign to force them from Palestine, London gave up and referred the matter to the newly formed United Nations. The UN revived the idea of partition, proposing a larger Jewish state made up of 56 per cent of Palestine, and an Arab state of 43 per cent, with Jerusalem remaining in international control. The Palestinian Arabs rejected the plan again, arguing that the Jews owned only 7 per cent of the land (20 per cent of the arable land) and made up only 33 per cent of the population.[9] The Zionist leaders formally accepted, declaring the state of Israel in 1948, though notably not agreeing to the UN's borders. Even before Britain's withdrawal, clashes erupted, with Palestinians living in the area allocated to Israel either fleeing or being forcibly evicted. Once Britain was gone, the situation worsened when the neighbouring Arab states all declared war on Israel. Though larger in size, the Arab militaries were poorly armed and trained and, though they claimed to be helping the Palestinians, their leaders secretly pursued their own agendas. The King of Transjordan occupied the West Bank of the River Jordan, allocated to the Palestinian state by the UN, as well the eastern part of Jerusalem, but then advanced no further. This freed Israel to take on the armies of Syria and Egypt. They defeated both and captured the north and southern parts of the Palestinian state, save for a strip of land around Gaza, which was retained by the Egyptians. By the time an armistice was agreed in 1949, Israel controlled 77 per cent of Mandate Palestine, including the western half of Jerusalem. With Egypt and the newly renamed 'Jordan' holding the remaining land, no Palestinian state was left. Palestinians would forever label the 1948 crisis as the 'Nakba' or 'disaster'.

For the next forty years, the Palestinian cause was expropriated by outsiders. First came the Arab nationalist governments of Egypt and Syria, whose anti-Israeli stance contributed to further wars in 1956 and 1967. The latter proved a disaster for the Arab governments, with Israel defeating the combined forces of Egypt, Syria, and Jordan in six days, and capturing Gaza, East Jerusalem, and the West Bank, as well as Sinai from Egypt and the Golan from Syria. In the aftermath, the UN passed Resolution 242, calling for Israel's withdrawal in exchange for peace with its neighbours. However, there was ambiguity about what 'withdrawal' meant. In the English version of the resolution, it stated that 'territories' should be evacuated, while in the French version it stated more specifically 'the territories'.[10] Israeli leaders have, ever since, insisted this means they only need to withdraw from some occupied territories, while their opponents have insisted it means all the land taken. This was notable, as the capture of all of Mandate Palestine, including all of Jerusalem, emboldened right-wingers in Israel, who insisted the land should be retained and settled by Jews, while Jerusalem should be Israel's 'united and indivisible' capital.

The blow of 1967 ended any hopes of reversing 1948 and the Arab governments adopted the more modest goal of recovering their lost territory. Egypt, which along with Syria fought another war with Israel in 1973 that ended in stalemate, made peace in exchange for

Sinai in 1979. Meanwhile, Jordan gave up its claim to the West Bank, making peace in 1994. Syria remained officially at war but, without allies, could do only limited damage. The retreat of Arab governments provided space for Palestinians living in exile to take up the fight. The Palestinian Liberation Organization (PLO) was a coalition of different fighting groups that launched raids into Israel and the occupied territories, first from Jordan and then from Lebanon. However, Israel launched reprisals on their host countries, culminating in the 1982 invasion of Lebanon, which caused the PLO to be evacuated to far-off Tunisia.

A Process but No Peace

With their external champions defeated, the Palestinians under occupation in the West Bank and Gaza led their own rebellion. From 1987 to 1991 a series of strikes and protests, known as the 'Intifada' or 'shaking off' gathered steam. The movement was largely non-violent but was met with force: Israeli defence minister Yitzhak Rabin ordered his troops to use 'force, power and beatings'.[11] This proved a misjudgement, as Israel's global reputation plummeted, with footage of villages being razed and boys throwing rocks against tanks broadcast around the world. Eventually Israel was pressured by its principal ally, the United States, to engage in peace talks, albeit reluctantly. This proved a lifeline to the PLO, which had little to do with the Intifada. Soon after the rebellion began, the PLO made a dramatic concession: recognising Israel's right to exist and giving up their claim to all of Mandate Palestine, instead lobbying for a truncated Palestinian state made up of the West Bank and Gaza, with East Jerusalem as its capital. This idea of a 'two-state solution' gained currency and formed the basis of talks between the PLO and Israel when they eventually came about. These secret talks, held in the Norwegian capital of Oslo, established accords that saw the PLO rule over parts of Gaza and the West Bank. Key areas of disagreement, such as the status of Jerusalem, whether the many Palestinian refugees could return home, and the degree of independence of the new Palestinian state, would be determined later. After decades in exile, the PLO leader Yasser Arafat returned in 1994 and was elected president of the newly created 'Palestinian Authority' (PA).

However, the PLO has been criticised for giving up too much for too little.[12] The Tunisia exiles were negotiating from a position of weakness. Instead of being the first step towards Palestinian statehood, the PA became an accomplice of Israeli occupation. Most of Gaza and the West Bank remained in Israeli hands. The PA was put in charge of the densely populated urban areas where Israel expected it to keep order. Peace talks between the two sides continued, but advanced little. It didn't help that Rabin, now prime minister and a convert to the need to negotiate, was assassinated in 1995 by a right-wing Israeli extremist opposed to the peace process. Even he had been reluctant to consider full Palestinian statehood. Most of his successors were even more cautious, especially after Palestinian Islamists, Hamas, initiated a campaign of suicide bombings against Israeli civilians. A final set of American-brokered peace talks collapsed in 2000 without agreement.

For Palestinians, conditions worsened after the Oslo accords. A small PLO elite benefited, but most people got poorer.[13] Checkpoints and guard towers sprouted up across the West Bank and Gaza, marking out the different areas controlled by Israel and the PA, denying the free movement Palestinians had previously enjoyed and crippling the economy. Meanwhile settlement-building and Israeli land expropriation continued. These frustrations, plus the lack of progress on peace talks, boiled over into a second Intifada, far more violent than the first. Islamists, and even some groups aligned with the secular PLO, increased the suicide bombings, prompting Israel in 2002 to re-invade the PA-held parts of the West Bank. Arafat's compound was surrounded and he, humiliatingly, was prevented from leaving until, two years later, his health failed, and he was permitted to fly to seek treatment in Paris, where he died.

Arafat's successor, Mahmoud Abbas, also failed, overseeing no peace process breakthrough while the Palestinians fragmented. Israeli domestic politics became dominated by right-wing political parties, who were, at best, sceptical of the peace process and, at worst, overtly opposed. A large separation barrier, including concrete walls 30 feet high, was erected around settlements and Jerusalem to keep out suicide bombers. But it also absorbed 8 per cent of the West Bank and separated many Palestinians from their families and property.[14] Successive US presidents led efforts to revive the peace process, but these proved either too pro-Israel for Abbas to accept or were derailed by Israel's leaders. Meanwhile the Palestinians divided. Hamas, surprisingly, won the PA's legislative elections in 2006. Because the Islamists did not recognise Israel and refused to renounce violence, Israel and its Western allies considered Hamas terrorists and refused to engage with a PA headed by it. With Western and Israeli encouragement, Abbas launched a botched coup. Hamas reacted by seizing control of the Gaza Strip, a region from which Israeli premier Ariel Sharon had unilaterally withdrawn all settlements a year earlier, concluding that its huge Arab majority made it unviable as a permanent Israeli holding. Hamas ejected all PA troops from Gaza and since then the Palestinian territories have remained divided. Gaza is controlled by Hamas but mostly sealed off by Israel and its ally Egypt. Hamas sporadically raid Israel, or launch rockets at civilians, prompting heavy Israeli military responses. This has caused massive damage and Gazans live in abject poverty. The West Bank, meanwhile, remains mostly controlled by Israel, with Abbas's PA back in charge of some urban areas. Abbas has not called presidential or legislative elections since 2006, overseeing an increasingly corrupt and autocratic rule.[15] Settlements continue to be built, while East Jerusalem is virtually cut off from the West Bank. Any kind of Palestinian state looks like a dim prospect.

Israel's Shift Rightwards

The Israeli government bears considerable responsibility for the failure of the peace process. There have been some serious engagements with the Palestinians. Rabin, before his assassination, tried to convince his Labor Party and the Israeli public of the merits of peace. Likewise, in 2000, one of his successors, Ehud Barak, offered Arafat a Palestinian state, albeit one that fell well short of the PLO's demands on borders, Jerusalem, and refugees. In the years 2006–8, another premier, Ehud Olmert, conducted secret negotiations that would have given the Palestinians a demilitarised state including most of the West Bank and Gaza, with Jerusalem shared, and a symbolic fraction of the refugees returning home.[16] Yet in all these cases, leaders were not able or willing to make sufficient concessions and undermined their own peace credentials. Rabin did not halt settlement construction. Barak only negotiated with Arafat once his earlier peace efforts with Syria had failed and with his government close to collapse, viewing peace as a route to domestic political survival. Olmert was unwilling to concede on dismantling key settlements as demanded by Abbas, and the talks collapsed after Israel launched a military strike on Gaza. These were the most 'dovish' of Israel's recent leaders, and they couldn't or wouldn't countenance the concessions needed. Yet recently, even the lengths these premiers were willing to go to have been rejected by successive Israeli governments.

Israel is a diverse and complex democracy and to characterise all 9 million of its citizens as 'right wing' is false. There is a long tradition of left-wing activism in the country, with the founding fathers of the 1940s and 1950s committed to a socialist Zionism led by a Labor Party that dominated the new state's early decades. Some Israelis are fiercely committed to peace with the Palestinians and oppose the occupation, with activist groups like B'Tselem playing a key role in documenting Israel's many human rights violations. That said, there has been a significant right-wing shift. The process began after the

1967 war, when right-wingers argued that the land captured should be kept and settled. They argued for a 'Greater Israel' to cover all of Mandate Palestine, and possibly more. Right-wing parties favouring settling the West Bank, which they called 'Judea and Samaria' after the ancient Jewish kingdoms that existed in those lands, have since come to dominate. The most successful has been Likud, which first came to power in 1977 and has displaced Labor as Israel's most successful party. Likud accelerated the growth of settlements and has helped derail the peace process.

There has not been a Labor government since Barak's in 2000, and by 2022 the party had been reduced to just 4 out of the 120 seats in Israel's Knesset (parliament). Two decades of right-wing leadership, both reflected and reinforced the rightward shift. Hostility to the peace process and Palestinians in general has increased. Most research suggests this owes much to the increase in suicide bombings and attacks on Israeli civilians from the second Intifada onwards, as well as two decades of education policy led by right-wing ministers.[17]

In recent years, the dominant force has been Likud's Benjamin Netanyahu, who was prime minister from 1996 to 1999, and then from 2009 to 2021, before returning to power again in late 2022. A skilled political survivor, Netanyahu has had a transformative impact on Israeli politics and the peace process. His arrival in power in 1996, so soon after the death of Rabin, put the brakes on Oslo, and he similarly abandoned Olmert's negotiations with Abbas when he became premier again in 2009. As prime minister he frustrated US President Barack Obama's attempts to freeze settlement activity. He then wooed the latter's successor, Donald Trump, arguably the most pro-Israel US president in history, encouraging his decision to move the US embassy to Jerusalem, effectively recognising Israel's annexation of the eastern half of the city.[18] Domestically, he contributed to the demonisation of Israel's Palestinian citizens, whipping up anti-Arab feeling during a 2019 re-election campaign.[19] Similarly, when Israeli politics became more fractious, with five elections held in four years, he brought even more right-wing parties into government in a bid to stay in power. In 2022 he took this further by partnering with a party led by a settler who argued for the deportation of Palestinians living in Israel and the West Bank.

For much of Israel's history, the Palestinian issue has played an outsized role in its regional foreign policy. Israel enjoys important relations outside of the Middle East and is expanding its ties to China and India, but its focus remains primarily on ensuring domestic security. After pacifying Egypt and Jordan, via peace treaties, Israel's regional priorities have shifted to minimising the threat from backers of Palestinian militants. Syria is one, having hosted Hamas for decades, as well as the more militant Islamic Jihad. Its collapse into civil war after 2011 (see chapter 1) has limited this threat, and strengthened Israel's grip on the Golan, with international pressure on Israel to give back the occupied heights reducing as the Syrian regime brutalised its own population.

A more serious threat is Iran. Since its 1979 Islamic Revolution, various Iranian leaders have called for Israel's destruction. In recent decades it has sponsored Hamas and Islamic Jihad, as well as using Lebanon and, after 2011, Syria, as a base for anti-Israel Shia militias like Hezbollah. While Israel has mostly tried to contain the threat through occasional incursions and air raids, it is alarmed that Iran's nuclear programme might change the balance of power. Netanyahu has therefore urged international action against Tehran's efforts to develop nuclear technology. He was livid with Obama for agreeing to a peaceful deal in 2015 (see chapter 5), believing Tehran couldn't be trusted, and successfully lobbied Trump to abandon the agreement. However, the Israeli security establishment is not convinced this has been wise, with Trump's actions playing into the hands of hardliners in Tehran, bringing to power hawks who may well seek nuclear weapons. While Israel has its own nuclear arsenal, developed secretly in the 1960s, and retains a close alliance with the US for further protection, Netanyahu and other leaders remain concerned that a nuclear break-out by Tehran will embolden it and its Palestinian, Lebanese, and Syrian allies.

However, a benefit of Iran's increased activism was a softening of Tehran's other regional enemies towards Israel. In 2020, under Donald Trump's stewardship, the UAE and Bahrain signed the Abraham Accords, normalising ties with Israel, later joined by Morocco and Sudan, further breaking the taboo about Arab states making peace with Israel before the Palestinian issue was settled. The UAE was especially keen to access trade and defence relations with Israel, and later encouraged its allies in Sudan to sign up. Morocco, which had long enjoyed not-so-secret ties to Israel due to the substantial Moroccan Jewish community, took the opportunity to bring its relationship into the open. Although Saudi Arabia did not sign itself, it was believed to approve given its very close ties to Bahrain. However, subsequent efforts to encourage Saudi Arabia to normalize ties with Israel, especially by the Biden administration, proved challenging. Firstly Riyadh agreed to a Chinese brokered rapprochement with Iran in March 2023, lessening its need for Israeli friendship. Later that year, Saudi Arabia further cooled its interest following Israel's heavy bombing of Gaza.

The Fragmented West Bank

The three decades since Oslo have left the Palestinians physically separated. Gaza is blockaded, East Jerusalem has been cut off from the rest of the West Bank, which itself has been fragmented into enclaves. Under the Oslo accords the occupied territories were divided into three areas, A, B, and C.[20] Area C is the largest, representing over 60 per cent of the land, and remains completely controlled by Israel. This includes all but one of the settlements, the border with Jordan and access to the Jordan River's water. The Palestinian Authority had direct control over security and administration in Area A, representing 18 per cent of the West Bank, while

Area B (22 per cent of the land) saw it control administration, but left Israel with security control. This is far from the statehood the PA thought it was signing up to in 1993. The PA administers 87 per cent of the West Bank Palestinian population in Areas A and B but controls barely 18 per cent of the land. These sectors are not contiguous, but dozens of tiny enclaves, resembling the Bantustans of Apartheid South Africa, with Israel controlling everything and everyone that goes in and out. Indeed, Human Rights Watch, Amnesty International, and a host of external critics have described the occupation as legally constituting apartheid, much to Israel and its supporters' outrage.[21] Yet near-constant footage of the Israeli military's heavy-handed treatment reinforces this characterisation, and it is one increasingly used by the Palestinians themselves. While Israel insists its collective punishment, widespread arrests, and house demolitions is necessary to defeat terrorism, Palestinians and their supporters argue this is meant to intimidate the native population to force them from the land Israel wishes to colonise.

The growth of West Bank settlements and the treatment of Jerusalem offers more evidence on this. According to the UN Office for the Coordination of Humanitarian Affairs (OCHA), in 2020 there were over 630,000 Israeli settlers living in more than 150 settlements in the West Bank and East Jerusalem.[22] All of these are in contravention of international laws against building on occupied territory, though Israel insists it is not 'occupied territory' since there was no internationally agreed sovereign, neither Jordan nor the Palestinians, before Israel captured the lands. Settlement numbers have risen *since* Oslo. In 1993, there were just over 250,000 settlers, representing 5 per cent of Israel's population, while today they represent 7 per cent. This is a growth from 17 per cent to 22 per cent of the entire West Bank population. Settlements vary in their character and purpose. The larger blocs are built by the government and house a mixture of ideological nationalists and those who are drawn to affordable housing.[23] Others are small outposts set up illegally by religious nationalists

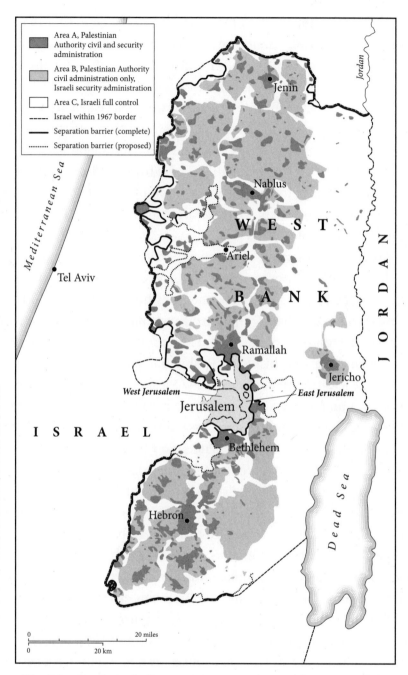

Legend:
- Area A, Palestinian Authority civil and security administration
- Area B, Palestinian Authority civil administration only, Israeli security administration
- Area C, Israeli full control
- Israel within 1967 border
- Separation barrier (complete)
- Separation barrier (proposed)

Mediterranean Sea

Jordan

Jenin

Nablus

WEST

Ariel

Tel Aviv

BANK

JORDAN

Ramallah

Jericho

West Jerusalem

East Jerusalem

Jerusalem

ISRAEL

Bethlehem

Dead Sea

Hebron

0   20 miles
0   20 km

The West Bank, including zones A, B, and C, settlements and the
separation barrier

whom the government often then feels obliged to defend. All Israeli governments, Labor, Likud, and others have been committed to holding onto East Jerusalem. A third of all settlers are in East Jerusalem, and there is a concerted effort to out-populate the Palestinians there. Major infrastructural works have been developed to make the city seem contiguous and many visiting tourists have no idea where West Jerusalem ends, and East Jerusalem begins. To Palestinians this is a constant battle. Those from East Jerusalem fight in the Israeli courts to avoid expropriation of land. Those from the West Bank have been cut off from the city, furthering its de facto separation from Palestine.[24]

This slow colonisation of occupied territory has been facilitated, whether intentionally or not, by the PA and external governments. It is important not to victim-blame the Palestinian leadership, and it is highly possible that Israel would have continued settlement activity whatever the response of the PA, but Mahmoud Abbas has led poorly. Palestinian-American historian Rashid Khalidi describes Abbas as 'one of the least impressive' of the PLO leaders surrounding Arafat, who only found himself as PA president because more talented alternatives had died, including some assassinated by Israel.[25] While the PA has limited power and is dependent on Israel to permit funds to be sent into its West Bank enclaves, Abbas has nevertheless floundered. With Western and Israeli encouragement, he attempted to illegally overthrow Hamas after it won the 2006 parliamentary election, leading to the Islamists' seizure of Gaza. He subsequently agreed to various reconciliation agreements, but they failed to revive the legitimacy of the PA because of Abbas's unwillingness to risk losing power. After he was elected president in 2005, a new election was due four years later, but ever since he has found excuses to delay the poll. Similarly, parliamentary elections were due in 2010, but they have also been postponed. Abbas was spooked by opinion polls suggesting Hamas would defeat his own Fatah party in both contests. He also fears younger Fatah rivals running against him as president, which partly prompted his decision to call off elections scheduled in 2021 barely a month beforehand.

Regional rivalries have exacerbated these tensions. Both Egypt and Jordan encouraged Abbas to postpone the 2021 elections, fearing that Hamas might win. The UAE, in contrast, pushed for the elections to be held, due to its support of one of Abbas' Fatah rivals, whom it hoped would do well. The UAE's interest was an attempt to outmanoeuvre its Gulf rival Qatar, which successfully established itself as a key external player. Qatar's influence is mostly financial, using its largesse to support both the PA and humanitarian aid in Gaza. This gives it leverage over Hamas, allowing it to act as an informal mediator between Hamas, the PA, and Israel. However, these regional attempts to influence West Bank politics are trifling compared to those of the major external player: the United States.

Since the early 1990s, the United States has positioned itself as the essential mediator between Israel and the Palestinians, at the time part of Washington's post-Cold War dominance of regional and global politics. The US hosted various peace talks, including the infamous handshake between Arafat and Rabin with Bill Clinton on the White House lawn. But Washington was never impartial, and heavily favours Israel, for various reasons. Historically, Israel was an ally in the Cold War. Ideologically, the US is a pioneering state that colonised its continent and has sympathy with the similar Zionist project, while many Americans view Israel as a fellow democracy that needs supporting in the mostly authoritarian Middle East. Meanwhile some Christian evangelicals believe a Jewish return to the Holy Land is fulfilment of a biblical prophecy. Domestically, the pro-Israel lobby in the US, led by organisations like the American Israel Public Affairs Committee (AIPAC) wields considerable political influence in a way no pro-Palestinian voices do.[26]

Consequently, most US presidents and their staff have viewed the peace process through a deeply pro-Israel lens. This has played a role in the failures of the process, given the absence of an honest broker, but it has also helped normalise Israel's de facto annexations. George W. Bush, for example, reversed the official US position against settlements by stating that any Israeli-Palestinian agreement should be based on 'facts on the ground', indicating for the first time that Israel might keep some of the West Bank. Donald Trump cut US funding for UNRWA – the UN agency that supports Palestinian refugees – which the PA depends on, and recognised Israeli control over East Jerusalem and the Golan Heights. He then proposed a 'Deal of the Century', which would have created a much-reduced Palestinian state on a portion of the West Bank and Gaza. This was rejected by Abbas and scrapped when Trump lost power, and his successor, Joe Biden, restored UNWRA funding. Some in Biden's Democratic party are less pro-Israel than in the past, and criticism is growing, especially among young Americans, but pro-Israel voices remain dominant. They are sufficiently powerful that Biden dared not reverse Trump's controversial shift on East Jerusalem, edging it further away from the Palestinians.

Gaza under Siege

However frustrating and disheartening life has become for Palestinians in the West Bank, it is nothing in relation to the misery of those in Gaza. Since Hamas seized power in 2007, the population have endured the dual pain of imposed Islamist rule, mirroring Abbas's own autocracy in the West Bank, and a siege by Israel and Egypt. This has shattered Gaza's economy, with unemployment doubling to over 50 per cent, while the availability of vital foodstuffs, building materials, and medicines is severely reduced.[27] Ironically, the blockade has enhanced Hamas's grip on power, as they control the maze of underground tunnels into Egypt (plus a handful into Israel) that are the primary entry point for goods and people. Israel's military operations against the strip have exacerbated the suffering. Three ground invasions in 2008–9, 2012, and 2014, alongside dozens of smaller attacks, were catastropic, while the 2023 war, discussed below, proved even more destructive. According to B'Tselem, between 2009 and 2022, 3,088 were killed in Gaza by Israeli security forces, two-thirds being civilians and nearly 700 being minors. In contrast, over the same period just under 200 Israelis were killed, mostly military personnel, but also civilians hit by the rocket fire that resulted in Israel's incursions in the first place.[28] Beyond the fatalities, the infrastructural damage has been enormous. In 2014 alone, 277 schools and 17 hospitals were damaged, and the destruction displaced nearly a quarter of Gaza's 2 million inhabitants.[29] The wars and siege have left over half of Gazans in a state of poverty, barely surviving in what has been described by many as the world's largest open-air prison.

While Israel characterises Hamas's rule as that of autocratic Jihadists akin to Islamic State, the reality is more complex. The group was inspired by Egypt's Muslim Brotherhood. Hamas, an Arabic acronym for 'the Islamic Resistance Movement', formed during the First Intifada and positioned itself as the true defender of Palestinian nationalism, in contrast to the PLO, which at the time was beginning the compromises that would lead to Oslo. In contrast to Arafat, Hamas leaders continued to claim all of Mandate Palestine as their homeland and refused to recognise Israel. They defiantly rejected the Oslo process and launched their first suicide bombings in the 1990s in a bid to derail it. This earned it particular ire from Israeli leaders and civilians, an ironic twist given the Israeli government had initially encouraged Hamas in the 1980s in the hope they would undermine the PLO.[30] While Israel's international allies, including the US and EU, have designated Hamas as terrorists, the group gained increased popularity among ordinary Palestinians. The failure of Oslo, continued oppression by Israel, and the corruption of Arafat, Abbas, and the PLO elite, made many sympathetic to Hamas's claims to be the true defenders of Palestine. This led to their 2006 election win.

Yet despite their claims of ideological purity, the group has proved pragmatic in power. While some Islamist policies have been put in place, many of the PA's secular institutions remained. Likewise, Hamas's relationship with other Islamists was nuanced. Despite being fellow travellers, Hamas brooked little opposition, and often used force to keep other Islamist groups in line. It viewed many as too radical, especially those sympathetic to Islamic State and Al-Qaeda. Similarly, despite Israel holding Hamas responsible for all rocket fire coming from Gaza, many rockets were fired by non-Hamas groups without its permission, prompting the ruling Islamists to crack down on such rogue activities for fear they would prompt unwanted Israeli incursions. Hamas even watered down some of its harsher stances, issuing a new charter in 2017 that accepted in principle the idea of a Palestinian state made up of Gaza, the West Bank and East Jerusalem. While this didn't recognise Israel or accept Oslo, it suggested the group might be open to a two-state solution. Its willingness to re-engage the PA and sign reconciliation agreements also suggests a pragmatic side.

Hamas's position in Gaza, including its relations with Israel and the PA, is significantly impacted by outside forces. Egypt controls the strip's only non-Israeli land border at Rafah. Being vehemently opposed to the Muslim Brotherhood and friendly with Israel, Cairo has mostly facilitated Israel's siege, keeping Rafah frequently closed. However, ties improved from 2018, with Rafah opened for an extended period after 2021. Partly this was because Hamas seemed to accept a two-state solution in 2017, and partly because Egypt and Gaza wished to improve cooperation against a shared enemy: Islamic State-aligned militants operating in Sinai (see chapter 6). Cairo also wished to break the influence of its then-rival Qatar. As in the West Bank, Qatar used its vast wealth to carve out influence in Gaza. Between 2012 and 2018 it spent over $1 billion on the strip.[31] This included rebuilding homes and infrastructure destroyed in the 2012 and 2014 wars. Less influential, though more vocal on Gaza, has been Qatar's ally Turkey. Turkish leader Recep Tayyip Erdoğan has repeatedly spoken out about the blockade, even severing ties with Israel in

2009. Yet, despite its symbolic support, Turkey has focused its energy and regional clout elsewhere. An indication of this lack of power and prioritisation came when ties with Israel were gradually restored after 2016 without requiring any policy change from Israel on Gaza.

Hamas's close ties to Qatar are partly reflective of its variable relations with Iran. Historically, Hamas and Iran had been close, with Tehran providing weapons, money, and training as part of its ideological opposition to Israel and its sympathy for fellow Islamists. However, Iran cooled its support when Hamas backed Syrian rebels against Tehran's ally, Bashar al-Assad, in the Syrian civil war. Assad had previously housed the Hamas headquarters in Damascus, but the Syrian dictator's repression of Sunni Islamist rebels caused a rupture, prompting the Palestinians to relocate to Qatar. However, as the Syrian rebels faced defeat, Hamas, once again the pragmatic player, reversed course. While it didn't sever ties with Qatar, it reconciled with Assad and welcomed the return of funds and weapons from Iran. Even so, the episode illustrated that Hamas remains an independent outfit and, despite some Israeli claims, is no Iranian proxy.

Palestinians in Israel and the Diaspora

While the focus of Palestinian politics and international relations is understandably the West Bank and Gaza, most of the world's Palestinian population live elsewhere. According to the Palestinian Central Bureau of Statistics, as of 2021 there were 14 million Palestinians in the world, only 5.3 million of whom lived in the occupied territories.[32] After the 1948 *Nakba*, refugees fled and their descendants make up communities of over a hundred thousand each in Chile, the United States, Saudi Arabia, Qatar, and the UAE, as well as smaller diaspora groups elsewhere. The two largest blocs of Palestinians outside the occupied territories, however, are closer to home: the 3–4 million living as permanent refugees in neighbouring states and the 1.8 million Palestinian citizens of Israel.

During Israel's war of independence, over 750,000 Palestinians fled the lands that eventually became the new state, but 150,000 stayed. They and their descendants now make up roughly 20 per cent of Israel's population. A small segment of this group, adherents of the Druze sect of Islam, opted to embrace the new Israeli state and became loyal citizens. The remainder, however, were wary and found themselves under deep suspicion from the new state that placed them under military rule until 1966. Some accommodations were made by Israel. Arabic became an official language alongside Hebrew and all citizens were allowed to vote, although Palestinians did not serve in the military. However, discrimination was routine. Arabs and Jews rarely mixed and Palestinians lived in the poorest neighbourhoods and towns, with less access to services and infrastructure. In recent years the situation has evolved. While some have moved away from their Arabic heritage, a more vocal majority have become increasingly politicised in their push for both better rights for Palestinians in Israel and for an end to the occupation of the West Bank and siege of Gaza. Electorally, after decades of disengagement, Palestinians have participated more. In 2022, 54 per cent voted, up 10 per cent on the previous election, contributing to more and more Arab parties gaining seats in the Knesset, and a say in Israel's politics.[33]

This increased politicisation has come partly in response to the shift rightwards among Israel's Jewish voters. The Zionist founders of Israel insisted the state would be both Jewish and democratic, but the growth of the internal Palestinian community has made those joint goals seem contradictory: with the Palestinian population growing faster than the Jewish, democracy could soon make Israel a non-Jewish state. Consequently, the Knesset passed the 2018 Basic Law on the Jewish Nation-State, which legally set down the state's Jewish character and also downgraded the official status of Arabic. Arab citizens and politicians were alarmed that this deprived them of any democratic route to equality, institutionalising their second-class status. At a popular level, the move reflected increased tensions between Israel's Jewish majority and the Arab minority. The International Crisis Group reported that 60 per cent of Israelis believed that Jews and Arabs should live separately, and reports of racial attacks towards Arabs increased.[34] In 2021, tensions exploded in spontaneous riots centred on the mixed city of Lod. Arab citizens rioted in protest at their treatment. Right-wing Jewish vigilantes responded, fighting both Arab residents and the police sent to calm tensions. Two people were killed, one Arab and one Jewish, and the crisis underlined the Palestinian Israelis' frustrations with their situation and, to many, the unsustainability of the status quo.

The 3–4 million refugees, meanwhile, are mostly based in Lebanon, Jordan, and Syria, facing very different circumstances. Jordan has treated its Palestinians most favourably, hosting the largest number. Officially 2 million of Jordan's 10 million citizens are Palestinian, but the number is likely far higher given the extent to which the original refugees integrated. Jordan was the only Arab state to offer Palestinian refugees full citizenship and, though refugee camps were built, they are now more like poor neighbourhoods. That said, for decades there was unofficial discrimination. The new arrivals, who tended to thrive in the business community, were excluded from top positions in government and the military and a Palestinian-Jordanian divide characterised politics and society for years. In recent decades the situation has improved, especially after the current king married a Palestinian, making their eldest son and heir of mixed heritage. However, informal discrimination remains in some places.

Syria officially hosts over 580,000 refugees, though the exact number remains unknown after some became double refugees, fleeing the country when it descended into civil war in 2011. Prior to that, Palestinians were not granted full citizenship as they were in Jordan, but were able to buy limited amounts of property, own businesses, seek employment, and serve in the military. However, their descendants could not become Syrians unless they had a Syrian parent, and they could not vote – no great loss in Syria's autocracy. Both Bashar al-Assad and his father Hafez made much of their support for the Palestinians and insisted that giving the refugees citizenship would represent a recognition of Israel. However, it left these refugees in a precarious position when many had to flee violence in the 2010s, some having difficulty gaining asylum elsewhere given their tenuous status in Syria.

In Lebanon, the situation has historically been the worst for Palestinians. The delicate sectarian balance of the state meant the Lebanese government not only denied the refugees citizenship but also prevented most from working or living outside of their squalid concrete refugee camps (see chapter 7). With the PLO using Lebanon as a base and playing a role in Lebanon's descent into civil war in the 1970s, there remains limited support for the refugees among Lebanon's population and its corrupt political class. With Palestinians fleeing Syria now adding to their number, the 400,000 or so descendants of the refugees in Lebanon remain stuck in deprivation, with few prospects. Given the Lebanese government's steadfast refusal to integrate the refugees, it is the Palestinians of Lebanon who appear most in need of a solution, and they are the most prominent group mentioned when the PA insists on refugees returning to Palestine. While the Syrians may accept some form of compensation to integrate the refugees they already have (Jordan has already made peace), the Lebanese will likely not. As nationalists, the Palestinian negotiators feel deeply for their brethren in refugee camps abroad, believing their plight should be alleviated by the Israelis who displaced them.

Two States, One State, Three 'States'?

On 7 October 2023 Hamas militants launched a massive, coordinated attack on Israel. After firing thousands of rockets, the security barriers around Gaza were breached allowing fighters to fan out into southern Israel. There they slaughtered over 1,400, mostly civilians, and took at least 220 more back into Gaza as hostages, before eventually being defeated by the shocked IDF. Israeli society was stunned. It was the bloodiest single day in Israel's history. Prime Minister Benjamin Netanyahu, who was criticised by some for being too complacent about the Hamas threat and for the intelligence failure of not anticipating the attack, vowed to, 'eradicate Hamas's military and governmental capabilities'. As after previous Hamas assaults, Israel initiated its own reprisals on Gaza, but far harsher than anything seen before. Gaza's power and electricity were cut off as the IDF pounded the strip. Within a month over ten thousand Palestinians were reported killed, mostly civilians, far more than the previous three Gaza wars combined. The strip faced what the UN called an 'unprecedented' humanitarian situation.

Foreign governments were jolted out of their previous disinterest in the Israeli-Palestinian conflict but responded in a familiar way. Western leaders were quick to emphasise their solidarity with Israel, though some also called for humanitarian ceasefires as the attacks on Gaza escalated. US President Joe Biden flew to Jerusalem and sent an aircraft carrier to the Eastern Mediterranean in a show of support, insisting on Israel's right to self-defence. While Biden privately urged caution on Netanyahu, in public he backed the Israeli premier, vetoing early efforts at the UN to push Israel on humanitarian pauses. The ferocity of Israel's response appeared to derail the move towards greater regional normalisation. Saudi Arabia, whom Biden had been lobbying to join the Abraham accords, was fiercely critical of Israel, while even the UAE condemned the Gaza bombings. Elsewhere Turkey's President Erdoğan continued his rhetorical support for the Palestinians, calling Hamas 'liberators', and cancelling a planned trip to Israel. Iran, who likely aided Hamas in acquiring weapons but, according to Israel, was not known to have planned the attack, praised its 'success' and condemned Netanyahu's response in equal measure. The renewed outbreak of hostilities demonstrated once again that, far from going away, this conflict can erupt with yet more unprecedented violence at any time and retains the potential to drag regional and international actors into the inferno. Moreover, the local and international responses, lacking as they frequently were in calls for moderation, empathy, or long-term solutions, illustrated how far all the actors remain from finding durable resolutions.

For now, then, a solution to the conflict looks highly unlikely. The two-state solution, the idea of an independent Palestinian state alongside Israel, which first emerged after 1967 and formed the basis of the Oslo Accords, looks increasingly improbable. Israeli governments that did engage seriously with the peace process were never willing to offer a deal close enough to the Palestinian leadership's minimum demands. More recently, Israeli politics' rightward shift has produced successive governments that are not willing to engage seriously with the process, preferring to manage the conflict while continuing with settlement building, annexation, expropriation, and reprisals. The Palestinian leadership has made the situation worse, with the rupture between Hamas and the PA leaving them weak and divided, enabling Israel to argue it does not have a realistic partner for peace, something seemingly confirmed by Hamas' targeting of civilians with suicide bombings, rockets, and kidnappings. Given the United States' supposed role as mediator in the peace process, it might be expected to step in to revive the two-state option, but Washington has never been impartial and its closeness to Israel means such an outcome is unlikely. While other regional powers have played a role in Palestinian politics in the past, today none is influential enough to shift the dial one way or the other. Even Iran, which Israel sees as its major threat, has better levers to Israel's north in Syria and Lebanon, and weaker ties to Hamas than in the past.

With the two-state solution dying, many supporters of the Palestinians, plus a few left-leaning Israelis, have argued that a one-state solution should be pursued instead. They recommend that Abbas should dissolve the PA and declare all Palestinians citizens of Israel, turning the conflict from one between two rival nations into a struggle for civil rights in a single state.[35] The logic behind this is that there are now, just about, more Arabs living in all of what was Mandate Palestine than Jews. This represents a 'South African' solution to the conflict, whereby compromise and reconciliation would lead to a single Israeli-Palestinian state that is democratic, shared, and a safe haven for both communities. Advocates like Rashid Khalidi argue that Palestinian activists need to work on convincing Israelis of the benefits of this.[36] However, worthy though such a project may be, it currently appears even more unlikely than the two-state solution. Both Israeli and Palestinian nationalisms are so deeply constructed among both peoples that it would likely take several generations to unpick them and rebuild trust. Unlike in South Africa, the Palestinians do not overwhelm the Israelis numerically and, from their position of advantage, it will be hard to persuade Israelis this is a concession they should make.

Most likely, therefore, is a grim continuation of the status quo, what might be termed a three-'state' reality, if not a 'solution'. The Palestinians remain divided in their enclaves of Gaza and a small part of the West Bank while Israel continues to colonise East Jerusalem and other parts of the occupied territories. The problem is that, as was seen with the First and Second Intifadas, the Palestinians have not been willing to remain passive for long, and the Gaza war could be the sign of things to come. Further violent struggle could simply reinforce the status quo, with the international community passively looking on, or somehow shift the dynamics among Israelis, Palestinians, or the outside world. If the history of the conflict has shown anything, it's that the more hopeless the situation feels for the Palestinians, the more likely they are to roll the dice and see where it lands.

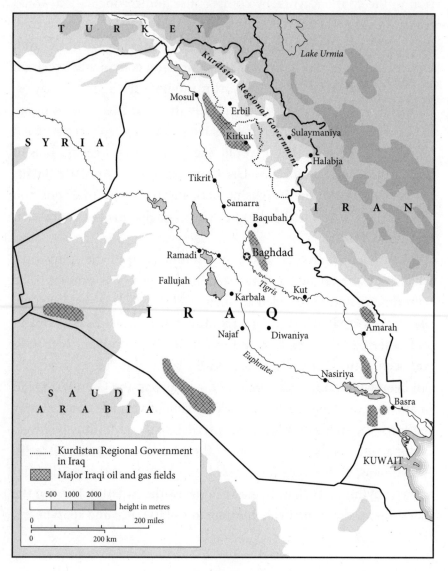

Iraq

5

Iraq
The Broken Republic

Few countries have endured as much as Iraq in the last forty years. Any Iraqi born in 1980 inherited citizenship within a prosperous modern economy. Oil wealth, industry, and advanced education had seen Iraq charge up global development tables during the 1970s, putting it close to some European states. But from that high point the decline was steep. That year Iraq's dictator, Saddam Hussein, invaded neighbouring Iran, triggering a gruelling eight-year war. Over half a million were killed and Iraq was bankrupted, prompting Saddam to launch another invasion in search of resources, this time of neighbouring Kuwait in 1990. But this provoked an even greater confrontation, with a UN-mandated international coalition led by the United States, which devastated Iraq from the air. Though Saddam retreated, his country was in ruins, the assault having destroyed what was left of industry and key infrastructure. What's more, the international community continued to punish Iraq for its invasion, maintaining the harshest set of trade sanctions ever devised. These reduced ordinary Iraqis to abject poverty, while doing little to dent Saddam's power.

This ended only in 2003, when the United States returned, this time to topple Saddam for good. Though they succeeded, it was far from the end of Iraq's suffering. Washington established a corrupt democracy based on religious and ethnic differences which, for the most part, served only a narrow elite. It also oversaw a massive outbreak of communal violence that neither the occupiers nor the new government was able to prevent, and often contributed to. A decade of instability, corruption, and sectarian violence was compounded by the rise of the Jihadist Islamic State, which captured a third of Iraq, including the second city of Mosul. Though Islamic State was eventually defeated, the battle with the Jihadists further damaged and fragmented an already fragile state, with little prospect of improvement. The Iraqi born in 1980, if they managed to survive the four decades of devastation without being killed or fleeing abroad like millions of others, might wonder how their country had fallen so far.

Certainly, Iraq has been ill-served by its leaders and elites. Saddam Hussein's dictatorship was disastrous. Not only did he provoke long conflicts, sanctions, and invasion, but his domestic policies created a climate of violence and fear, exacerbating sectarian and ethnic tensions that would erupt horrifically after he was toppled. His successors were little better. Though less megalomaniac, the (mostly) exiles empowered by the American invasion were self-serving and oversaw a miserable blend of corruption and violence. Grassroots leaders who challenged the elite were culpable too, often encouraging division further.

However, Iraqi leaders have not acted alone and much has been facilitated by foreign governments, also pursuing their own agendas. Historically, Britain left a toxic legacy when it first established Iraq. More recently, regional governments like Turkey and Syria have each meddled at different times. However, the two most consequential modern players have been the US and Iran. Washington led the anti-Saddam campaigns of the 1990s, culminating in his ouster in 2003, and then oversaw a poorly conceived and executed occupation. Iran has become the most powerful regional power in post-2003 Iraqi politics. Taking advantage of the sectarian system established by

Washington, Tehran has deeply infiltrated its neighbour to the west, transforming what was once its enemy into a key ally – some would say client. However, while these two players have dominated Iraqi politics, often using it as a proxy battleground for their own rivalry with each other, the picture, as ever, is complex. External players have had a deep impact, but via their interaction with domestic dynamics, rather than directing Iraqis to their will.

The Rises and Falls of Iraq

The state of Iraq is barely a hundred years old, but it was built on the site of some of the world's oldest and most developed civilisations. Not far from Baghdad can be found the ruins of ancient Babylon, one of humanity's earliest cities, or the remnants of the Persian capital Ctesiphon, once the world's largest settlement. Baghdad also once boasted that title, when it was capital of the Abbasid Caliphate and home to the most advanced science and learning during the 'Islamic Golden Age' of the eighth and ninth centuries. Yet from this pinnacle Iraq suffered centuries of invasion and decline, beginning with the Mongols in 1258, who permanently destroyed the irrigation networks that had helped the region flourish for millennia. Thereafter Baghdad and its environs became something of a backwater, absorbed into the Ottoman empire but of marginal economic, political, or cultural importance. However, the discovery of oil in the early twentieth century changed this, prompting Britain to capture the region after it defeated the Ottomans in the First World War.

London fused together three Ottoman provinces: Basra in the south, Mosul in the north, and Baghdad in the centre, to forge a new country, 'Iraq', which it ruled on behalf of the League of Nations, theoretically preparing it for independence. But Britain's rule was self-interested and left a damaging legacy. Most of the inhabitants were Muslim, but with sizeable Christian and Jewish communities, until the 1950s when the latter were forced to emigrate, mostly to Israel, after a surge in hostility following the Palestinian *Nakba* (see chapter 4). But the Muslim majority was not homogeneous. Most were Arab, but the mountainous north was dominated by Kurds (see chapter 8) as well as a sizeable Turkmen community. Most of the Muslims were Shia, with the holy Shia cities of Najaf, Karbala, and Samarra in the centre of the new country, but Sunnis were the ruling elites under the Ottomans, dominating government, commerce, and the military. Differences among these three largest ethno-religious groups, Shias, Sunnis, and Kurds, need not have led to division, but London exacerbated tensions. After a country-wide rebellion against its rule within a year of taking over, London concluded it needed a local puppet and so imported a foreign prince from the Arabian Peninsula, Faisal, to be king. But Faisal favoured and empowered fellow Sunnis rather than those from the Shia majority.[1] He similarly marginalised Kurds, denying requests for cultural and educational recognition, provoking a series of rebellions that Britain ruthlessly helped crush. The king did gain nominal independence for Iraq in 1932, but remained Britain's client, granting it extensive military bases and, most importantly, the right for the London-based Iraq Petroleum Company (mostly owned by the precursors of BP, Shell, Total, and ExxonMobil) to have exclusive rights to extract oil without paying royalties until 1950.[2]

Britain's power was weakened by the Second World War and the 1956 Suez Crisis, but the death knell for its influence in Iraq came in 1958, when military officers overthrew the pro-British monarchy and murdered the king, Faisal's grandson. Though this marked the start of forty-five years of dictatorial rule it also catalysed a wave of social and economic transformation.[3] Traditional tribal life was discouraged, with tribal courts abolished and women's rights improved. Education expanded, as did the middle classes, as Iraq rapidly urbanised and industrialised. These trends continued when the Arab nationalist Ba'ath party seized power in 1963. They nationalised the Iraq Petroleum Company, prompting Iraq's wealth and prosperity to surge forward during the 1970s oil boom. By the end of that decade, Iraq was on the brink of matching the level of industrial development of some Western states, but this was soon confounded by the rise of Saddam Hussein.

Saddam was a relative of the Ba'ath party leader who led a further coup in 1968 and, over the next decade, he became the most powerful figure in the country. In 1979 he declared himself president and initiated a reign of terror, purging dozens of leading Ba'athists at a televised party congress that saw alleged 'traitors' removed from their seats and led out to be imprisoned or executed. Under Saddam, the Ba'ath party dictatorship became even more sinister. An admirer of Stalin, he emulated his idol's police state and instituted an omnipresent personality cult.[4] Brutal though these policies were, it was his foreign policy that ultimately doomed the Ba'ath regime and unleashed decades of suffering and regression.

Barely a year after becoming president, Saddam defied the advice of his military leaders and ordered an invasion of Iran. He hoped to weaken the Islamic revolutionary regime that had just come to power, while also capturing and annexing some of Iran's oilfields. But the blitzkrieg he envisaged soon stalled and Iran fought back. The result was a stalemated conflict that dragged on for eight years, causing widespread death, destruction, and, ultimately, no territorial change. Having nearly bankrupted Iraq's economy with one war, Saddam sought to solve his financial woes by launching another: invading and annexing the wealthy Gulf state of Kuwait in 1990 (see chapter 9). But this provoked international outrage. The UN mandated a military mission led by the United States to forcibly eject Saddam from Kuwait. This was achieved in early 1991, when Washington launched Operation Desert Storm, not only forcing Saddam's retreat, but also destroying much of what was left of Iraq's developed infrastructure.

The US president, George H.W. Bush, declined to pursue Saddam's army into Iraq, but had urged the Iraqi people to rise up and overthrow their oppressor.[5] Many attempted this. Saddam, like most leaders since Faisal, was a Sunni and favoured the minority group, particularly those from his native Tikrit and its local tribes. Shia, who had long been marginalised, had little love for him and reacted to George H.W. Bush's calls by launching a rebellion in the Shia-dominated south. At the same time the Kurds in the north also rebelled. They had been oppressed even more. Saddam regarded them as potential fifth columnists during the Iran–Iraq war after Kurdish militia fought with Iran against Baghdad. Saddam responded with a campaign of oppression against civilians that culminated with the gassing of up to 5,000 Kurds in the 1988 Halabja massacre. Because of this recent history, Washington and its allies feared Saddam would use chemical weapons on Kurds again and so created a no-fly zone over the northern mountains. This prevented Saddam's forces from entering the area, effectively cutting it off from the rest of Iraq for the next decade. Western forces offered the south no such support, however, and Saddam crushed the uprising there, leaving many Shias feeling both a deep sense of betrayal by the West and by their Sunni countrymen who had stayed loyal to Saddam.

Anti-Western feeling was further fuelled by the sanctions that remained on Iraq for the decade after Desert Storm. The UN had forbidden any state to trade with Iraq, so no food, medicine or vital supplies were allowed to enter, and Iraq could not sell its oil to raise funds. The logic of keeping these in place was to prevent Saddam from re-arming and some vague notion that it would prompt the military to overthrow him. Instead, Saddam stayed in power while poverty, malnutrition, and illness soared. More than the wars and Saddam's brutal rule, the decade of sanctions accelerated Iraq's decline and had a deep impact on the country's national psyche.[6]

Invasion and Aftermath

Iraq's fortunes were to change, for better or ill, because of a series of terrorist attacks, 6,000 miles away. Al-Qaeda's slaughter of nearly 3,000 people on 11 September 2001, had nothing to do with Iraq, with whom the Afghanistan-based Jihadists had no direct ties.[7] Even so, the United States government, now headed by George W. Bush, son of H.W., was dominated by a clique of neo-conservative idealists determined to link the attack to Saddam Hussein. The US and some of its allies, especially Britain, accused Iraq of retaining weapons of mass destruction (WMD) from the Iran–Iraq war that might be used to either attack the West or be given to Al-Qaeda. Several years later, a British inquiry revealed these claims to be based on questionable intelligence, but at the time the White House used the WMD threat to justify removing Saddam by force.[8] In contrast to Desert Storm in 1991, the UN refused to endorse America and Britain's actions, which many believed made the invasion illegal and, alongside the inability later to find any WMD, gave it an air of illegitimacy from the start. The military operation, when it came, was swift. US-led forces invaded from Kuwait in March 2003 and captured Baghdad within three weeks. Saddam fled but was later captured hiding near his hometown of Tikrit. The new Iraqi government put him on public trial and sentenced him to death by hanging in 2006.

The end of Saddam's dictatorship left a power vacuum. Though the Bush administration insisted it would liberate Iraq from Saddam's tyranny, it had outlined few plans of what post-Ba'ath rule would look like. In the northern mountains, Iraq's Kurds had been governing themselves since 1991 under the protection of the Western no-fly zone and transitioned to the post-Saddam era relatively smoothly. Elsewhere the situation was more chaotic. The White House based many of its policies on the counsel of Iraqi exiles who had spent decades abroad and returned in 2003 to find the country unrecognisable.[9] The invaders were not greeted as liberators, despite the exiles' beliefs they would be. A handful of Baghdadis joined American soldiers in symbolically pulling down a statue of Saddam, but beyond this, most viewed them with suspicion – after all, these were the forces that had bombed and sanctioned Iraq for years. The US and Britain made matters worse by committing a series of errors with lasting consequences. First, they failed to keep order. The US admitted it had too few troops to police Iraq, next to none of whom spoke Arabic, and so could do little to stop the widespread looting that broke out immediately after Saddam's fall.[10] Ministries and museums, with decades of records, property deeds, and vital administrative documents essential for running the country, were torched. In contrast, sufficient US forces were found to guard the Ministry of Oil, which remained unscathed. Faced with a security vacuum, local militias began to form.

Second, they abolished the Ba'ath party and began a process called 'de-Ba'athification'. After thirty-five years in power, membership of the party was a necessity for anyone hoping to enter state employment, rather than a conscious endorsement of Saddam Hussein. Yet de-Ba'athification saw thousands of competent administrators, doctors, and teachers, among others, fired overnight, defenestrating Iraq's bureaucracy. Third, in a similar vein, the US abolished the Iraqi army. This decision was made by Paul Bremer, the White House-appointed governor of occupied Iraq, and came as a surprise to both George W. Bush and the US military commanders on the ground, who had expected Saddam's army to be reconfigured and used to keep order.[11] But Bremer was instead influenced by certain exiles who saw Iraq through a sectarian lens and believed that Shia soldiers would not serve under Sunnis who they wrongly believed to make up most of the officer corps. Yet by abolishing the army Bremer worsened the security vacuum that was being filled by criminals and armed militias that intimidated the local population. He also created a mass of unemployed former soldiers with military training to join them. It took four years of chaos and violence before a new Iraqi army, built from scratch by Washington, was able to keep order again.

Finally, the post-Saddam political system the US created was highly dysfunctional. The occupation officially transferred sovereignty back to an interim government in mid-2004, while a year later an elected assembly hastily drafted a new constitution that was approved by referendum. However, despite this democratic veneer, much was decided in backroom deals by a handful of politicians, with considerable influence from the US embassy.[12] The key players were the two parties representing the Kurdish north, who secured continued autonomy for their region and the role of kingmaker in Iraqi politics, and several Shia parties, mostly dominated by exiles from either the West or Iran. Sunni parties, and the many who did not want ethnic or religious identity to be the defining characteristic of Iraq's politics, were marginalised. The result was a parliamentary democracy in theory but a corrupt sectarian oligarchy in practice.

Elections to parliament were relatively free, but the elite parties all agreed to implement a 'Muhasasa Ta'ifia' or 'sectarian apportion-ment' to allocate office. This idea, first proposed by exiled opposition Iraqis, was endorsed wholeheartedly by the US and returning Iraqi exiles after 2003. It views ethno-religious identity as the key feature of politics in Iraq and allocates jobs according to demographic repre-sentation. The prime minister, the most powerful office, is always a Shia; the (largely ceremonial) president is always a Kurd, and the Speaker of Parliament is always a Sunni. All other offices are similarly distributed. The system seemed modelled on a similar confessional ruling bargain established in Lebanon (see chapter 7) and, unfortu-nately, led to similarly weak and corrupt governance. The system encouraged elite leaders to seek benefits only for their own commu-nities, whom they depended on for power, rather than the country as a whole. Elections led to months of bargaining between the elites over who got which jobs, paralysing the government. Even after agree-ments were made, the exiles who dominated high office were more interested in using their ministries to enrich themselves and their allies than in governing.

Washington's failures to bring either order, good governance, or prosperity contributed to the years of violence that engulfed Iraq after the fall of Saddam. The violence had two parallel, sometimes overlap-ping, strands. First was an insurgency launched against the US-led occupation. Various Iraqi militias targeted US positions through suicide bombings, ambushes, or roadside bombs aimed at making the occupation unsustainable. Shia militias, often armed and financed by Iran, took the lead in Shia-dominated areas. Most Sunni fighters, many of whom had originally been Saddam loyalists, fought the US separately, with some eventually joining Al-Qaeda in Iraq. It is a sad irony that, despite US claims, prior to 2003 there was no recorded Al-Qaeda presence in Iraq. Yet, after the invasion, branches did form to fight the occupation and attracted Jihadists from around the world.

Second was the eruption of communal violence between Sunni and Shia militias. As Iraqi scholar Zaid Al-Ali notes, prior to Ba'ath rule there had only been three notable instances of large-scale Sunni–Shia violence in 400 years, while mixed neighbourhoods and even inter-communal marriage had grown from the 1960s.[13] But the final years of Saddam's rule and the imposition of a sect-based political system after 2003 heightened tensions. As Saddam's state collapsed and the Americans left a security vacuum by abolishing the army, sectarian Sunni and Shia militias formed, increasingly with the aim of ethnically cleansing rival communities. Mixed neighbourhoods in Baghdad were purged and religious sites were targeted, notably the Imam Al-Askari Mosque in Samarra (one of Shia Islam's holiest sites), which was bombed in 2006. Often this violence was led or encouraged by the political elite. Several militias were the arms of leading political parties, while Nouri al-Maliki, the prime minister from 2006, was frequently anti-Sunni in many of his policies. Hundreds of thousands were killed, while millions had to flee their homes, often abroad. Among the worst affected was Iraq's Christian community. Persecuted by both sides and with few safe havens, most of the once-substantial Christian population fled abroad. In Saddam's final years an estimated 1.5 million Christians were living in Iraq. Today the number is believed to be a tenth of this.[14]

The violence eventually eased from late 2007. Partly this was down to a 'surge' of US troops deployed to tackle the insurgency. Partly it was down to Washington's accompanying 'Awakening' policy of collaborating with Sunni tribes that had been sidelined by Shia and Kurdish politicians since 2003.[15] Partly it was due to burn-out, with few mixed neighbourhoods left to cleanse and the erection of huge concrete barriers to permanently separate the communities. Partly it was down to the new Iraqi army finally being able to keep some degree of order. However, this proved a temporary respite. The aftermath of the 2003 invasion and the political system that it created ensured little stability.

Iran in Iraq

The US and Britain were not the only foreign powers responsible for the instability, and others sought influence in the chaos of post-Saddam Iraq. Turkey, which borders Iraq to the north, became a significant partner to the newly autonomous Kurdish region, known as the Kurdistan Regional Government (KRG). It greatly increased trade with the enclave, which boomed with energy wealth while the rest of Iraq stagnated. At the same time, it launched military raids on positions it claimed were safe havens for Turkish Kurdish separatists. Syria, Iraq's neighbour to the west, also interfered, cynically allowing Syrian and other Jihadists to pass through its territory to join Al-Qaeda's insurgency.[16] Though Damascus loathed Jihadism, it wanted to bog down the US occupation to deter Washington from turning to Syria after Iraq. Interestingly, Iraq's wealthy southern neighbour, Saudi Arabia, did not get involved. Though it opposed Saddam, who had threatened Saudi oilfields after invading Kuwait in 1990, it urged its ally Washington not to invade, correctly predicting that it would benefit its regional nemesis, Iran. Yet when the US spurned this advice, Riyadh opted not to use its wealth to buy influence in Baghdad's new politics, despite having historical ties with some Iraqi exiles. Exactly why is unclear. Some claim they didn't want to endorse the new Shia-dominated political system, while others argue Riyadh knew they would have only limited influence, so didn't bother.[17] Perhaps this is true, given Iran's starting advantages, but they still left the field open for Tehran. By the time the Saudi leadership realised their mistake and started to engage fully from the late 2010s it was too late: Iran had become the most powerful regional player in the new Iraq.

Iran and Iraq share their longest land borders, nearly 1,500 km, which thread from the northern Kurdish mountains down to the oil fields of the Gulf. They have deep historic cultural ties, particularly religion. The Islamic Republic of Iran that was declared in 1979 placed Shia Islam at the centre of its political identity and ideology, making neighbouring Iraq's Shia majority and its holy shrines even more important to Tehran. But Iraq is also vital to Iran's security and regional ambitions. Saddam's invasion in 1980 had exposed how vulnerable Iran was if Baghdad was ruled by an enemy. Though the new regime survived the war, Saddam's continued presence acted as a physical barrier to Tehran's wider ambitions of becoming a dominant player in the Middle East. America's overthrow of Saddam therefore represented both a threat and an opportunity. Saddam was not mourned in Iran, but his replacement by a US occupation was terrifying. Like its allies in Damascus, Tehran worried that America would want to move onto the Islamic Republic next. The Bush administration's declaration in 2002 that Iran, along with Iraq, North Korea, and later Syria, Libya, and Cuba, represented an 'axis of evil' that posed a threat to world peace, seemed to suggest such a goal. Yet simultaneously, the invasion represented an opportunity for Iran. The sect-based system established by the US after 2003 favoured Shia politicians, many of whom had close links to Iran. If it played the situation correctly, Iran could flip Iraq from a long-standing enemy to a close ally. Similarly, with Saddam gone, the road was open for greater influence beyond Iraq, in the wider Middle East, provided the Americans could be pushed out.

Though often characterised by Western critics as a dictatorship, Iranian politics is more complex than this simple caricature suggests.

The presidency and parliament are elected, though candidates must be approved by an unelected clerical council. Major political decisions, especially foreign policies, are ultimately decided by the religious Supreme Leader, Ayatollah Khamenei, though decision making is influenced by a mixture of elected and unelected figures. Ever since 1979, Iran's approach to the world has generally oscillated between hard-line and moderate wings of the establishment. The events of 9/11 occurred during an era when moderates held sway and Iran was trying to improve its ties with the West, prompting Tehran to help the US defeat Al-Qaeda and its defenders, the Taliban, in Afghanistan in late 2001. It therefore proved quite a shock to be labelled an 'enemy to world peace' by George W. Bush, and the subsequent Iraq invasion triggered conservative hawks to become more ascendant in Iran, led by the paramilitary Islamic Revolutionary Guard Corps (IRGC). Believing that influence in Baghdad was now vital to Iran's interests, they poured energy and resources into Iraq's post-war politics.

To do this Iran played a long game built on three overlapping strategies. First, it built close ties with Iraqi politicians. This was not difficult given that many of the new leaders had spent considerable time in exile in Iran and were fellow Shia Islamists. These included Prime Minister Maliki, whose party received funding from Tehran.[18] Old alliances with Iraqi Kurds from the Iran–Iraq war were also reactivated, notably with Jalal Talabani, who became Iraq's first post-Saddam president. Tehran further tried to forge links with new Iraqi actors, particularly Muqtada al-Sadr, a young cleric who formed a popular grassroots movement in Baghdad's poor Shia-dominated suburbs. Second, it cultivated the growth of Shia militias. This often overlapped with its sponsorship of political actors, providing money, weapons, and training for the armed wings of its clients including, at first, al-Sadr's 'Mahdi Army'. But over time Iran grew frustrated with some of these groups, especially as the insurgency against the US and anti-Shia Jihadists intensified, and so Iran built its own militia groups from scratch. Among the most prominent of these was Kata'ib

Hezbollah, an Iraqi Shia group modelled on the Lebanese Shia group Iranian forces had helped establish in the 1980s.[19]

Third, it built a deep cultural presence in Iraq to facilitate its political and military links while simultaneously promoting its image and ideology to ordinary (Shia) Iraqis. Within weeks of Saddam's fall, the Quds Force, the IRGC's elite military and intelligence unit, led by Qassem Suleimani, helped set up the 'Centre for Restoration of the Sublime Gates' in southern Iraq.[20] This organisation was primarily tasked with restoring and protecting Iraq's various Shia shrines, but it also formed the base of operations for the Quds Force in Iraq. From here Suleimani was able to lobby politicians, run guns, and eventually set up militias. But its original religio-cultural task was not a mere front: Iran genuinely did support long-neglected Shia religious sites, charities, and media, earning goodwill from many in the community.

This strategy had mixed results. On the one hand it achieved its main goals. Post-Saddam Iraqi politics became dominated by Shia leaders such as Maliki, who were close to Iran. Despite Bush's 'Surge' stifling some of the insurgents, the occupation proved too costly for the United States, which ultimately abandoned any fantasies of further regime change in Iran or Syria, and withdrew all troops under Bush's successor, Barack Obama, in 2011. Moreover, Iraq did prove a platform for deepening Iran's presence elsewhere in the Middle East, with Suleimani enhancing ties with Lebanon, Syria, and Yemen in the years immediately after Saddam's fall. But on the other hand, Iran's meddling did not go unnoticed. Washington under both Bush and Obama was particularly concerned over Iran's pursuit of nuclear power, which it had begun to develop when the hardliners returned to power. Convinced Tehran was developing a nuclear weapon, the Bush administration pushed for UN sanctions, squeezing the Iranian economy. Obama expanded these, crippling Iran's finances further, to the point that frustrated voters elected moderates back into power in the form of President Hassan Rouhani in 2013, who promised to negotiate with the US. These negotiations eventually became Obama's 2015 deal between Tehran and the Western international community to end sanctions in exchange for Iran suspending its nuclear programme.[21] This proved the key context to understand the two governments' responses and surprising collaboration over Iraq's next tragedy: the rise of Islamic State.

The Islamic State Crisis

In early June 2014, just over a thousand fighters from the Sunni Jihadist group Islamic State in Iraq and Sham (Greater Syria) captured Mosul, Iraq's second-largest city. Inside they found a vast cache of money, weapons, and equipment, including 2,300 Humvees left by the Iraqi army, which had disintegrated and fled.[22] A few days later its leader, Abu Bakr al-Baghdadi, announced from Mosul's Great Mosque that the territory he controlled, spanning eastern Syria and western Iraq were part of a new 'Caliphate', Islamic State, that sought to unite all Muslims under its rule. The declaration prompted a wave of Syrian, Iraqi, and international Jihadist volunteers to join this 'Caliphate'. Meanwhile the weapons and money acquired enabled Islamic State to push deeper into Iraq and Syria, threatening both Baghdad and the Kurdistan Regional Government. Suddenly, this once marginal Al-Qaeda offshoot looked capable of sweeping through not only Iraq and Syria but the whole Middle East.

Only a few years earlier, Al-Qaeda in Iraq had been close to collapse. The American 'surge' of 2007–8 had decimated the group, as had Washington's accompanying 'Awakening' policy. But Baghdadi, who in 2010 took over leadership of the group – now rebranded Islamic State in Iraq – pulled it back from the brink. First, he took advantage of Sunni disaffection with Prime Minister Nouri al-Maliki, who had become more anti-Sunni after securing a second term in 2010. He undid much of the work done by America's 'Awakening', marginalising Sunnis once more. This was exacerbated by Obama's withdrawal of all US troops in late 2011, leaving many Sunnis fearful as to their fate, driving some into the arms of Baghdadi. Second, Islamic State recruited into its ranks former Saddam-era officials, who had been similarly excluded from the new politics, adding valuable military expertise. Finally, Baghdadi took advantage of the civil war that erupted in neighbouring Syria from 2011 (see chapter 1). Many Syrian Sunnis were similarly disaffected with the dictatorial rule of President Bashar al-Assad, an Alawi Shia, creating some ready recruits for Baghdadi. The chaos there also allowed Islamic State to cross the border and capture territory in eastern Syria, giving it a base for launching attacks back in Iraq.

While Iraqis like Maliki and Baghdadi were ultimately responsible for Islamic State's rise, their actions were facilitated by foreign governments. The United States was especially culpable. By invading Iraq in the first place, the US created conditions for Al-Qaeda's emergence – previously it had had no substantial presence in the Middle East. Thereafter the US helped radicalise a generation of Sunni Iraqis by detaining thousands in prison, some of whom were subject to torture. Baghdadi was one such former inmate. After sowing the seeds of chaos, the US then withdrew too quickly. Obama placed too much faith in Maliki, ignoring the evidence of his growing corruption and sectarianism. Maliki had taken personal control of the new Iraqi army, which he packed with corrupt cronies, undermining its reliability. As a result, Obama left a weak but well stocked army that collapsed in the face of Islamic State's Mosul assault. Iran also shoulders some blame. It too supported Maliki, with Suleimani encouraging his anti-Sunni approach and providing him with sectarian Shia militia. Some Sunnis' support for Islamic State was partly a backlash against this. Finally, Turkey and Qatar played a role. Both supported the opposition to Assad in Syria's civil war and sent money and weapons to an array of fighters in an imprecise way, meaning a lot ended up in the hands of Islamic State. Turkey was especially lax, leaving its long border with Syria open for foreign fighters to cross back and forth.[23] This was the primary route for foreign Jihadists heading to Iraq.

The fall of Mosul proved a moment of crisis for the new Iraqi state and the two key external players most deeply involved: the US and Iran. Though Maliki had been increasingly authoritarian in his later years, he was no dictator, and his bungling campaign against Islamic State caused all his allies to turn on him: parliament, his party, the US, and Iran. By August 2014 he was forced to resign, replaced by Haider al-Abadi, a more conciliatory figure. Meanwhile a military response to Islamic State was launched. Obama, having initially dismissed Islamic State as insignificant, was alarmed by the fall of Mosul and launched a full military campaign against the Jihadists. This meant returning to Iraq at the invitation of al-Abadi to retrain and reorganise the Iraqi army, alongside a massive air campaign to 'degrade and destroy' Baghdadi's ability to wage war in Syria and Iraq. Washington further cooperated with Kurdish fighters in Iraq and Syria, seeking to repel Islamic State from their homelands.

Iran also belatedly realised the extent of the threat, fearing it might prompt the collapse of the friendly Iraqi state it had helped construct and usher in a wave of anti-Shia ethnic cleansing. Suleimani therefore took the lead in the campaign on the ground, ironically placing him on the same side as the Americans whom he had spent nearly a decade fighting. Suleimani brought the Iraqi Shia fighters he had sent to Syria to help Assad back to Iraq and built new militia specifically to take on Baghdadi. These Popular Mobilisation Units (PMUs) or the 'Hashd al-Shabi', emerged immediately after the fall of Mosul, when Iraq's leading Shia cleric, Ayatollah Sistani, who was independent of Iran, issued a religious edict or 'fatwa' calling on citizens to defend the country. An array of PMUs formed, many of whose members would go on to dominate Iraqi politics. Most were aligned with Iran and under Suleimani's command, but some were independent, especially those linked to Muqtada al-Sadr.[24] Using PMU militias to support and supplement the US-backed Iraqi army, Suleimani energetically crisscrossed northern Iraq, including the Kurdish areas, directing battles, and helping to halt Islamic State in its tracks. Such was Suelimani's significance that the Iranian general earned plaudits from Western media, with *Newsweek* featuring him across a front cover under the headline, 'First he fought America, now he's crushing ISIS [Islamic State]'.[25]

The US and Iran campaigned against Islamic State separately, but with the same goal of destroying the so-called Caliphate. Despite checking Baghdadi's advance, it was years before the Iraqi military could recapture Mosul. When this came about, in 2016–17, it took nine months to dislodge the Jihadists and left the city devastated. After they were eventually ejected, the historic Great Mosque from which Baghdadi had declared his Caliphate had been reduced to rubble. By 2019, the last Islamic State stronghold had been captured and Baghdadi himself was hunted down by American special forces in western Syria and killed. The Jihadists had been defeated for now, but their rise and fall had left a deep scar on Iraq's politics. Moreover, now that their common enemy was defeated, the US and Iran had fewer reasons to cooperate and tensions soon re-emerged.

After Islamic State

As Islamic State retreated, Iraq's many problems that were either obscured or exacerbated by the struggle with the Jihadists, bubbled back up. One was the fate of Iraq's Kurds. Since 2003 the KRG had been operating more and more independently of Baghdad, even agreeing separate oil and defence deals, prompting some of its leaders to push for full independence.[26] The fight with Islamic State emboldened them further after Kurdish fighters expanded the areas under their control to include the oil-rich city of Kirkuk. This prompted tension with the Baghdad government, which wanted the city returned. Things came to a climax in summer 2017, when Kurdish leaders called an independence referendum, which was won by over 93 per cent but dismissed by Baghdad as illegal.[27] A few weeks later, to reassert their authority, the Iraqi army and supporting PMU units moved into Kirkuk, prompting the Kurdish forces to withdraw without a fight. The move pushed the KRG back to its original borders and tempered Kurdish ambitions for independence, but also shattered any illusion of Kurdish–Arab cooperation and unity that might have been present during the fight with Islamic State.

A second problem was the power of the PMUs. They varied hugely in character. Though mostly Shia, there were numerous Sunni units and some Christian and Turkmen militias. Many had been forged by Suleimani and were loyal to Iran, but others were independent. Some acted as loyal and disciplined fighters, supporting the army, and then keeping order in liberated areas, while others were sectarian zealots or thugs, terrorising Sunni neighbourhoods. The future of these units began to be debated. On the one hand, a growing street protest movement that challenged the corruption at the heart of post-Saddam politics complained that the PMUs were unelected armed groups, often more loyal to Iran than Iraq, and too powerful. On the other hand, many of the political leaders supported the continued presence of PMUs. Most of the elite had close ties and alliances with various PMUs, putting them on the state payroll. Others feared it would be too difficult to either abolish the units or fold them into the army: that they or their Iranian backers would violently resist any such move. The PMUs thus became a permanent feature, provoking resentment from many and adding yet more unaccountable (often violent) actors into Iraqi politics.[28]

A further feature was renewed conflict between the US and Iran. Obama's successor as president, Donald Trump, completely rejected his predecessor's dialogue with Tehran. Heavily influenced by Israel and Saudi Arabia's enmity towards Iran, in summer 2018 Trump pulled out of the nuclear deal agreed by Obama, initiating a new series of sanctions. This, though, only swung the pendulum in Tehran back to the hardliners, mandating Suleimani to step up his activities against the US in Iraq. The informal truce that operated while both were focused on Islamic State was shattered. Kata'ib Hezbollah and other pro-Iranian PMUs began hitting American units in Iraq. Suleimani's reach was greater than ever. On his orders, the Houthis in Yemen in 2019 (see chapter 3) launched an audacious drone attack on Saudi Arabia's largest oil facility, provoking panic in Riyadh and Washington.[29] Israel even began to become directly involved, attacking Iranian bases in Iraq, which was again becoming a battleground for external rivalries.[30] Nowhere was this more evident than when Donald Trump ordered the assassination of Suleimani at an Iraqi base in January 2020.

The order came in response to Kata'ib Hezbollah marching on the US embassy in Baghdad, a few weeks after they had killed a US contractor during a missile attack on Kirkuk. Few expected such a dramatic response from the US, but Trump was famously unpredictable and willing to break conventions. The drone strike targeted Baghdad airport, killing Suleimani and the leader of Kata'ib Hezbollah, Abu Mahdi Muhandis. Trump's audaciousness provoked rage in Baghdad and Tehran, with even the independent-minded Sadr ordering his followers onto the street to demand the US withdraw its remaining troops from Iraq. Many in Iraq and the wider region feared Iran would escalate, provoking all-out war with the Trump White House. As it was, Khamenei opted instead to defuse the situation. A US base in Iraq was attacked but, seemingly deliberately, no American soldiers were killed. Declaring that Suleimani had now been avenged, Tehran opted to move on, recognising that it couldn't risk open conflict with Washington. However, while Iran retained its ability to operate in Iraq and the wider Middle East, the loss of Suleimani and, in Iraq, Muhandis, was a blow. Their successors lacked charisma and organisational ability, emboldening a new group of Iraqis who had started to protest Iran's dominance.[31]

Iraq's 'Tishreen' (October) protest movement erupted in October 2019 and rumbled on for years thereafter, despite disruptions caused by the 2020–21 Covid-19 pandemic. Tens of thousands poured onto the streets of Baghdad and southern Iraq, led by largely uncoordinated groups, unattached to the existing political elite. They were mostly young, unsurprising given that 60 per cent of Iraq's population was under 25 and therefore did not remember the Saddam era or earlier, but all agreed that what had replaced it was not working. They had much to complain about. The economy was stagnant. Little industry developed after 2003, and unemployment was rife, especially among the young. The government relied almost entirely on the oil sector for income but used this to pay off allies and cronies rather than build public services or infrastructure. Despite having the fifth-largest oil reserves in the world, Iraq has an electricity grid that provides only 5–8 hours of power a day, a decrepit education system, potholed roads, and inadequate healthcare.[32] Added to this, environmental disaster was looming. Poor water management by the government (and Iraq's neighbours) had prompted horrendous dust storms across Iraq that worsened health and contributed to the desertification of former agricultural areas, forcing many farmers to migrate or give up. This was all especially felt in Basra, where a combination of little water, limited electricity for air conditioning and 50-degree heat in the summer made it the epicentre of the protest movement.

The protesters blamed the whole corrupt elite for these woes and demanded political reform that ended the 'sectarian apportionment' system. These protesters, the majority of whom were Shia, rejected the sectarianism of most of the political parties and wanted a system that served the Iraqi people rather than a small elite. Similarly, despite being Shia, they frequently complained about Iran's undue influence and the PMUs they had built – objections that grew after the death of the charismatic Suleimani. The protesters were frequently met with force from the government. The police or PMUs were sent in to disperse the demonstrations, often violently, with hundreds of protesters killed. Leading activists were assassinated, with fingers pointing to Iran and its Iraqi allies. This deterred some, while questions over tactics, such as whether to take part in parliamentary elections or boycott them, fractured the movement further. Meanwhile some of the elite attempted to co-opt the protesters for their own ends. Leading parties set up youth wings or new entities led by prominent protesters that were cynically intended to take the sting out of the movement.[33]

The most significant intervention though, came from Sadr. The cleric did not initiate the movement, but many of his supporters from poor Shia areas took part and so it was relatively easy for him to weigh in behind the protesters once they had started to act. Sadr's position was complicated. On the one hand, unlike most Iraqi politicians, he did genuinely have some grassroots support and might not be considered as elitist as others. However, his critics argue that he simply used the protests as a route to power. If this was the case, the strategy had some success. In the October 2021 parliamentary elections, the first since the advent of the protests, Sadr's party did very well after pledging to fulfil the protesters' key demands: ending 'sectarian apportionment' system and reining in Iranian-aligned PMUs. However, the Iraqi system meant Sadr did not have a majority and had to negotiate with other parties to form a government. As always in post-Saddam Iraq, negotiations took months, leaving the government paralysed for over a year until a new premier was agreed. Sadr complicated matters further by dramatically ordering his MPs to resign in June 2022 because negotiations were not going in his favour. To up the pressure, the next month Sadr ordered his supporters to (peacefully) twice storm the parliament building – though this led to violent clashes with opposition PMUs. The result was yet more paralysis. Sadr and his followers claimed this was in the pursuit of fulfilling the protesters' demands of reforming the Iraqi system, but his opponents saw it as a cynical ploy to engineer himself into power. When a government was finally agreed in October 2022, Sadr refused to take part.

The Broken Republic

Such long periods of paralysis typify the extent to which the post-2003 political system is failing. The US fantasised that it could create a prosperous democracy in Iraq but, like the British before them, prioritised their own imperial ambitions, informed by pre-existing prejudices over the construction of a functioning and viable state. Iran and, to a much lesser extent, Turkey have similarly prioritised their own interests in Iraq's new politics, making matters worse. The system has been built for Iraqi politicians, whether Shia, Sunni, or Kurdish, who conceive of themselves as representatives of their ethnic or religious group, rather than legislators serving the country as a whole. This has exacerbated divisions, sometimes leading to violence. Moreover, the elites empowered by the US and Iran have been dominated by corrupt exiles, further decreasing the chances of effective government. The result is a broken republic that it is hard to fix. The protest movement that began in 2019 is no surprise – indeed it is remarkable that such frustrations at the system did not emerge earlier. But the failure of the movement to translate widespread frustration into political change is an indicator of how embedded the system and its elites have become.

Meanwhile, Iraq's problems continue to grow. It regularly comes near the top of lists of the most corrupt countries in the world, and the worst in which to do business.[34] Its economy is stagnating, while environmental damage gets worse. The question of Kurdish independence remains unanswered while the Kurdish region continues its de facto separation from the rest of Iraq. Violence remains a possibility, with the twin threats of ethno-sectarian violence and Jihadism far from defeated. Iraq's weak government is prey to external influence, so it remains likely that foreign players will continue to interfere in its politics, seeing Iraq as a convenient battleground for wider regional and international competition. As has been the case for at least the past forty years, if not longer, the Iraqi people could suffer once more from these external and internal machinations, with all the negative consequences they bring, for some time yet.

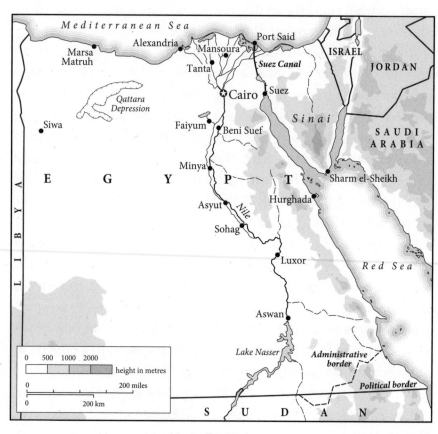

Egypt

6

Egypt
Fallen Giant

Egypt is the most populous country in the Middle East by some way. At over 103 million, it outdoes its nearest rivals, Turkey and Iran, by more than 15 million, and towers over other regional powers like Saudi Arabia (34 million), the UAE (9 million), and Israel (9 million). It similarly boasts the largest city in the region. Cairo, with its 21 million inhabitants, is more than double the size of London or New York, and a good 6 million larger than its nearest regional competitor, Istanbul. Egypt has the largest standing army in the Arab world and wields considerable cultural heft.[1] Cairo is home to the Arab movie industry, the ancient Al-Azhar Islamic university, and the headquarters of the regional cooperation organisation, the League of Arab States (known as the Arab League). Unlike many Middle Eastern states, it has a long history as a homogeneous country, avoiding some, but not all, of the divisive identity politics that have destabilised others. Because of these many advantages, Egypt has historically been among the most powerful countries in its neighbourhood. Ancient Pharaohs, Islamic Caliphs, Ottoman governors, and nationalist dictators have all been able to harness Egypt's potential to project power far beyond the Nile. But those days appear long gone. Cairo holds many monuments to Egypt's more prosperous past: the pyramids of Giza, the Islamic old city, the late nineteenth-century Parisian-esque downtown, and the modernist Cairo Tower, which during the 1960s was the tallest building in Africa. But today visitors to the city are struck more by the overcrowding, the gridlocked traffic, the polluted river, and the vast urban sprawl. The capital, like much of Egypt, far from emulating its past successes, is barely struggling to survive.

In the late nineteenth century Egypt was a more developed country than Japan, and even as late as the 1960s it was more prosperous than countries that have since overtaken it like South Korea and Taiwan. It has likewise fallen behind most Middle Eastern and North African states, where once it was the most advanced. Twenty-first-century Egypt has the sixth lowest regional GDP per capita and fourth lowest literacy, while nearly 30 per cent of Egyptians live below the poverty line.[2] A marker of this decline has been Egypt's changing regional role. Once it was the pre-eminent Arab power in the Middle East, intervening militarily or politically in its neighbours' affairs, but today an enfeebled Egypt is dependent on neighbours and allies further afield – like the US – for economic support. While its autocratic governments have mostly avoided the extent of foreign meddling found in contemporary Yemen, Syria, or Lebanon, its politics did briefly become an arena for regional competition in the 2010s. When a popular uprising overthrew the stagnant thirty-year dictatorship in 2011, a wave of optimism, fear, instability, and political activity was ushered in. Ultimately this ended in 2013, when the military deposed the elected Islamist government, establishing an autocracy even harsher than the one toppled two years earlier. The new military dictator, Abdel Fattah El-Sisi, while no puppet, was strongly backed by the UAE and Saudi Arabia in this move, and implicitly endorsed by Washington. Meanwhile the Islamists' allies, Turkey and Qatar, were outraged. While Sisi has since sought to move beyond any obligations to these external backers and reassert Egypt's independence, he has had mixed results. Where once it dominated the region, Egypt today is at best a medium power.

EGYPT

The Wealth of the Nile

Ninety-five per cent of Egyptians live along the banks of the Nile and its delta, and the world's longest river is the main reason Egypt exists. In an otherwise desert environment, the fertile land along the Nile has provided rich agriculture since the earliest human civilisations. Surpluses and wealth from agriculture, and the strong central governments and bureaucracies that developed with it, enabled Egypt's rulers often to project power beyond the Nile. But at the same time these bounties, alongside Egypt's strategic location at the gateway of two continents, have made the country an attractive prize. Egypt's history seems to oscillate between eras of dominance and those of subjugation. Several millennia of pharaonic rule were finally ended by defeat and annexation, by the Persians, Greeks, and then the Romans, as Egypt became the breadbasket for Rome and its eastern Byzantine successor. Islamic conquest in the seventh century eventually led to Egypt's return to pre-eminence when a Shia Caliphate, the Fatimids, used Cairo as the base for an empire spanning the Levant, North Africa, and Arabia. Egypt would remain independent for the next 500 years, with the Fatimids' various successors extending their rule over much of the Middle East, until they were once again defeated and absorbed into another empire by the Turkish Ottomans, in 1517.

As elsewhere in the Middle East, the Ottomans' decline in the nineteenth century brought European empires swooping in. First came the French under Napoleon, who briefly conquered Egypt in 1798 but were defeated by the British, allowing the Ottomans to reconquer. One of the Ottoman commanders, an Albanian called Muhammad Ali, emerged as the de facto ruler, modernising much of Egypt's agriculture and military, and challenging Istanbul's rule by capturing Sudan, Syria, and Arabia. While Ali was forced back, he secured recognition of Egyptian autonomy and his family's control of it. But his successors' rule was undermined when they ran up huge debts to Britain, which took an increased interest in Egypt after

143

the construction of the Suez Canal. This led to London invading in 1882 and declaring an Egyptian 'protectorate' within the British empire.

British rule saw the continuation of many of the modernisation trends begun under Muhammad Ali. Infrastructure, education, urbanisation, and agricultural reforms all continued apace, as did the modernisation of the military. Egypt became increasingly cosmopolitan as first Ali's fellow Albanians and then western Europeans acquired land and established businesses. But foreign rule fuelled nationalism, particularly among Egypt's growing intellectual and artisan classes, which was heightened when Britain massively increased its military occupation during the First World War. This exploded into popular unrest in 1919, forcing London to grant Egypt nominal independence in 1922, though it retained control over key aspects of defence and the Suez Canal.[3] The hollowness of independence was exposed during the Second World War, when Britain once again dispatched its military to Egypt and then humiliated the king, Farouq, by surrounding his palace with tanks, demanding he appoint a new government of London's choosing. Though the 1920s and 1930s were times of relative liberalism, when Egyptians enjoyed press freedom, a cultural renaissance, and a (mostly) functional parliamentary democracy, economic inequality grew.[4] The masses and middle classes grew frustrated at the aloofness of Farouq and the ruling elite, especially what they saw as an unwillingness to force Britain out for good. The military emerged as the leading voice for these concerns, drawing many officers from humble or lower middle-class backgrounds. They were further enraged by the army's humiliation in Palestine in the Israeli war of independence in 1948–9, the poor conduct of which was blamed on government incompetence. One group within the military, the Free Officers, ultimately ended royal rule and British influence when they staged a bloodless coup in 1952. A few days later they sent Farouq into exile and within two years had Britain agree to withdrawing its last troops.

The leading player among the Free Officers, soon to become president of the newly created republic, was Colonel Gamal Abdul Nasser. To many, Nasser remains a hero who stood up to the West and gave Egypt and the Arab world back its pride. At home, Nasser smashed the old order. His socialist policies saw land requisitioned from the elite and distributed among the peasantry, industry and other enterprises nationalised, women's rights improved, and increased access to healthcare and education. The economic disparities of the monarchical era lessened, making Nasser especially popular among the masses. Abroad, Nasser eclipsed even Mohammad Ali in making Egypt the most prominent state in the Middle East. When Britain made a last-ditch attempt to claw back influence in Egypt by invading the Suez Canal with France and Israel in 1956, it was forced into a humiliating climbdown when its ally, the US, insisted London withdraw. Though he had done very little in the crisis, Nasser claimed responsibility for Britain's retreat and was hailed across the Arab world as an anti-imperialist hero. Thereafter Nasser embraced Arab nationalism, positioning himself as the Middle East's Bismarck, promising to unite the Arab world that had been artificially divided by European empires. Egypt began to interfere across the region: inspiring military coups against Arab monarchies, backing players in Lebanon's sectarian politics, temporarily uniting with Syria, and sending the Egyptian army into North Yemen's civil war. Nasser's colossal reputation extended even beyond the Middle East as he became a leading player in the anti-Cold War Non-Aligned Movement alongside India and Yugoslavia.

But Nasser's critics argue these temporary foreign successes were outweighed by later failures. Egypt's moment in the sun was fleeting. The 1960s saw the collapse of the union with Syria, a costly quagmire in North Yemen followed by catastrophic defeat to Israel in the Six Day War that saw Sinai occupied and the Suez Canal closed. Bankrupt, Nasser had to abandon both Arab nationalism and non-alignment to beg Arab monarchies for funds and the Soviet Union for weapons.

This came on top of failures in the socialist policies that saw his bureaucratic economy struggle. There was also a dark side to Nasser's rule. He swept away the liberalism of the interwar years, constructing a dictatorship. In his first weeks in power, the leaders of a labour dispute in the textile industry were hanged, underlining the break with the past. While Nasser's was not as brutal as the subsequent Middle Eastern dictatorships of Hafez al-Assad or Saddam Hussein, press freedom was ended, parliamentary democracy abolished, and there were regular crackdowns on political opponents. Nasser also oversaw the end of Egypt's cosmopolitanism. Foreign landowners and businessmen were dispossessed and encouraged to leave, as was Egypt's ancient Jewish community, as hostility towards Israel intensified. While millions of his supporters took to the streets to mourn Nasser when he died in 1970, and the Egypt he left behind may have temporarily flourished, it was beset by problems.

Nasser's successor was another Free Officer, his vice president, Anwar Sadat, who lacked his comrade's charisma and oratorical gifts. Even so, Sadat attempted to consolidate power by addressing the challenges left at the end of Nasser's reign. Internationally, he launched a new war against Israel in 1973 that ended in stalemate but paved the way for a negotiated peace that saw Sinai returned and the Suez Canal re-opened. It also enabled Egypt to switch sides in the Cold War, ditching the Soviet Union for the US, which offered $1.5 billion in aid every year.[5] Domestically, Sadat promised more political and economic openness, initially allowing more dissent and press freedom and abandoning socialism for market economics. However, though the economic reforms brought wealth to the elite and some in the middle classes, the masses suffered, and poverty increased, while Cairo once again started running up major foreign debts. Moreover, Sadat backslid on his political liberalisation when the rapprochement with Israel prompted domestic opposition. Eventually this contributed to Sadat's assassination in 1981, when radical Islamists who felt betrayed by the peace treaty gunned him down during a military parade.

Sadat's death ushered in what became the thirty-year reign of Hosni Mubarak. Mubarak was also a military man, an air force commander during the 1973 war, but a generation younger than his two predecessors and less swayed by the ideological currents they lived through. He continued on the domestic and international path set by Sadat: peace with Israel, alignment with the West, and capitalist autocracy at home. Yet though this proved stable in the medium term, it perpetuated a decline that had begun in the Nasser era, with Egypt becoming poorer, more unequal domestically, and increasingly diminished abroad.

Officers and Islamists

Like all states and societies, modern Egypt is complex, with multiple groups and institutions playing a role in politics, international relations, and everyday life. That said, two bodies stand out for their disproportionate influence on contemporary Egypt: the military and the Muslim Brotherhood. The military is most important, dominating politics, the economy, and society. Since the end of the monarchy, all but one of Egypt's presidents have been military men. Professor Yezid Sayigh has described Egypt as 'the Officers' Republic' because of the extent of the military's role.[6] Serving or former officers not only hold major offices of state like ministries and governorships, but also key positions in leading industries and business. However, the government is no military junta, and many leaders have tried to maintain the army's privileges while keeping it from intervening too heavily in politics. Nasser, for example, discarded his uniform for a suit. Though he drew on the military for prime ministers and other key positions, he was also fearful that the army might seek to overthrow him – as it had King Farouk – and so tried to dilute its influence, with only limited success. Sadat likewise feared a military coup, especially after peace with Israel gave it no external focus. His solution was to offer the military a greater slice of the newly opened-up economy. These privileges continued and expanded under Mubarak, who attempted to keep the military out of politics (though not individual military personnel) in exchange for access to huge wealth.[7]

On the one hand, these strategies largely worked. Though the military remained the most powerful component of the ruling regime, it did not intervene in politics directly. In contrast to the Turkish military, a similarly powerful 'deep state' body that launched four coups d'état between 1960 and 1997 (see chapter 8), Egypt experienced no such army intervention for nearly sixty years after 1952. The flipside was that by granting the military so much wealth and status, it became fiercely protective of its privilege. This ultimately led the army to overthrow Mubarak in 2011, sacrificing the president to retain its own privileges. But long before then it regularly interfered in many aspects of government and the economy: pushing to expand its control, squeezing civilian business out or demanding a cut. This helped create competitive 'fiefdoms' within the already cumbersome bureaucracy, making governance and service delivery even slower and more inefficient.[8] For those on the inside, the rewards were considerable. Senior officers lived in resort-style compounds in the suburbs of Cairo, separated from the rest of society. Due to conscription, they had access to up to a million men under their command to provide cheap labour for various business enterprises. These included army-run cement factories, farms, steel companies, water bottling plants, pasta plants, and of course defence industries. These activities grew even more after 2011.

The army was among the few beneficiaries of the later years of Mubarak's rule, when the economy struggled. The reforms of the Sadat era ushered in an era of crony capitalism, in which a private sector emerged alongside the huge state-run enterprises, but one that was deeply corrupt. Though Mubarak initially benefited from Egypt's limited supply of oil and gas, these resources, like much of the economy, were depleting and mismanaged, forcing Egypt to start importing both. Likewise, despite its long agricultural history, lack of investment and mismanagement meant Egypt had to import huge quantities of wheat. While Nasser had encouraged family planning, these measures were de-prioritised and Egypt's population boomed, leaping from 27 million in 1960 to 87 million in 2010.[9] By way of comparison, the UK's population grew by only 10 million in the same period. This created a huge labour force that the struggling economy simply couldn't satisfy, leaving widespread unemployment, under-employment, and frustration.

One of the main beneficiaries of this economic decline was the other major force in Egyptian politics: the Muslim Brotherhood, an Islamist organisation formed in the 1920s. Its founder, Hassan al-Banna, insisted they were not a political group, instead wanting to work at grassroots level to encourage people to adopt a more religious way of life. However, their widespread activities meant they were frequently viewed as a threat, first by the monarchy and then by Nasser, who outlawed the group and arrested its leaders. Sadat was more lenient and legalised the Brotherhood, encouraging religion more than Nasser did in the hope that Islam might substitute for the Arab nationalism that his foreign policy was moving away from. This came alongside a general increase in piety among Egypt's population. By the 1970s, as Egyptians travelled to work abroad, many were influenced by the conservative Islam they experienced in the Gulf states and were simultaneously disillusioned by the left-wing secularism of Nasser that had ultimately delivered little.[10] As Sadat's and then Mubarak's economic policies shrank some state services, more and more were drawn to the Brotherhood, who provided alternative services like education and health clinics in deprived areas.

Despite regular crackdowns, by the 1980s the Brotherhood had become a political force, standing in elections to the relatively power-less parliament, and fielding candidates for professional syndicates and university unions. They did especially well in the first round of the 2005 parliamentary elections, which the US pressured Mubarak to allow to be freer than usual, prompting the president to introduce new restrictions for the second round to ensure the Brotherhood didn't triumph. However, despite Mubarak's fears, the Brotherhood were far from an unstoppable force. There were internal divisions over ideology and strategy as well as between older and younger generations. Moreover, despite their widespread support, the leadership was dominated by a small, closed group of conservatives who would ultimately prove lacking in political skill. Though the events of 2011–13 would be characterised as a struggle for Egypt between the Brotherhood and the military, the Islamists had nowhere near the influence and resources of the officers and would fall short.

The Uprising and the Coup

That confrontation, when it came, took both the military and the Brotherhood by surprise as it emerged from a popular uprising that neither initiated. In January 2011, after mass protests had toppled nearby Tunisia's dictator, angry Egyptians took to the streets demanding the fall of their own tyrant. After thirty years of Mubarak's autocratic rule, coupled with economic decline and the regular humiliations doled out by the security forces, anger boiled over Millions eventually took to the streets of Cairo and other cities demanding 'the fall of the regime'. Despite Mubarak repeatedly insisting he would not stand down, after eighteen days of protest the matter was taken out of his hands. The army, after some nudging from the US, deposed the 82-year-old leader and dispatched him to his villa in Sharm el-Sheikh.[11] In his place the military declared that a Supreme Council of the Armed Forces (SCAF) would rule until elections were held within six months.

The Brotherhood were not heavily involved in the protests and only joined the calls for Mubarak's ouster late in the day. Instead, the protesters were a more organic, disorganised collection of the middle classes, youths, labour activists, and students. But once Mubarak was gone, they proved ineffective at forming united political parties, lacking both a unified voice and the grassroots networks to organise. In contrast, the Brotherhood had these in abundance, and soon emerged as the main beneficiary of the new era. At first, the Brotherhood chose to be conciliatory. They insisted they would not seek to impose Islamic *sharia* law if elected and would not dominate politics, declining to field a candidate for the presidential elections and only contesting 30 per cent of parliamentary seats.[12] However, by the time the SCAF agreed to elections (later than promised), the Brotherhood had undergone some internal changes, expelling many of the reformists and youth activists who had been involved in the protests, and adopted a harder line. They stood for more than half of the parliamentary seats, winning the largest representation with 37 per cent of the vote. More controversially, they then entered a candidate for the presidency, Mohamed Morsi, who narrowly defeated the SCAF's chosen candidate. For the first time in the history of the Egyptian Republic, the president was not a military man, but a democratically elected Islamist.

Democratic Egypt lasted just over a year. Morsi was ill-suited to the role of president. He had been the Brotherhood's second choice candidate, thrust into the election when the preferred nominee was disqualified. Neither a great speaker nor an effective administrator, Morsi was chosen for his long loyalty to the Brotherhood rather than his presidential qualities.[13] In power, Morsi proved rigid and unaccommodating, exacerbating the divisions in Egyptian politics rather than bridging them and consolidating the democratic revolution. He alienated the liberal activists who had brought about the 2011 uprising. While many disliked the Brotherhood, a large number had backed Morsi rather than the SCAF candidate, fearing the alternative was a return to military dictatorship. But once in power, Morsi and the Brotherhood ignored the liberal deputies in parliament, instead working only with other religious parties or accommodating the military's demands. He further outraged liberals with autocratic measures in the name of 'protecting the revolution' that were seen by some as an Islamist power grab.[14]

Morsi also alienated the military. The SCAF had been reluctant to give up power but had eventually permitted elections. Senior military commanders at first hoped they could work with the Brotherhood, but the Brotherhood's failure to find a compromise presidential candidate dispelled this. There were some instances of collaboration, such as the constitution passed through by Morsi in 2012, which gave the military considerable autonomy and protected its privileges, and an electoral law that heavily favoured the Brotherhood over liberals. Naively, the Brotherhood believed this would neutralise the army. Likewise, Morsi handpicked an army man, Abdel Fattah El-Sisi, as defence minister, believing the pious general would be his man in the military. Instead, it was Sisi who led the eventual coup. By summer 2013, Morsi was widely unpopular except among his core Brotherhood supporters. Not only liberals and pro-army voices, but also Egypt's Christians (5–10 per cent of the population) were fearful of Egypt becoming another Iran, where a popular revolution was taken over by Islamists. Throughout the early summer, protests were held against Morsi, secretly encouraged by intelligence agencies on Sisi's orders.[15] In early July, Sisi then used the protests to justify a move against the Brotherhood. The military gave Morsi forty-eight hours to meet the demands of the protesters. The tin-eared president refused and apparently was completely surprised to be placed under arrest a few days later.

Sisi ushered in a new era of dictatorship and repression far worse than Mubarak's. A sign of this came just over a month after the coup, when almost a thousand Morsi supporters were massacred by the military during a peaceful sit-in in Cairo's Rabaa Square. Despite the sporadic violence of Nasser, Sadat, and Mubarak, such mass killing was not familiar to Egyptians, who had largely avoided the horrors seen in Iraq or Syria. Soon afterwards the Brotherhood was outlawed once again, part of a wider campaign against all possible opponents to the new regime, including liberals and leftists. Thousands were arrested and hundreds sentenced to death.[16] Morsi himself was put on trial and was given the death penalty for trumped up spying charges, a sentence later commuted to life imprisonment, though he died in prison in 2019. His defence minister, meanwhile, assumed power. After drafting a new constitution that granted the presidency and the military even more power, Sisi was elected president in May 2014. The election took place amid a climate of fear following the crackdown, and several liberal activists boycotted the poll. Sisi won 96 per cent of the vote in what seemed a sham contest against a single pliant competitor. While the 43 per cent turnout was lower than the 52 per cent who voted in Morsi's election two years earlier, Sisi did seem to enjoy some genuine popularity among those who felt he had saved Egypt from the Brotherhood. In contrast, Brotherhood supporters and liberals were desolate at the failures of the 2011 revolution.

Scholars and analysts have offered a range of reasons why Egypt failed to build a successful democracy after 2011 and fell back into authoritarian dictatorship two years later. Professor Robert Springborg, among others, has argued that Egypt faced several obstacles to developing a functioning democracy after Mubarak was toppled.[17] Egypt's population was much younger, more rural, undereducated, lacking in a sizeable middle class, and overly dependent on the state for sustenance compared to other countries that have seen successful democratic revolutions. A further structural disadvantage was the pre-existing position of the military within the Egyptian state. Given the privileged position afforded the army by Nasser, Sadat, and Mubarak, it was always going to be difficult for democratic forces to keep the officers in their barracks, especially if they felt threatened. It is plausible that elected leaders with greater political skill than Morsi and the Muslim Brotherhood might have been able to placate the military and act in a conciliatory manner to gradually embed democratic practices. However, the Islamists completely failed at this, blundering repeatedly, and alienating all but their core support. Finally, all the domestic players were aided by foreign actors. As will be discussed below, most foreign assistance came from forces uninterested in or actively opposed to democratic transition. Qatar and, to a lesser extent, Turkey supported the Brotherhood, while the UAE and Saudi Arabia backed Sisi's coup. The United States, which might have been a key advocate for democratic forces in an allied state, was notably silent in 2013, a de facto endorsement of the military takeover.

Buying Influence

For all its flaws, Egypt is far more stable than many of its Middle Eastern contemporaries, having avoided the civil wars of Syria, Libya, and Yemen, and the political chaos of Iraq and Lebanon. But this has not made it impervious to foreign influence. In the later years of the twentieth century, and especially since 2011, Egypt's weakness has been its economy, and the ruling elite's need for funds. This has allowed foreign actors to buy influence. While prior to the uprising this was mostly friendly Gulf states and the US pouring money into Mubarak's crumbling regime, the disruption of 2011 prompted competing regional and international governments to back different factions. Most of the Gulf states were shocked by Mubarak's fall. They had assumed that their mutual ally, the US, would support the ailing Egyptian regime, and were appalled that President Barack Obama helped facilitate his departure by urging the military to oust him. The exception was Qatar, whose Al Jazeera news station had provided wall-to-wall coverage of the uprising, inspiring more Egyptians to join the protests.

Qatar had long connections with the Muslim Brotherhood, while the UAE and Saudi Arabia both opposed the organisation, but all were distracted in the immediate aftermath of the uprising: Doha and Abu Dhabi by Libya (see chapter 2) and all by Bahrain (see chapter 9). Gradually, these three Gulf states started to show more interest in Egypt. In the 2011 parliamentary elections, the Salafist al-Nour party, Islamists who are more conservative but less revolutionary than the Brotherhood, gained the second-largest number of seats, partly due to Gulf-based funding.[18] Saudi Arabia helped facilitate this, possibly hoping that the Salafists would split the Islamist vote and weaken the Brotherhood. From the other side, once the Brotherhood formed a government, Qatar stepped in to boost Egypt's floundering economy, offering $7 billion in aid. Meanwhile Al Jazeera continued to offer favourable coverage of the Brotherhood, including through a new Egypt-focused channel. Turkey, Qatar's close ally and a fellow backer of the Brotherhood, similarly agreed a $2 billion loan.[19]

But foreign aid couldn't save Morsi, whose government was on the brink of economic crisis – a further factor prompting the coup. Sisi, meanwhile, was strongly supported by the UAE and Saudi Arabia. He had a personal relationship with the Saudi leadership, having once been defence attaché at the Egyptian embassy in Riyadh. He was similarly close to UAE Crown Prince Mohammed Bin Zayed (MBZ). As the military started plotting their coup, leaked recordings have since suggested that the UAE was involved early on.[20] This included funding some of the anti-Morsi demonstrations and promising to cover any losses in US aid should Washington oppose the ouster. Within days of Morsi's toppling, Saudi Arabia, the UAE, and their Gulf ally Kuwait announced a $12 billion aid package for the new government. MBZ further endorsed the action by visiting Sisi in Cairo barely two weeks after the Rabaa Square massacre. In total, these three Gulf states provided $30 billion in aid over the next three years.[21] In contrast, Qatar was frozen out by the new regime. Al Jazeera had some of its channels banned, while its journalists were arrested and tried, including Western correspondents for their English station.

Financial and diplomatic support came with some strings attached. The UAE and Saudi Arabia became increasingly activist against their two main, separate, regional enemies, the Muslim Brotherhood and Iran, and now expected Sisi to join their efforts. Sisi though, was no puppet, and engaged selectively. He enthusiastically joined Abu Dhabi in supporting rogue general Khalifa Haftar, who was fighting a democratically elected Muslim Brotherhood-aligned government in neighbouring Libya. He also joined the Saudi–UAE coalition against Iranian-backed Houthi rebels in Yemen but sent just a token naval force. Similarly, though Cairo agreed to blockade and isolate Qatar in 2017 alongside Riyadh and Abu Dhabi, Egyptian involvement was restrained. No Qatari investors in Egypt were expelled, while the 250,000 Egyptian citizens in Doha stayed put.[22] Sisi also refused to be drawn into the Syria conflict, where Saudi Arabia was sponsoring rebel forces against Iran's ally, Bashar al-Assad. With many of the rebels aligned with the Muslim Brotherhood, Sisi was not especially keen for Assad to be defeated and quietly kept channels open with the Syrian leadership, a practice shared by the UAE.

Indeed, of the two Gulf states, the UAE has proven the closer ally. Tensions with Saudi Arabia were sparked when power transitioned in 2015 to Prince Mohammed Bin Salman (MBS), who ousted Sisi's closest ally from the Saudi court and later arrested him.[23] Cairo sought to build bridges, including granting Saudi Arabia control over two uninhabited Red Sea islands, despite considerable domestic objections, and the two remain allies despite some disagreements. Sisi was able to regain some autonomy from his Gulf backers in 2016, when he secured a $12 billion loan from the IMF, allowing greater financial independence. However, the precarity of Egypt's finances was exposed once again, first during the Covid pandemic and then the 2022 Ukraine war, from which Egypt imports much of its grain. This prompted Cairo to gratefully accept a $22 billion aid package from Saudi Arabia, the UAE, and a newly rehabilitated Qatar.[24] Once again Egypt's weak finances had left it prey to outside leverage.

Arguably the US has the most influence over Egypt but has proven less effective than the Gulf states at using it. Since Sadat swapped sides in the Cold War, Egypt has been a key American ally in the

Middle East. As Egypt is the most populous state, with the largest army, and home to the Suez Canal, through which 10 per cent of the world's trade flows, ensuring the country is stable and aligned with the US has been a strategic priority.[25] This is closely linked to Washington's deep commitment to Israel: maintaining the peace deal that the White House brokered and utilising Cairo's connections to Palestinians in the neighbouring Gaza strip to defuse tensions when necessary (see chapter 4). The alliance, like Egypt's with the Gulf states, is oiled and maintained by money. The 1979 peace brought with it an annual grant from the US, currently $1.3 billion, most of which is military aid, and Washington also provides billions more in arms sales. However, America's power and priorities have changed in recent years, reducing the importance of the relationship to both parties. After overextending in the Middle East with the occupation of Iraq and getting stuck in a two-decades-long quagmire in Afghanistan, the US public and its leaders lost enthusiasm for overseas adventures. At the same time, the 2008 financial crisis weakened the US, while the rise of China ended the post-Cold War era of unchallenged American global dominance. This was the context in which Egypt's uprising and coup took place: with Washington's leaders far less interested in Egypt and the wider Middle East and having less of a free rein to act than in the past.

Successive presidents have dealt with these changing circumstances differently. Barack Obama, who was president during the uprising and coup, had been elected partly after a popular backlash against his predecessor George W. Bush's failed interventions in the Middle East. As such, he was reluctant to get involved in Egypt when the uprising broke out, and some of his advisers, such as Secretary of State Hillary Clinton, urged sticking by Mubarak.[26] However, Obama eventually recognised Mubarak's position was unsupportable and urged the Egyptian military to intervene against him. Though the US had no pre-existing relations with the Brotherhood, the White House frantically sought to build ties in the next year, with Obama speaking to Morsi to help broker a ceasefire between Hamas and Israel in Gaza in 2012. Morsi naively believed this personal endorsement would ensure Obama would prevent the Egyptian military from over-throwing him, over-estimating both America's influence in Cairo and its commitment to the Brotherhood government. As it was, US intelligence were aware of the likelihood of a coup months before it occurred but did little. Obama reportedly asked the Pentagon to urge Sisi against intervening, but his defence officials disliked the Brotherhood and did not act.[27] Obama then came under pressure from lobbies supporting Israel, the UAE, and Saudi Arabia to not oppose the ouster when it came, meaning he chose not to describe the events of 2013 as a 'coup', which legally would have required the US to suspend its aid to Egypt. Even after the Rabaa massacre, the White House only suspended payments, before restoring them soon after. Despite his initial support for the uprising, ultimately Obama prioritised security and stability over democracy and showed himself unwilling or unable to stand up to pressure from Israel and the Gulf.

Obama's successor, Donald Trump, also favoured stepping back from Middle Eastern involvement. But while Obama struggled to marry his strategic preference for less involvement with his personal commitment to freedom and democracy, Trump had no such hang ups. While Obama had refused to invite Sisi to the White House as the human rights situation in Egypt deteriorated, Trump invited him within months of assuming office, later referring to him as 'my favou-rite dictator'.[28] Trump's four years improved US–Egypt ties, as the bombastic president embraced Sisi, MBS, MBZ, and Israeli premier Benjamin Netanyahu, endorsing their anti-Iran and anti-Brother-hood regional policies. This culminated in the Trump-brokered Abraham Accords that saw Israel sign peace agreements with the UAE, Bahrain, Morocco, and Sudan, paving the way for closer ties between Egypt and Israel as the regional stigma around working with the Jewish state diminished. However, ties with Washington did not simply slip back into the close alliance of the late Cold War. Trump remained lukewarm on the region and generally took a more isolationist, transactional approach to foreign relations. When Joe Biden succeeded Trump in early 2021, he also de-prioritised the Middle East, focusing instead on events in East Asia and later the 2022 Russian invasion of Ukraine. Maintaining cordial ties with Egypt was important, but Biden was under more pressure than Trump from Congress and his Democratic base to speak out against Sisi's human rights record. Biden held back a token $150 million of a $1.3 billion aid package in 2022, but also held the first Strategic Dialogue with Egypt in six years, indicating that Sisi's autocracy would not obstruct the alliance.[29]

For Sisi's part, he preferred to diversify his foreign ties rather than become dependent on the US. This meant getting close to Vladimir Putin's Russia, which became a source of arms procurement, energy collaboration, tourism, and diplomatic collaboration in Libya and the eastern Mediterranean. Sisi wasn't replacing the American alliance with a Russian one, but diluting his dependence allowed him to have multiple sources of external funds, arms, and aid. In a sign of a broader shift for Egypt's view of the US, while 75 per cent of its arms came from the US in the 2000s, only 23 per cent did in the 2010s, the remainder mostly coming from Russia, Germany, and France.[30] The US remained important to Egypt but was no longer the most essential ally it once had been. This was seen in 2022, when Egypt joined fellow Arab states, and Israel, in refusing to join Western allies in condemning Russia's invasion of Ukraine, instead pursuing a neutral position.

Sisi's Egypt

While Sisi may have overseen the kind of stability his foreign allies appreciate, it has come at a cost to ordinary Egyptians. In the years since the coup Sisi has consolidated his rule in a brutal manner. He gained re-election in 2018 by a similarly high margin of 97 per cent, before amending the constitution to permit him to remain in power until 2030. Other amendments gave him the power to appoint all chief justices and the public prosecutor, effectively putting the courts in his hands. He empowered the army even more than his predecessors, granting it near-complete immunity and autonomy from the law, while giving officers an even bigger slice of the economy.[31] Meanwhile crackdowns have continued. What began as repression of the Brotherhood was extended to include all political opposition: journalists, activists, labour leaders, and students. A year after the coup 40,000 people had been detained and 3,000 killed. Among those detained, tortured, and murdered was an Italian PhD student, Giulio Regeni, but the Egyptian government denied involvement in his killing. In 2016, Amnesty International reported that 'hundreds of students, political activists and protesters, including children as young as 14, vanish without trace at the hands of the state'.[32] While elections to parliament were permitted, in a return to the Mubarak days, they heavily favoured regime loyalists who dominated the mostly powerless talking shop. Formerly disgraced Mubarak cronies were rehabilitated, while in 2017 the ex-president himself was released from the prison he had languished in since the uprising and was granted a state funeral when he died peacefully in 2020.

Sisi's Egypt is a more violent and polarised place than before 2011. Communal violence between Muslims and Christians has increased. The increased piety of both communities had raised tensions in the past, especially Christian objections to restrictions on building new churches, but 2011 had seen both communities protest against Mubarak together. However, the Coptic Christians' broad support for the coup, illustrated when the Coptic Patriarch stood alongside Sisi days later, made the community an increased target for persecution, including suicide bombings on cathedrals and mob attacks that killed over 100 people. Violent crime in general increased under Sisi's rule, as did sexual harassment and assaults on women, which was already a major issue under Mubarak. A 2017 survey showed that over 60 per cent of Egyptian men have sexually harassed women in public.[33] While Sisi has publicly made gestures in support of Christians and women, under his rule they have been less safe. Further divisions exploded into violence in peripheral regions. Members of the long-neglected Nubian community in southern Egypt clashed with Arab tribes in 2014, leaving twenty-five dead. Meanwhile a major insurgency broke out in Sinai, another marginalised region, where a terrorist group allied with Islamic State was able to recruit from the disaffected Bedouin population. Sisi, who saw Islamic State Jihadists and the Muslim Brotherhood as one and the same, escalated the pre-existing campaign on assuming the presidency, deploying over 25,000 troops into Sinai. This came with heavy-handed tactics, including indiscriminate air strikes and the bulldozing of villages. Over 3,000 soldiers and more than 1,000 civilians were killed.[34] Though the Jihadist forces have been reduced, due to military operations and some much-needed economic investment in the Sinai, they remain active and sporadically attack army positions.

Sisi had some initial success in stabilising Egypt's economy. The 2016 IMF loan came after Cairo agreed to a harsh economic reform programme, including a 50 per cent currency devaluation that disproportionately impacted the poor. However, it did help cut the government's spiralling deficit and reduce public debt to 90 per cent of GDP – still a considerable amount – and GDP per capita surpassed 2016 levels within four years. Yet the 2020 Covid pandemic and Ukraine war two years later added new economic pressures. Further IMF loans were sought, prompting austerity measures and, in 2022, a further currency devaluation that again hit the poor hard, increasing resentment at the Sisi regime.[35] The economic problems were further hampered by Sisi's grandiose infrastructure projects. A parallel canal alongside the Suez Canal was built at the cost of $8 billion to boost usage, though the increase in revenue proved less spectacular than promised. Similarly, 2015 saw construction begin on a $58 billion new capital city to move government out of traffic-clogged Cairo, and presumably away from another potential popular uprising, but building proved slow and many questioned the need for this, and its value. Egypt also invested heavily in military hardware after 2013, becoming at one point the world's third-largest importer of weapons. Military spending had fallen considerably under Mubarak, and equipment needed replacing, but the scale of Sisi's investment suggests he was prioritising satisfying his own army and arms dealing allies like the US and Russia over the needs of his own people.[36] In the meantime, Egypt's education and health services declined further and there was little investment in human capital. After a temporary bounce, Sisi's economy still didn't provide enough jobs, with large employers like the tourism sector struggling to return to pre-2011 levels.

One area of relative success for Sisi has been foreign policy. While he remains close to the Gulf states, he has sought to carve out a distinctive approach in his neighbourhood. As well as supporting Haftar in Libya, there has been greater involvement in the eastern Mediterranean than under Mubarak. Egypt has developed its offshore natural gas and modernised its navy to protect those platforms. Likewise, Sisi has improved ties with fellow eastern Mediterranean allies, Israel, Greece, Cyprus, and Italy. In contrast, ties with Turkey have soured. This was primarily over Ankara's backing of the Muslim Brotherhood, but it manifested itself further in the two countries backing opposite sides in the Libyan civil war, and Sisi supporting Cyprus and Greece's claims to gas fields over those of Turkey and North Cyprus. After several years of hostility, 2022 saw some improvement in Turkish–Egyptian ties. In contrast, relations remained strained with southern neighbours. Sisi has sought to deepen his involvement in Sudan's increasingly violent politics after the overthrow of its dictator in 2019, with mixed results. Meanwhile relations with Ethiopia are increasingly tense over Addis Ababa's plans to build a Grand Ethiopian Renaissance Dam that will cut the flow of Nile water into Egypt (see chapter 10). Elsewhere, Sisi has sought to enhance Egypt's influence in the Middle

East, becoming the first Egyptian president in thirty years to visit Iraq, while agreeing a gas deal for Lebanon in 2022 to help mildly ease the economic crisis there. However, these are relatively minor interventions and, though they put Egypt at the table again, the country is a long way from holding the dominant position over the region it did in the past. Sisi has successfully stopped Cairo from being the arena for regional competition it temporarily became in the early 2010s, but his foreign policy has not returned Egypt to the top tier of regional powers. A 2023 invite to join the 'BRICS' bloc of developing non-western economies alongside five other new members pointed to Egypt's potential future clout. However, at present, it lacks the capacity to influence much beyond its immediate neighbourhood.

An Unsustainable System?

Despite all the changes since 2011, many of the causes of the uprising that ousted Mubarak have not been resolved, and in many ways conditions have worsened. The demographic pressures are increasing, with Egypt's population expected to hit 160 million by 2050. The economy continues to be mismanaged by Sisi and his military partners, and is nowhere near providing the mostly youthful population with the jobs they need. Added to this are environmental concerns. Despite a superficial embrace of green politics, including building one of the world's largest solar plants and hosting the 2022 Global Climate Change Conference (COP27), Egypt has suffered from decades of under-investment. Agricultural products have been returned from foreign buyers due to contamination, while pollution in the Nile and poor water quality have had considerable health impacts.[37] Meanwhile, as too little of the state's resources are being spent on ordinary people, lavish amounts are being distributed to the elite, especially the army, which now controls over a quarter of the budget. Resentments against Sisi continue to grow, although his regime enjoys two differences from the Mubarak regime that was overthrown in 2011. First, the president retains some popularity. While Mubarak was widely disliked after thirty years in office, Sisi won the genuine endorsement of a large segment of the population when he came to power. That said, the true extent is hard to gauge given the lack of truly free elections, and he seemed to lose much goodwill during the economic troubles of the early 2020s. Second, Sisi has constructed a far more fearsome police state than Mubarak, arguably more so even than Nasser, making the consequences of rebelling far greater. For now, these two factors suggest that a repeat of 2011 is not on the cards, despite considerable poverty. However, events in Egypt and elsewhere during the 2011 Arab Uprisings suggest that such factors can't deter disappointed populations forever, and future unrest against Sisi's regime cannot be ruled out.

But things have changed, and a future rebellion may not mean another stab at democracy. It is highly plausible that the powerful army would jettison Sisi and find a replacement leader were his popularity to wane further, or that Egypt's powerful backers in the Gulf might again sponsor a substitute dictator. Alternatively, given the fierce nature of his rule, Sisi might respond to unrest violently like Bashar al-Assad in Syria, possibly triggering a civil war or state collapse. With the Muslim Brotherhood enjoying significant grassroots support and Islamic State having a base in the Sinai, there is a chance of violence involving militant Islamists. Such an outcome is the nightmare scenario for the US, Europe, and fellow Middle Eastern capitals, who desperately crave stability in the region's largest state. Western countries fear state collapse will prompt yet more mass migration and people trafficking, as occurred when civil wars broke out in much less populous Libya and Syria. Meanwhile, Israel and the Gulf states want Egypt to remain placid. Most foreign governments therefore are quite content to back Sisi's dictatorship. Even though they recognise the potential combustibility within Egypt, they fear that tinkering with democratic reforms, as occurred in 2011, could spark the instability they most fear. As such, it is incredibly difficult for those opposing Sisi's rule, given they face repression at home and no real support abroad. The problem, of course, is that this course may prove unsustainable. Egypt has fallen a long way but seems still to be falling.

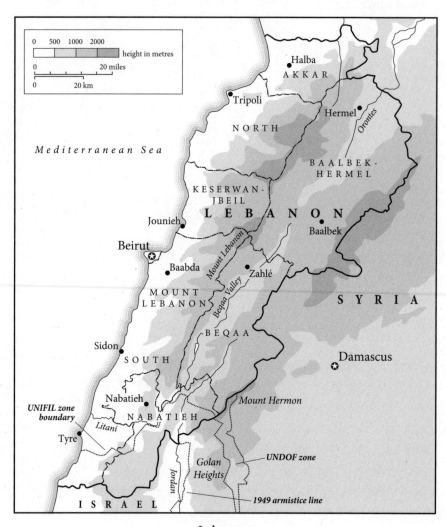

Lebanon

7

Lebanon
A Crumbling State

The blast was huge. Just before 6 p.m. on a typically warm summer evening on 4 August 2020, Beirutis coming home from work noticed a trail of smoke rising from the port area of Lebanon's capital. Twenty minutes later there was an explosion, then another, much bigger than the first. It sent an enormous red and orange mushroom cloud into the air and a vast shockwave across the city. It was one of the largest non-nuclear explosions in history, causing the ground to shake as far as distant Cyprus, 150 miles away. The scene in Beirut was devastating; 218 people were killed, over 7,000 were injured. The houses and shops in the vicinity of the port, trendy bars favoured by the city's hipster youth and restaurants frequented by the well-to-do elite, lay in ruins. The fronts of Ottoman-era mansions, that had somehow survived Lebanon's civil wars and invasions, crumbled. A nearby hospital was so badly damaged that patients had to be treated in the street. Meanwhile a 100-metre-wide crater now blighted the capital's coastline.

As people rushed to make sure loved ones were safe and emergency services scrambled to tend to the victims, fear and panic momentarily set in. What had just happened? Lebanon's violent history meant there was no shortage of possibilities. Perhaps this was an attack from Israel, which had invaded five times since the 1970s, and regularly flew its fighter jets over Beirut's skies to intimidate its neighbour. Perhaps it was an attack from the Jihadists who had bombed civilians and battled the army in recent years. Maybe this was the first skirmish in a renewed civil war, given the recent tensions between Lebanon's different factions. Alternatively, maybe it was the accidental detonation of one of the many caches of weapons hidden around the country by Hezbollah, the most powerful militia. It soon transpired that all these hypotheses were off the mark, but the reality was no less tragic. The blast came not from an aggressive neighbour, a terrorist group, or squabbling factions, but rather an accidental fire at the port that ignited a huge quantity of ammonium nitrate. Despite it being so close to a densely inhabited area, the highly flammable chemical had been stored there by government officials without proper safety measures for over six years, with no one taking responsibility for its safe disposal. In essence, 218 people had been killed, 300,000 displaced, and a large part of the capital devastated because of government incompetence and neglect.

The ruling elite made matters worse by obstructing attempts to investigate the explosion and hold those responsible to account. Lebanon enjoys one of the most liberal political climates in the Middle East, with a free press, regular elections, and a tradition of public protest. But it also suffers from a deeply corrupt sectarian ruling elite that, while claiming to represent Lebanon's diverse religious communities, largely serves its own interests. That they sought to bury scrutiny of the 2020 blast is consistent with the same attitude they and their predecessors have taken through much of Lebanon's modern history.

This is Lebanon's great tragedy. It has the potential to be a beacon of freedom and prosperity. Within a compact space it is blessed with rich agricultural land, luscious orchards, stunning mountains, and sumptuous beaches – in the 1960s brochures boasted that tourists could ski in the morning and swim in the sea in the afternoon. Beirut is a creative and vibrant city, sometimes labelled the 'Paris of the Middle East', for its fashionable boutiques and cafes, art scene and intelligentsia. It has an industrious, well-educated population, many of whom emigrate to become leaders of industry and professions elsewhere. But Lebanon's history and present is not the story of success and prosperity, but rather conflict and instability. In the 1970s it erupted into a fifteen-year civil war between different religious and ideological factions. Though a peace was eventually agreed, it ultimately transformed the armed warlords into suited oligarchs who divided state resources among themselves. Despite professing unity, the elites, and many Lebanese, remained divided, as this was built into the design of the post-war political system. These tensions were exacerbated, as they had been before and during the civil war, by the elites' relations with foreign powers. Ever since Lebanon's conception factions have courted external patrons to outmanoeuvre domestic rivals, frequently turning the country into a battleground.

A Sectarian State

Lebanon's constitution recognises eighteen different religions among its 5 million or so inhabitants. Such unusual diversity in confession is a product of the region's particular history and geography. At the heart of the country stands Mount Lebanon, whose craggy and imposing peaks proved a refuge for Maronite Christians fleeing first Byzantine then Islamic domination. Though a separate church, the Maronites grew close to Rome when European Crusaders invaded in the 1090s, and eventually entered full union with Catholicism. As a result, the Maronites have long looked to foreigners for protection, especially France in recent centuries. The mountains also proved a refuge for another religious group who arrived in the eleventh century, the Druze, a small, nominally Shia Muslim sect that had been persecuted by the region's Sunni rulers. While the Maronite and Druze inhabitants coexisted peacefully for most of the millennium that followed, in 1860 Mount Lebanon descended into civil war. Bloody fighting between Druze and Maronite fighters culminated in a Druze victory and the ethnic cleansing of some Christians.[1] External players stepped in, with France backing the Maronites and Britain allied to the Druze, and they pressured the increasingly weak Ottoman empire that ruled the area into granting Mount Lebanon special status. With European governments acting as protectors, the region was given semi-autonomy and ruled over by a Christian governor aided by a council that had to include representatives of all the region's religious groups. This singling out of religion as the key identity in politics was to cast a long shadow.

When the Ottoman empire collapsed after the First World War, France pushed for control of Mount Lebanon, citing its historic role as protector of the Maronites. While Maronite leaders embraced this, others were less enthusiastic, most telling an American fact-finding mission that they favoured incorporation into a larger independent united Arab state.[2] These appeals were ignored by Britain and France as they carved up the Ottoman lands between them. France opted to partition the northern Levant, creating two new states: Syria and Lebanon. But the Lebanon it created was far larger than the tiny semi-autonomous enclave of Mount Lebanon, bringing in many non-Maronites. Sunni Muslims, who had been the ruling elite under the Ottomans, dominated the cities of Tripoli and Sidon, as well as much of Beirut. Shia Muslims, historically the marginalised peasant class in this area, formed a majority in the south near Tyre and the fertile eastern Beqaa valley. Many Orthodox Christians, a different confession to the Maronites, were also absorbed into the new state. Many of these non-Maronite groups resented France separating them from family, friends, and co-religionists in Syria – barely 100 km from Beirut – and were aggrieved that Paris intended to establish the Maronites as their new ruling elite. To placate these concerns, France returned to the religion-based political formula of the Mount Lebanon protectorate. It created a democratic constitution that made religion the primary political identity, distributing offices according to sect. The powerful president was always a Maronite, the prime minister a Sunni, the speaker of parliament a Shia, while Druze and Orthodox Christians were also to be represented in cabinet.

This formula was retained and formalised when Lebanon was granted independence in 1943. Under a 'National Pact' agreed by the elite leaders, allocation of high office and parliamentary seats was based on the demographic size of each sect. Christians were awarded more parliamentary seats than Muslims by a ratio of 6:5, and the president was always a Maronite. The years after independence brought prosperity and an open political society that saw Western tourists flock to Lebanon's beaches and ski slopes, while Arab dissidents became regulars in Beirut's coffee shops. But in the background the sectarian political system struggled. Many were unhappy with the National Pact, arguing that it failed to accommodate shifts in demographics. While Christians made up a majority in the past, many suspected this was no longer the case, a suspicion increased by successive governments' refusal to conduct a new census – the last being held in 1932. Others rejected the National Pact all together. As Beirut became a hotbed of intellectuals and militants in the 1950s and 1960s, many Sunnis, Druze, and Orthodox Christians argued that Lebanon should abandon its colonially imposed sectarian system and create a true democracy based on one person one vote.[3] Such voices were often aligned with the Arab nationalist movement growing across the Middle East at the time, inspired by the Egyptian President Gamal Abdul Nasser (see chapter 6). They wanted to reverse France's partitions, reuniting with Syria and, possibly, the rest of the Arab world. This stance made them sympathetic to the 110,000 Palestinians who had fled to Lebanon when Israel was created in the late 1940s, and to the militant Palestine Liberation Organization (PLO) that set itself up in in the south after being expelled from Jordan in 1970 (see chapter 4). In contrast, many Maronites, though not all, feared the Palestinians. Since Palestinians were mostly Sunni Muslims, the Maronites worried that were they to remain in Lebanon and become citizens, the delicate sectarian balance would swing against them. They loathed the PLO's presence and the attacks from Israel on south Lebanon it provoked.

These tensions boiled over into civil war. First for a few months in 1958, and then more seriously between 1975 and 1990. The sectarian political system had ensured that the Lebanese state was weak, allowing independent militias to develop that the army was powerless to curtail. These armed groups were usually centred around powerful families or a particular ideology, like Arab nationalism or communism, and were mostly sectarian in character. In 1975 an alliance of Maronite Christian militias faced off against the PLO and its Lebanese allies, mostly Sunni and Druze militias, prompting ethnic massacres on both sides. The weak state contracted further, and the army disintegrated as soldiers deserted to join militias from their own religious group. Militias and warlords became the dominant players, with neighbourhoods ruled over by armed gangs, extracting payment from the residents for protection and controlling the flow of goods and people into their fiefdoms. Fighting became as much about spoils of war as ideology. Maronite, Sunni, and Shia militias all fought their co-religionists as well as each other, either in turf wars or with the encouragement of foreign patrons.[4]

These foreign governments intervened from the start of the war and their involvement escalated. Some Maronite militias received weapons and money from Israel to fight their mutual Palestinian enemies.[5] When this failed to defeat the PLO, Israel directly invaded, first occupying a small area of south Lebanon in 1978, and then making a massive incursion in 1982 that took Israeli troops all the way to Beirut. This was a short-term success as the international community intervened and arranged the evacuation of the PLO from Lebanon, never to return. However, it did not stabilise Lebanon, as the Maronite ally whom Israel had hoped would rule, Bashir Gemayal, was swiftly assassinated. This precipitated one of the bloodiest episodes of the war when Gemayal's enraged Maronite militiamen massacred up to 3,500 Palestinian refugees, now left unprotected, which the occupying Israeli military did little to prevent. Its grand designs in tatters, harassment from guerrilla fighters soon forced Israel to retreat south. The invasion ironically removed one enemy from Israel's northern border but created a new one. Shias had not been major players in the early stages of the war, but the occupation of Shia-dominated south Lebanon prompted armed resistance. The Shia Islamist government that came to power in Iran in 1979 declared Israel its enemy and sent militants to build a new Shia Islamist group in Lebanon: Hezbollah – 'the party of God'. It soon became Israel's chief tormentor, forcing the army back to a narrow strip of the south, which it eventually evacuated in 2000.

Other states intervened more briefly. A multinational force led by the US, France, and Italy was deployed to Beirut in 1982, but withdrew a year later after a series of bomb attacks killed hundreds of Western peacekeepers. Later in the war Saddam Hussein's Iraq sponsored Maronite militias to scotch its rival Syria's plans in Lebanon. But it was Syria that ultimately proved the most consequential intervener, and its government came out on top when the war ended. The president, Hafez al-Assad, played a cynical game regarding his western neighbour that he, as an Arab nationalist, believed should never have been severed from Syria in the first place. He wanted to prevent his enemy, Israel, from succeeding, but he also wanted to ensure that Lebanon remained weak and subservient to Damascus. To do this, Hafez sent troops in 1976, which remained there until long after the war's end. He also backed an array of militias of all sects, cultivating a Rolodex of clients he could call on. When more powerful players like Israel and the US intervened, Syria couldn't challenge them directly, but acted as spoiler – likely arranging the assassination of Gemayal and facilitating Iran's development of Hezbollah.

Hafez was also willing to wait until circumstances turned in his favour. By 1990, with the Cold War winding down, the US was more favourable to pro-Soviet Syria, and courted it to join the international coalition to push Saddam Hussein from Kuwait (see chapter 5).

Hafez, who loathed Saddam anyway, agreed on one condition: he was to be given free rein in Lebanon. Washington leant on its Israeli allies, battered by a decade of failure in the south, to accept this. By this point Lebanon's warlords and elite leaders, also exhausted and aware that the world was changing, had already been persuaded to explore peace options, signing a deal in the Saudi Arabian city of Taif in 1989. With Washington's approval, the war finally came to an end in 1990, with Syria permitted to deploy its army across Lebanon, chasing down any militants who refused the Taif compromise and the new overlordship of Damascus.

The Taif System

The Taif Accord, as it became known, was a grand bargain made by the ruling elites, similar to the National Pact of 1943 and, like its predecessor, it would shape Lebanon for the next thirty years. The accord saw the warlords of the civil war, often the leading families that had represented their religious communities for decades, agree to disarm and re-enter a reconfigured sectarian political system. Now Christians and Muslims would have equal numbers of parliamentary seats and, though the president remained a Maronite and the premier a Sunni, the former lost power. Yet this still didn't address many of the original grievances that sparked conflict. The state remained weak and sect-based, disappointing those who wanted Lebanon to become a non-sectarian republic. It also failed to address the question of changing demographics. With censuses still effectively forbidden, most estimates suggested the religious balance had dramatically altered during the war.[6] With many Christians and Sunnis emigrating, Shias, who were mostly too poor to flee, became the largest religious group. Yet Taif still left them under-represented. Hezbollah, which refused to disarm like the other militias, arguing it was still fighting Israeli occupation in the south, played on these feelings of dispossession to build a powerful popular support base.

But for all the deal's flaws, it was still a peace and came alongside a wave of post-Cold War optimism that saw war-torn Beirut rapidly rebuilt. At the heart of this was a Sunni Lebanese businessman called Rafiq Hariri who made his fortune in Saudi Arabia during the war years and returned to become prime minister for much of the 1990s and early 2000s. Hariri wanted to transform post-war Lebanon into a neoliberal playground for tourists and investors.[7] Despite Hariri not having been a militia commander, nor having come from an ancient ruling family, the other elites welcomed his plan, transforming themselves from warlords into businessmen. They used their high offices to award themselves and their followers government contracts. Elites who once fought over control of checkpoints now squabbled to secure the ministries with the juiciest budgets to plunder. Hariri, meanwhile, transformed downtown Beirut from a war zone into a pleasure palace, creating a sanitised commercial district packed with up-market restaurants, apartments, and boutique shops. Unfortunately, like much of post-war Lebanon, this appeared designed for wealthy tourists and the ruling elite, and was beyond the economic reach of most ordinary citizens.

If elite graft was one continuity in the new Lebanon, another was outside interference. Iran maintained its sponsorship of Hezbollah and Israel persisted with raids against it, including two brief invasions in 1993 and 1996. Meanwhile Saudi Arabia's close relationship with Hariri meant it too began to see Lebanon as an arena for its regional ambitions. The most important player, however, remained Syria. The head of Syrian military intelligence in Lebanon was effectively a governor, using Syria's military presence to keep leaders in line while taking a cut from most economic ventures. At first Hariri and others accepted this, seeing Syria's presence as stabilising. But by 2004 the premier had fallen out with Damascus, now ruled by Hafez's inexperienced son, Bashar al-Assad (see chapter 1). Assad's insistence on extending the term of Lebanon's pro-Syria president against Hariri's wishes caused a fatal rupture. A few months later, on

Valentine's Day 2005, Hariri was assassinated by a huge car bomb that rocked Beirut, and fingers immediately pointed at Syria. Public displays of mourning by Hariri's supporters soon swelled into angry demands for Syria's immediate withdrawal from Lebanon. They were encouraged by the United States, France, and Saudi Arabia, all Hariri allies and antagonistic towards Damascus, having recently sponsored a UN bill that demanded Assad's withdrawal.[8] On 14 March, a month after the assassination, over a million Lebanese gathered in Beirut against Syria. With pressure growing, Assad conceded, ending Syria's twenty-nine years of military presence in Lebanon.

But Syria's departure only brought more division, instability, and external interference. Opposition to Assad was far from unanimous. A week earlier, on 8 March, Hezbollah had hosted a rival demonstration, supporting Syria and, notably, opposing the UN resolution which also called for the disarming of all militias – a veiled attack on Hezbollah. These rival demonstrations soon gave their names to the two political coalitions that dominated post-Syria politics. The March 14 alliance was led by Hariri's son, Saad, and included most of the Sunni and Druze political parties, plus many Christian ones.[9] On the other side was March 8, led by Hezbollah, other parties claiming to represent Shias, and some claiming to represent Christians, including that of former army chief Michel Aoun. In a sign of the cynicism of Lebanese politics, Aoun had made his name in the civil war as a sworn opponent of Syria but now returned after years of exile in a pro-Syrian alliance. The Taif system promoted unity governments, meaning though March 14 won the first elections after Syria's departure, March 8 parties, including Hezbollah, still held plenty of seats in the cabinet.

But tensions ran high. More assassinations followed Hariri's. Car bombs targeted anti-Syrian politicians and journalists, leading some to blame Damascus and, by extension, its March 8 allies. In summer 2006 Lebanon suffered a devastating thirty-four-day war with Israel. After Hezbollah guerrillas kidnapped two Israeli soldiers, Israel responded with a ground incursion and a brutal bombing campaign, killing over 1,000 people. Hezbollah fought back surprisingly effectively, allowing it to claim 'victory' once the war was eventually stopped by a UN-brokered ceasefire. This brought Hezbollah and its leader, Hassan Nasrallah, huge popularity across the Arab world, emboldening them at home.[10] A few months later, they tried to collapse the government by resigning March 8's seats in cabinet. When this didn't work, the alliance ordered supporters to peacefully occupy downtown Beirut. The result was a sit-in that lasted over a year and paralysed the city centre. Hariri's playground was occupied by cloth tents while the army put razor wire around government buildings to deter further encroachment. Tourists and investors stayed away, and the economy nosedived. Worse was to come. In May 2008 riots broke out in areas with mixed Sunni and Shia populations, escalating into direct armed fighting. The contest was one-sided and the veterans of Hezbollah and other March 8 militias defeated the inexperienced March 14 fighters within a week. A peace was brokered, and March 8 returned to the cabinet, with the tent city taken down and downtown Beirut finally re-opened, but Hezbollah had exposed how precarious the Taif peace was. For all the talk of unity and reconciliation, fighters could be mobilised to turn on their countrymen within moments.

Fear of a return to civil war loomed especially large when Syria itself collapsed into internal strife in 2011. It first heightened tensions between Lebanon's communities. In Syria, Bashar al-Assad's government was mostly supported by members of his own Alawi sect, a derivative of Shiism, along with most of Syria's other Shias, its Druze and Christians, as well as some Sunnis. Consequently, many of Lebanon's own Shia and small Alawi population were sympathetic to Assad, especially after Hezbollah sent its own forces to help the beleaguered dictator. Alongside confessional solidarity, Hezbollah feared losing its vital supply line from Iran through Syria were Assad to be defeated. In contrast, many of Lebanon's Sunnis were more supportive of the anti-Assad rebels, largely drawn from Syria's under-represented

Sunni majority. Lebanon's Christians were more muted. Many aligned with March 8 openly supported Assad, arguing that the radical Islamists that had emerged among Syria's opposition would persecute Christians if victorious. Those aligned with March 14 loathed Assad but also feared a Sunni Islamist neighbour should he fall. The various political leaders of all stripes insisted Syria's war would not spill over into Lebanon, but violence still occurred. Sunni and Alawi neighbours fought in Tripoli; a series of bombs killed dozens in Sunni- and Shia-dominated areas; while Hezbollah, in alliance with the army, fought Sunni Jihadists in Sidon and along the Syria border.

A second challenge came from the war's economic impact. While Lebanon was flooded by international NGO (non-governmental organisation) workers using it as a base to engage with the conflict, other revenue ceased. After the 2008 reconciliation deal and re-opening of downtown Beirut, tourists and investment had slowly returned, but now with fears of renewed instability the revival ground to a halt. Exacerbating this was the influx of Syrian refugees. As the situation in Syria worsened more and more fled to the relative safety of Lebanon. By 2014 over a million refugees had arrived, meaning a quarter of Lebanon's population was now Syrian.[11] But the government was a reluctant host. With memories of Palestinian refugee camps forming the cornerstone of PLO militarism in the 1960s and 1970s, the cabinet refused to permit the new arrivals to set up formal camps like their countrymen elsewhere. Instead, wealthier refugees rented private accommodation while poorer arrivals lived in squalid informal tent cities. Their presence added further tension and economic strains, with political leaders often scapegoating them for various woes, prompting sporadic attacks.

Yet despite the potential combustibility, Lebanon did not return to civil conflict. The elite managed to cut various deals and bargains to de-escalate every time it looked like the country might be close to the precipice. This included delaying parliamentary elections by over five years and a stand-off over the presidency that saw Lebanon have no head of state for twenty-nine months. Even so, conflict was avoided. Yet, as ever, these were elite bargains, and did little for the ordinary population, who chafed in frustration over the years of paralysis and decline.

Regional, American, and European Involvement

The factionalism encouraged by the constitution has meant generation after generation of ruling elites have looked abroad for support, taking advantage of the major regional and global rivalries of the day. This was true of Britain and France's competing efforts to influence the declining Ottoman empire, the Arab-Israeli conflict, and the Cold War. Today is no different, with geopolitical battles played out either on Lebanese soil or via Lebanese politics, particularly the various attempts to roll back Iran. Iran now has a major presence in Lebanon, based on Tehran's religious, ideological, and strategic concerns. Religiously, Iran's leaders wish to aid and protect Lebanon's fellow Shias. Ideologically, its opposition to Israel and support for what it calls the 'resistance' against American designs for the Middle East has led to sponsorship of Hezbollah. Strategically, keeping Hezbollah armed gives it both defensive and offensive capability. It can use the Lebanese militia to attack Israel either from Lebanon or the positions in southern Syria it took during the Syrian civil war. Defensively, Hezbollah's rocket arsenal, which wrought havoc on northern Israel during the 2006 war, acts as a deterrent to Israel striking Iran itself. While Iran started off as the junior partner to its ally Syria in Lebanon, as Damascus became weaker, Tehran's role has grown. This included sending its senior military commander, Qassem Suleimani, to help direct Hezbollah's war effort in 2006, and then paying for much of the reconstruction of bombed-out Shia-dominated neighbourhoods afterwards.[12] Billboards in southern Beirut proudly display images of Hezbollah and Iranian leaders boasting that it was Tehran that funded much of the reconstruction efforts. While Nasrallah is his own man and no Iranian puppet, his militia has become an important tool of Tehran's regional policy. It was deployed in Syria for its own interests, but also to Iraq and Yemen (see chapter 3) at Iran's request.

On the other side, Israel's role in Lebanon has evolved. Where once it too backed local allies, it was scarred by the invasion of 1982 and the next eighteen years of gruelling occupation. Any grand designs it once had of transforming Lebanon into a friendly neighbour are long past and it now prefers a direct response, launching military strikes on Hezbollah or other militants. Many Lebanese and outside observers worry this might provoke another Hezbollah–Israel conflict like 2006.[13] Any such war would be even more destructive, given that Hezbollah forces are far better armed and battle-hardened after a decade fighting in Syria, meaning Israel would have to deploy even more force. The counter-argument is that neither side wants a war. There is a 'balance of terror' on both sides of the border, with leaders recognising that a destructive war is in neither of their interests. Indeed, Hezbollah and its Iranian allies only occasionally respond when Israel attacks its positions, viewing them as warning shots or 'hair cuts' designed to limit their expansion rather than remove them altogether.[14] In addition, Russia's presence in Syria after 2015 diminishes the chances of accidental war, given that Moscow enjoys good relations with Iran, Hezbollah, and Israel and could mediate should any escalation occur. That said, this delicate balance could easily change; calculations could shift, for example if Russia was to withdraw from Syria, or if a more hawkish Israeli leader were to be elected, or through a weakening of Hezbollah's position in Lebanese politics. Similarly, as seen by the 2023 Gaza war, clashes between Israel and Hezbollah (and Iran)'s ally Hamas also hold the potential to alter dynamics.

Iran's other opponents, Saudi Arabia and the United States, historically took an active role in Lebanese politics, but their interest has cooled. After the civil war Saudi Arabia backed Rafiq Hariri and the

March 14 movement led by his son, Saad, arming and training the militias that were quickly defeated by Hezbollah in 2008.[15] But since the coming to power of Prince Mohammed Bin Salman (MBS) in 2015, this support has diminished. MBS was distracted by developments closer to home – his intervention in Yemen and the Qatar blockade (see chapter 9). While he did initially see Lebanon as another arena in which to outmanoeuvre his regional rival, Iran, this interest waned after a disastrous move in 2017. Saad Hariri, who was serving as Lebanon's prime minister, was invited to Riyadh, and a few days later announced that he was resigning due to continued interference by Iran and Hezbollah. This was bizarre given he was enjoying cordial ties with Hezbollah at the time and had met an Iranian official only days earlier. It transpired that the Saudi Crown Prince (after 2017) was forcing Hariri's hand, hoping to replace him with a more pliant pro-Saudi leader, and was effectively holding him hostage. But this backfired spectacularly. Anti-Saudi feeling erupted in Beirut, with protesters from all political parties demanding Saad's release. Riyadh's Western allies urged MBS to relent, which he did, allowing Saad to leave. Saad eventually returned to Lebanon where he rescinded his resignation. His poorly-thought-through coup in tatters, MBS stepped back from Lebanon, pulling funding from Saad's party and calling on all Saudi citizens to leave Lebanon.[16] While this kept Saad in office, it crippled his political career, stripping his party of a key external backer and ultimately led to the slow demise of March 14.

Washington has also retreated. Initially it was a key supporter of Taif, engineering Syria's post-war takeover, then supporting the March 14 movement against Damascus. But as Washington lost interest in transforming the Middle East after the failures of George W. Bush, its commitment to Lebanon similarly diminished. Barack Obama was careful not to get too involved in case he derailed his nuclear deal with Iran. Donald Trump was even more disengaged, viewing Lebanon primarily through an anti-Iran, pro-Israel, and pro-Saudi Arabia lens. This included placing sanctions on Hezbollah and some of its March 8 allies as part of a wider anti-Iranian sanctions programme.[17] But beyond this Trump was muted, allowing France to lead Western aid efforts after the 2020 Beirut explosion. His successor, Joe Biden, similarly sent aid to Lebanon during the crises of the early 2020s, but with little fanfare or effort to help solve the problems.

This has left the EU as the most prominent Western actor, with France taking the lead. Europeans had harsh memories of the Lebanese civil war when dozens of its journalists were taken hostage for years and images of massacres in the (relatively close) eastern Mediterranean were broadcast to shocked audiences. It therefore was eager to help in rebuilding after the Taif peace and has since been the largest provider of aid alongside the United States. But the EU is a cumbersome foreign policy operator. Despite representing the largest single economic market in the world and having vast resources, its twenty-seven member states (twenty-eight before Brexit) often have different agendas, making it difficult to construct and pursue effective policies. In the Middle East and North Africa, its flagship approach, 'the European Neighbourhood Policy', was designed to enhance ties with its Middle Eastern neighbours, promoting growth and stability via trade. There was some success in the early 2000s with all Middle Eastern and North African states with a Mediterranean shore, except Syria and Libya, signing association agreements that brought free trade.[18] However, this was a high point and Brussels proved unable to translate it into either stability or significant influence. Since then, Brussels has tended to allow its larger member states that have stakes in certain arenas to take the lead: France, Italy, and Spain in North Africa; Germany in Israel; and France and Britain (prior to 2021) in the rest of the Levant, Egypt, and the Gulf. But on the many occasions when member state interests clash, as was the case between Italy and France on Libya (see chapter 2), the EU is rarely able to subordinate these differences to a wider 'European' policy. This often leaves the EU impotent, having a theoretical approach to a region or issue that is being undermined or ignored by leading member states.

In Lebanon there was thankfully less disagreement on approach. The EU routinely agreed to large funding packages for Beirut to keep its economy afloat. This included a major bailout in 2001 when the government was close to bankruptcy, and further donor conferences arranged in 2002, 2007, and 2018, as well as extra funds to help with Syrian refugees after 2012.[19] France took a lead in all of these, hosting the conferences in Paris. The French government, as the former colonial ruler, takes a special interest in Lebanon. Its interest receives mixed responses in Lebanon. Many in the ruling elite and middle classes, especially among some Christians, speak French and retain a cultural tie to France, aided by the large Lebanese community that moved there during the civil war. Others, notably Hezbollah and its allies, see France as a meddling former imperialist.[20] Recent French leaders have varied in the importance they assign to Lebanon. Jacques Chirac was close friends with Rafiq Hariri and took a personal interest in bringing his assassins to justice. Emmanuel Macron, meanwhile, saw in the 2020 Beirut blast an opportunity to emphasise his statesmanlike credentials, rushing to the scene long before other Western leaders, where he was greeted warmly. Macron followed up by raising yet more aid to repair the damage and proposing a reform programme for Lebanon's struggling economy and politics.

But Western grants have been counter-productive. The vast sums raised were handed over to Beirut with few controls over how the money was spent. As such it simply flowed into the pockets of the elites, who used it to shore up their allies and supporters but didn't let it filter down to the wider population. Indeed, many in Lebanon's growing opposition movement began to criticise the EU and other donors for sustaining the corrupt elite.[21] Belatedly, in both 2018 and 2020, Brussels tried to attach conditionality, but Lebanon's leaders were unable or unwilling to reform. This obstinacy ultimately doomed Macron's 2020 efforts, with most elites steadfastly refusing to make the changes needed. He was also scuppered by geopolitics. His plan engaged with Hezbollah, recognising that it was a key player in Lebanon, but this brought fierce criticism from the US, Saudi Arabia, and Israel. With little domestic or international support, the Macron initiative swiftly collapsed – yet another victim of the internal and external machinations that have troubled Lebanon throughout its recent history.

The Brink of Collapse

The 2020 explosion and attempted cover-up was sadly not unique, but rather the latest in a series of catastrophes precipitated by the ruling elite. A year earlier Lebanon had entered an economic crisis that, at the time of writing, shows no sign of ending. Before then, in 2015/16 a dispute over waste collection had seen Beirut's garbage pile up for months, rotting in the streets while the ruling parties bickered over responsibility. These years of near-permanent crisis have pushed the post-war Taif system and, indeed, the Lebanese state, to the edge. Public faith in Hariri's neoliberal economics, the sectarian power-sharing system, and the ruling elite that benefits from both is at a record low, as a disparate protest movement has grown to demand change.[22] However, the elites are so entrenched, and still receiving significant outside support, that many would seemingly rather oversee disaster than risk their privileged position.

The 2015 garbage crisis exposed the lengths the elites would go to protect themselves. The question of where to deposit Beirut's waste had been put off by successive ministers since the civil war. They had been relying instead on a temporary landfill on the city's outskirts. The nearby residents repeatedly complained that the private company contracted to manage the site was neglecting their duties, leading to rats and flies infesting their homes. The landfill was meant to be closed in 2008 but kept being extended as ministers, typically, kicked the can down the road. In July 2015 the village residents snapped, blocking the site entrance. Within days garbage was piled all over the city and surrounding countryside as citizens fly-tipped in the absence of waste management. The garbage festered in the summer heat, filling the capital with a vile stench. Enraged citizens turned their fury on the government, setting garbage piles on fire and protesting across the country. Their slogan, '#You Stink', flooded social media, rallying tens of thousands onto the street. The protesters soon moved beyond just garbage and targeted the elite as a whole, attacking their inability to provide services, the sectarian system, and the failure of their neoliberal economics. But their efforts ultimately failed as the ruling elite circled the wagons. Some of the activists had hoped to elect new political leaders in the 2016 Beirut municipal elections: non-sectarian experts who would rule justly. But, incredibly, the rival March 14 and March 8 blocs allied on the same ticket to stop them. Despite gaining 32 per cent of the vote, the activists gained not one council seat and were locked out of office.[23]

If the garbage crisis rocked public faith in the ruling elite, the economic crisis four years later shattered it. Since the end of the civil war, the Lebanese economy has been dependent on regular injections of foreign currency, mostly from tourism, foreign investment, aid, deposits in its discreet banking sector, and remittances from Lebanon's huge diaspora. This allowed the Central Bank to keep the Lebanese lira pegged to the US dollar, creating a degree of economic and financial stability. Incoming foreign currency also funded the government's growing trade deficit and public debt.[24] But this was a house built on sand. Lebanon produced very little, with a negligible manufacturing sector, but had high consumption rates, with the fashionable middle classes thirsting for imported foreign goods. When the Syrian civil war scared away tourists and investors, the foreign currency dried up and there were no alternative exports to claw dollars back. Meanwhile no effort was made to deter consumption of foreign goods. Indeed, many of the elites had import businesses that encouraged the practice. The Central Bank attempted some financial engineering, but it only staved off the impending crisis, and ultimately added more to public debt.[25]

By 2019, there were no tricks left to play. It became clear that Lebanon was going to default and that the peg on the dollar was unsustainable, prompting the black-market exchange rate to inflate. To prevent a run on deposits, commercial banks suddenly closed for two weeks, and when they re-opened, they restricted account holders' access to foreign currency. Such a move was illegal, but ministers declined either to force the banks to release people's funds, recognising the banking sector would collapse, or take action to protect people's savings. Making matters worse, the Central Bank printed more liras to compensate for the lack of dollars available. The result was a disaster. The lira rapidly devalued from the pegged rate of 1,500 lira to the dollar in 2019 to 35,000 lira by 2022, as citizens frantically sought the security of foreign currency. Life savings were decimated. Inflation skyrocketed, with the cost of some basic staples like rice rising by over 1,000 per cent.[26] Businesses folded, unemployment grew, while vital imported medicines became prohibitively expensive. Within a few years over 80 per cent of the population were below the poverty line – a sharp drop for an historically middle-class country.[27] In one illustrative episode, a desperate man charged into a bank armed with a shotgun, not to rob it, but to demand a small portion of his own savings to pay for his father's medical bills. This garnered considerable public sympathy, not condemnation, and several copycat 'robberies' soon followed.

As with the garbage crisis, the collapsing economy sparked furious protests. From October 2019 until 2022 there were regular demonstrations across Lebanon, sometimes small, sometimes gathering hundreds of thousands. Economic woes were the prompt, particularly cuts in subsidies on fuel and food, but the protesters soon demanded the same as in 2015: an end to sectarian politics, the ejection of the corrupt ruling elite, improved public services, and a functioning economy. But the elite dug their heels in. Occasionally protesters were met with violence, with government security forces or thuggish supporters of certain parties sent in. More often the government simply ignored the crowds: offering a few words of support or promising change but doing very little. Indeed, outside funders like the EU grew increasingly frustrated at the ruling elite's unwillingness to make even minor reforms, blocking recovery funds and sanctioning certain leaders in an effort to force their hand. The IMF likewise agreed a $3 billion bailout loan in 2022, but only on the condition of reforms that the elite were reluctant to make.[28] In contrast other foreign governments encouraged intractability. Iran especially continued to provide Hezbollah with vital funds, making the militia reluctant to consider any reforms. Hezbollah's rivals had benefited from banking and tourism, so the economic crisis hit them harder than Nasrallah's party. As government services, including the security sector, corroded, Hezbollah was able to use Iranian money to keep providing medical, educational, and security support to its constituents, thus maintaining support and insulating the organisation from some of the anger.[29] But this in turn deterred Nasrallah from considering change. Ironically the Islamist militia, which first formed as a radical revolutionary party, had become an arch-defender of the status quo.

And they were not alone. Despite the scale of the crisis: the billions of dollars being lost, the number of deaths caused by the 2020 explosion, and the huge rise in poverty, the established elite proved nearly impossible to budge. The protesters were enthusiastic, but disparate, and, as in 2016, found it hard to turn street activity into electoral success. In the 2022 parliamentary elections a handful were successful in gaining seats, but most went to the established parties once again. This is not that surprising. The elite parties still had core supporters whom they provided with services and economic support – which they now desperately needed – and the sectarian electoral system made it hard for mixed religious groups like the street protesters to overturn concentrated blocs of pro-establishment voters. Despite their best efforts and hopes, the protesters were left saddled with a self-serving elite. Western governments and NGOs also faced the paradox that if they wanted to help the Lebanese survive the crisis, they had to work with the corrupt leaders who had caused it.

Where is the State?

'*Wayn al-dawla*?' Where is the state? A common polemical question asked by Lebanese at protests, in fuel queues, or in dark homes when the electricity cuts out (as it frequently does for hours every day).[30] They are right to ask. Lebanon is not historically a poor country. Beirut is home to shining towers hosting opulent apartments, designer nightclubs with retractable roofs, luxury sports cars, and Gucci boutiques. But the lights don't stay on for twenty-four hours a day and trash collection is sporadic. A short walk from the bright lights of downtown will take you to neighbourhoods of poor Shias who could never afford to sit in its overpriced restaurants. A little further and you'll find Palestinians whose grandparents fled to Beirut seventy-five years ago but still live in concrete 'camps' because they are denied Lebanese citizenship. Alongside them live Syrian refugees in a similar predicament. The state, for all those who have missed out, is absent. This has been the norm since the end of the civil war ushered in a particular form of sectarian neoliberal economics that created clear haves and have-nots, but in recent years successive crises have greatly swelled the latter group. Now the middle classes, who once paid private companies to generate electricity or provide medical insurance, are also keenly feeling the missing state, as they are denied access to their bank accounts while the cost of living spirals.

But what can be done? It's not as if efforts haven't been made. In the 1970s, the Palestinians in their camps fought for recognition and inclusion but failed. Some Shias likewise joined militias to better their standing, but those movements ended up being absorbed by the system itself. Now the middle classes are trying to peacefully protest their way into change, only to find themselves locked out by the ruling elite. Lebanon was created as a weak, sectarian state that has deeply entrenched generation after generation of elites who have little interest in changing that situation. Indeed, they have fought and killed to preserve a form of the status quo countless times. This structure of weakness and sectarian factions has encouraged the elites to look outside Lebanon for help, pulling in whatever regional or international rivals of the day might seek advantage in promoting their allies in Beirut. Where once this meant Britain, France, Egypt, and Syria, today it means Iran, Israel, the US, the EU, and Saudi Arabia. Tomorrow it could be others. As long as the system remains in place, Lebanon will remain fought over, with the active encouragement of its self-serving elites. Yet history shows how hard it is for Lebanon to move on. The Taif system may yet collapse in this current crisis or the next but, as was seen after the civil war, elites and their outside backers will look to find new sectarian grand bargains that keep them in power.

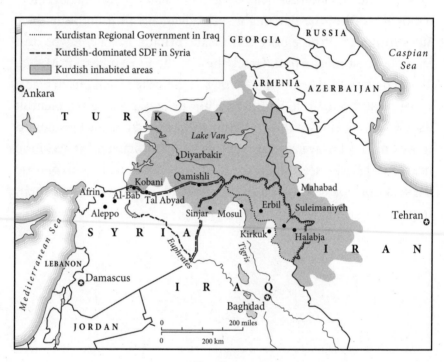

Kurdistan

8

Kurdistan
The Struggle in the Mountains

The Kurds have a good claim to being the largest stateless nation in the world. Estimates suggest there are at least 30 million Kurds living in the Middle East.[1] 'Kurdistan', the mountainous area where Kurds form the majority population, is substantial, stretching from western Iran through northern Iraq, northern Syria and almost all of south-eastern Turkey. Were all this territory ever to be amalgamated as a single independent Kurdistan, it would become the fifth-largest state in the Middle East. So why has this nationalist dream not become a reality? Historically, the Kurds missed out when Britain and France carved up the Ottoman empire after the First World War. While some Kurdish leaders lobbied for independence, instead the region was partitioned, with Kurds becoming a minority in four different states. At this point Kurdish nationalism was far weaker than the rival Turkish, Arab, and Iranian nationalisms that it was competing with, and 'Kurdishness' was not especially strong among the mostly rural and tribal population. However, this changed over the course of the twentieth century as government discrimination and violence within all four states prompted Kurdish identity to harden, sparking several nationalist movements.

Similar nationalism elsewhere has often led to secession and independence, but no such liberation came for the Kurds. Partly this was due to internal divisions. Kurds have multiple fault lines among themselves. They speak various different dialects. While 75 per cent are Sunni Muslims, there are other religious groups, including Shia, Christian, Alevi, and Yazidi communities. There are significant ideological differences, with some nationalists favouring leftist, secular solutions, while others prefer conservative, tribal politics. Moreover, many who may be Kurdish by birth reject ideas of Kurdish nationalism altogether. The division of the Kurds into four states meant nationalist movements developed distinctly in different places, based on the challenges for the Kurds of each country. Such internal divisions have been exploited and exacerbated by external players. The governments of Turkey, Iran, Syria, and Iraq, all of whom firmly reject any kind of Kurdish independence as it would mean losing valuable territory, have all sponsored Kurdish groups in others' states to further their own agendas. Powers from further afield have also weighed in, whether Britain, Israel, Russia, or, most significantly, the United States.

Added to internal divisions and foreign machinations, the Kurdish cause has been further undermined by poor leadership. Whether it be the uncompromising brutality of leftists in Turkey or the corruption of Iraq's KRG, even when Kurdish nationalists have managed to overcome the many obstacles in their path, their leaders have failed to make breakthroughs. As a result, Kurdistan has frequently been the scene of violence, misgovernment, and poverty.

A Divided People

Some Kurds claim ancient roots in the Kurdistan mountains reaching back to Abraham.[2] Tribes from this region were certainly around in the seventh century when they were absorbed into the Islamic Caliphate. They provided some of the fiercest Muslim warriors, among them Saladin, the twelfth-century vanquisher of the crusaders. Yet, despite his Kurdish origins, he probably did not view himself as a

'Kurd', given that religion was the primary identity at this time. A specific Kurdish identity did not emerge until the nineteenth century.[3] Most Kurds at this point lived in the Ottoman empire, though some lived over the border in Persia. As the cosmopolitan empire began to decline, many of its communities were drawn to nationalist ideas coming from Europe and pushed for independence. But the Kurds were slow to follow this trend, being a mostly rural and tribal society, lacking the urban centres and intelligentsias that had developed nationalism elsewhere.

But the world was moving around them. When the Ottomans were defeated in the First World War, the victorious allies sought to partition their territory into European-style nation-states, to be ruled or influenced by a great power patron. With Kurdish nationalism less developed than its Arab, Armenian, or Greek counterparts, few pushed for a Kurdish state that incorporated all of Kurdistan. The southern regions were allocated to Syria and Iraq, to be ruled over by France and Britain respectively, while the eastern region remained in Persia, soon renamed Iran. Initially the allies agreed to an autonomous Kurdish region within Turkey, with the possibility of future independence, as part of the punishing Treaty of Sèvres they imposed on the defeated Ottoman Turks.[4] However, this treaty was shredded almost before the ink was dry when the rebel Ottoman general, Mustafa Kemal, fought a successful war of independence against the Sèvres vision. The allies and Kemal instead agreed on the Treaty of Lausanne, which acknowledged the creation of a new country, Turkey, from the Ottoman Turkish lands, rejecting Greek, Armenian, and Kurdish claims. All talk of independence or even autonomy now extinguished, the Kurds were divided between four states: Turkey, Iran, Syria, and Iraq.

At this point, aside from a handful of nationalists, most Kurds did not feel a strong sense of Kurdish identity, with tribe and religion more significant ties. This would change in the coming decades in response to the repression and forced assimilation they faced.

Nowhere was this worse than in Turkey. Kemal, who took the name Ataturk (Father of the Turks) oversaw a strict programme of homogenisation in his new state. The once sizeable Christian community had already been removed, first by his Ottoman prede- cessors via the horrific Armenian genocide and then by his exchange with Greece of millions of Turkish Christians for Greek Muslims in 1923.[5] This left Turkey as an overwhelmingly Muslim country. But Ataturk was a staunch secularist and wanted the Turkish language rather than Islam to bind his new country together. This meant trouble for the Kurdish speakers in the east.

A systematic effort was made by Ankara to supress Kurdish iden- tity with the goal of turning the Kurds into Turks. All references to Kurdistan were removed from official documents, Kurdish was banned from schools, and Kurdish place names were replaced by Turkish ones. Thousands of villages were cleared, and their inhabit- ants deported west, where the plan was for them to be outnumbered by, and integrated with, Turks. Thousands of Kurdish children, both boys and girls, were forcibly sent to boarding schools to be built into good Turks. Increasingly even the term 'Kurd' was dropped, with 'Mountain Turk' preferred instead.[6] These measures, alongside Ataturk's anti-religious policies such as abolishing the Islamic Caliphate in 1924, provoked numerous rebellions by Kurdish tribes, many led by conservative and religious chiefs. These in turn prompted more state repression, leading to a vicious cycle: the army inflicted heavy casualties; the Kurds grew more resentful and agitated; and Ankara became even more determined to supress their identity.

The Turkish Kurds' plight was worsened by economic conditions. In the nineteenth century the Kurdish region was only marginally poorer than western Turkey, but during the twentieth it became significantly so. Literacy rates in 1950 were half the national average – not helped by the fact that Kurds weren't allowed to study in their own language.[7] Economic weakness prompted migration and many Kurds left the mountains for cities, either in Kurdistan or western metropolises like Istanbul. But far from integrating as Ankara hoped, these migrants formed Kurdish communities in Turkey's cities. Now Kurds had become a more urban population, nationalism developed and spread rapidly, and several nationalist groups emerged from the 1960s, quite different from the tribal-based rebels of the past. Some were conservative groups, but leftist organisations dominated, most significantly the Partiya Karkeren Kurdistan – the Kurdistan Workers' Party (PKK), which launched a major guerrilla campaign in eastern Turkey in 1984. With the Turkish army deployed to crush the insurgency, the result was a state of near civil war in Turkey's east. By the time the PKK's leader, Abdullah Ocalan, was captured in 1999, more than 40,000 people had been killed, with widespread destruction across the region.[8]

Iraq's Kurds fared little better. The Kingdom of Iraq established as a British Mandate in 1921 was dominated by Arabs, though divided between Sunnis and Shias, and the monarchy generally held a chauvinistic view of Kurds, who comprised roughly 18 per cent of the population. Successive revolts were launched by Kurdish tribes. In 1922 a short-lived 'Kingdom of Kurdistan' was declared then destroyed by British forces, followed by another revolt in 1931 before that was again crushed. The most significant rebellion came in 1943, led by Mulla Mustafa Barzani, who united most Kurdish tribes against Baghdad demanding Kurdish autonomy. He held out for two years before eventually being defeated after Baghdad persuaded some tribes to abandon him.[9] He fled to Iran and became something of a folk hero to Kurds before eventually being invited to return to Iraq when the monarchy was overthrown in 1958. Kurdish autonomy was promised and Kurdish political parties legalised, allowing Mulla Mustafa's party, the Kurdistan Democratic Party (KDP) legal status. But Barzani fell out with Baghdad again in 1960 when autonomy talks broke down, prompting another decade of rebellion, followed by yet more autonomy talks that failed to deliver, and more fighting.

The Ba'athist government that came to power in Baghdad in 1968 shared the anti-Kurdish, Arab nationalist chauvinism of previous rulers, but also sought to actively displace Kurds from strategic positions. They embarked on an 'Arabisation' programme: burning down Kurdish villages and deporting 600,000 Kurds to other locations within Iraq, while settling Arabs in traditionally Kurdish regions.[10] There was a particular effort to settle more Arabs in Kirkuk, the site of significant oilfields, and an area contested by the mixed Kurdish, Arab, and Turkmen population. The situation worsened when President Saddam Hussein launched the Iran–Iraq war in 1980. Saddam targeted Shia Kurds along the Iranian border, believing them to be aligned with Tehran. He then ordered mass executions of civilians in Erbil, home of the KDP, now led by Mustafa's son, Masoud Barzani, who had aligned with Iran. Then came the *Anfal* campaign of 1988, when Saddam instructed his cousin, 'Chemical' Ali Hassan al-Majid, to loot Kurdish lands. Ali used killing squads, chemical weapons, aerial bombing, and mass deportation, culminating in the infamous 1988 gas attack on Halabja. In total a further 100,000 Kurds were killed, prompting many to label the campaign a genocide.[11] The one silver lining was that when the Kurds rebelled again in 1991, after Saddam's disastrous invasion of Kuwait, the international community were so fearful they'd be targeted by chemical weapons that they provided a protective no-fly zone. The result was Iraqi Kurdistan's first experience of real autonomy: an internationally protected region finally outside Baghdad's control, which would shape how Iraq's north developed after Saddam was finally toppled in 2003.

Iran's Kurds were similarly discriminated against by successive governments, though arguably suffered less than their counterparts in Iraq or Turkey. Iran's demographics are complex. Just over 50 per cent of the population are ethnically Persian, with the remainder made up of sizeable Azeri, Kurdish, Baloch, Lurs, and other communities. The Kurds make up around 10 per cent, but what distinguishes them from most Iranians is not their different ethnicity and language, but their religion. Most are Sunni Muslims, compared to the 90–95 per cent of Iranians who are Shia.[12] This distinction, alongside inspiration from fellow Kurdish nationalists in other states, saw Iran's Kurds become increasingly rebellious against Tehran's rule, which was attempting to centralise control. An early high point came in 1946 when an independent Kurdish republic of Mahabad was declared with Soviet support at the end of the Second World War. However, this was swiftly extinguished by Iranian forces once the Soviets withdrew.

Thereafter the ruling Shah's Savak secret police cracked down harshly on Kurdish culture, language, and political organisations. Contrarily though, the Shah happily sponsored Iraqi Kurdish parties like the KDP to undermine his rivals in Baghdad.[13] Iran's Kurds generally celebrated when the autocratic Shah was toppled in the 1979 revolution, and Kurdish fighters rushed to take control of the region as the army melted away. However, the new Islamic Republic proved no better and, in many ways, replicated the Shah's approach: it backed Iraqi (and Turkish) Kurdish groups abroad to undermine its regional rivals but cracked down hard on Kurds at home.[14] While the end of the Iran–Iraq war led to more leniency from Tehran, allowing cultural publications and events like celebrating Kurdish new year, *Newroz*, political groups remained banned and repressed.

Syria's Kurdish community is the smallest of the four and was the least politically active for much of the twentieth century. Syria's Kurds were in the furthest region from the mountains, mostly located along the border with Turkey, many having fled to its relative safety in the face of Ankara's oppression in the 1920s and 1930s. Hostility towards the Kurds from the Syrian government grew as Arab nationalism reached its height in the 1950s, and Damascus started challenging the Kurds' right to the fertile plains many now lived on. In 1958 Kurdish publications were banned, while three years later Syria was renamed the 'Syrian Arab Republic', suggesting little place for the 9 per cent of the population who were Kurds. In 1962, over 120,000 Kurds had their citizenship removed due to spurious claims that they were illegal migrants from Turkey, when in fact many had been settled for generations but lacked the paperwork to prove it.[15]

When Hafez al-Assad became president in 1970, he increased discrimination at home, while mimicking other countries in sponsoring Kurdish rebels abroad. Like Saddam he settled Arab communities in Kurdish areas to dilute their concentration and banned Kurdish from being spoken at work.[16] Yet at the same time he was the principal foreign sponsor of the PKK, providing them with weapons, training, and money to launch attacks on his Cold War enemy, Turkey. These policies had two lasting effects on Syria's Kurds. First, as elsewhere, repression led to an increased sense of Kurdish identity, but later than in other states and weaker. Most looked abroad for a foreign sponsor, meaning nationalists in Syria were generally backed by other Kurdish groups from either Iraq or Turkey. Second, Hafez's support for the PKK meant it developed a significant presence inside Syria. This would prove key when Syria erupted into civil war in the 2010s.

Turkey and its Kurds

Roughly half of the world's Kurds live in Turkey and consequently Ankara's policies have had a deep impact on the community's fate. In turn, because Kurdish nationalism is such a concern for Turkey, the issue has shaped Ankara's relations with its neighbours. Changes in the Turkish capital in the 2000s therefore raised hopes that the new century would be more peaceful than the last. The shift came in 2002 when the conservative, mildly Islamist Justice and Development Party (AKP in Turkish) was elected, ushering in over twenty years of unbroken rule. Ataturk and his ideological successors, known as Kemalists, had adamantly opposed Islamists, and used legal and extra-legal means to deprive them of office. After Ataturk's death in 1938, the army acted as the defender of 'Kemalism', frequently intervening in politics to prevent Turkey's elected politicians from deviating too far from what they felt was Ataturk's secular nationalist vision. It was the army that was most hawkish on Kurdish issues.[17] The AKP's election therefore represented something of a revolution. Not only were they able to hold on to power longer than previous Islamist-leaning politicians, but they outmanoeuvred the army to eventually break its grip on politics.

The key figure was Recep Tayyip Erdoğan, who co-founded the party and became prime minster in 2002. Erdoğan, an ex-professional footballer from the Black Sea coast, was driven by both ideology and ambition. Ideologically, he was a Turkish nationalist but opposed to Kemalist secularism. A devout Muslim, he believed that the secular elites of Ankara and Istanbul who had ruled since 1923 did not represent the many religious provincial Turks. Indeed, it was support from this constituency that helped sweep the AKP to power. Unlike the Kemalists, he also took pride in the legacies of the Ottoman empire. Turkish foreign policy since 1923 had been west-ward facing: the country had joined NATO in the 1950s and largely disengaged from the Middle East regions the Ottomans once ruled. But the AKP instead pursed a 'neo-Ottoman' approach that saw Turkey become a major player in former Ottoman lands.[18] Initially the goal was to have 'zero problems with neighbours', but after the Arab Uprisings of 2011, Turkey took sides. Erdoğan was also very ambitious. After being re-elected in 2007 and 2011, he sought to get around a limit on the number of terms he could serve as prime minister by amending Turkey's constitution. This would allow him to be elected to a newly beefed-up presidential office for longer. To achieve this, Erdoğan proved a canny, pragmatic, and ruthless leader, and tried to use the Kurdish question to achieve his goals.

The AKP's emergence came during a period of relative calm for Turkish Kurdistan. The army had finally gained the upper hand in a gruelling war with the PKK. After Turkey threatened to invade Syria in 1998 due to its close ties to the PKK, Damascus ejected the PKK and its leader Abdullah Ocalan, who was apprehended a year later in

Kenya. Though he was sentenced to death by Turkish courts, under pressure from the EU, which Ankara then aspired to join, this was commuted to life imprisonment. From prison Ocalan, who had previously advocated an uncompromising Marxist separatist ideology, rapidly changed tack, calling for a ceasefire and revising his views in favour of local autonomy rather than full independence. A long ceasefire held, providing an opening that Erdoğan took advantage of when he came to power.

The premier's hope was to woo Kurdish voters over to the AKP with a new national identity that emphasised Turks' and Kurds' common religion rather than their ethnic differences. Securing Kurdish support might deliver permanent parliamentary majorities and facilitate his constitutional reforms. The plan had some merit. Many Kurds were religious, some even Islamist, as seen by the emergence of an Islamist rival to the PKK, Hizbullah (not to be confused with the Lebanese Hezbollah, despite both being supported by Iran). Likewise, many opposed the AKP's Kemalist rivals, whom they blamed for the decades of repression. Erdoğan also promised reforms and improvements to Kurdish cultural rights, partly to placate the Kurds and partly to satisfy criteria set by the EU. He visited the region in 2005, saying publicly that Kurds should be able to call themselves Kurds, abandoning the Kemalist mantra of 'Mountain Turks'. He also permitted the use of the Kurdish language in education, though only in private institutions for over-18s, and Turkey's first Kurdish television channel was launched.[19] Despite the ceasefire with the PKK breaking down in 2004, Erdoğan still opened a dialogue with Ocalan. From 2009 there were several meetings between Turkish intelligence and PKK representatives, with the hope of a breakthrough raised. Erdoğan also softened Turkey's stance to Kurds abroad, forging close ties with the KRG in Iraq. This was primarily an economic relationship, but it helped Erdoğan to promote a more pro-Kurdish image. His plan had initial success, with the AKP winning a landslide re-election in 2007, including winning most of the Kurdish-dominated provinces.

But 2007 proved an aberration, and most Kurdish voters abandoned the AKP in the parliamentary and presidential elections that followed. Why did Erdoğan's strategy fail? First, he didn't deliver on his promises. The cultural measures introduced were half-hearted and piecemeal. The television station, for example, was dull and unwatchable. Meanwhile the Kurdish language was legalised, but key letters absent from Turkish remained prohibited, making something of a mockery of the legalisation. Engagement with the PKK was equally lacklustre, with Ocalan's peace proposals ignored and Erdoğan frequently abandoning talks when he felt his domestic position was stronger. Crucially, hawks on both sides, PKK field commanders and the Turkish military, seemed uncommitted to peace, with raids and reprisals constantly undermining what few efforts there were.

Second, Erdoğan's message of bridging the Turkish–Kurdish divide was taken up more effectively by another party, the centre-left People's Democratic Party (HDP), led by a charismatic Kurd, Selahattin Demirtaş. Drawing support from Kurds and Turks, the HDP overcame Turkey's harsh electoral criteria – designed to exclude Kurdish parties – to gain representation in parliament for the first time in 2015, winning most Kurdish provinces in the process. Finally, Erdoğan's foreign policy became increasingly harsh towards Kurds abroad, which turned off Kurds at home. While he may have been friendly to Iraq's KRG, he was openly hostile to Syria's Kurdish militants as Turkey's southern neighbour exploded into civil war in 2011. This culminated in 2014, when the Jihadist Islamic State besieged the Syrian Kurdish town of Kobani and Erdoğan refused to open the Turkish border to help. With Kobani held by the Syrian allies of the PKK, Erdoğan seemed to be content to let the Jihadists wipe them out. Eventually international pressure forced Ankara to facilitate some relief, allowing Iraqi Kurdish fighters to pass through Turkey into Syria, but the damage was done: Turkey's Kurds saw that Erdoğan was no friend after all.

The Kobani episode represented something of a fork in the road. On the Kurdish side, it sparked renewed activism. Kobani had prompted riots in Kurdish cities and then, inspired by their Syrian brethren who had carved out an autonomous zone, the PKK's youth wing declared autonomy in multiple Turkish Kurdish cities in late summer 2015. This outraged Erdoğan and he deployed the military once more. Over 600 people were killed in harsh urban fighting, and up to half a million displaced, but the Turkish military had retaken all the cities by spring 2016.[20] For Erdoğan, Kobani saw him abandon his Kurdish strategy, and marked a shift to a more autocratic form of rule. This was facilitated by an attempted coup in June 2016 against Erdoğan by disgruntled military officers, which was bungled and quickly failed. Erdoğan used the plot as a pretext to repress multiple domestic enemies. His former allies, a group of Islamists known as the Gulenists, were blamed, but they were not the only ones targeted. Kemalists and Kurds also fell victim. Hundreds of thousands of state employees were dismissed from their posts, including over 20,000 military officers, turning the once independent army into an institution loyal to Erdoğan. Thousands of journalists were arrested, judges were dismissed, as were academics at universities.[21] The result was a complete purge from Turkey's state institutions of anyone suspected of not backing Erdoğan. Demirtaş was among those rounded up and imprisoned.

The purge empowered Erdoğan, impacting the Kurds in two ways. Domestically, he pushed ahead with his plans to revise the constitution, calling a referendum in 2017. Having given up on securing Kurdish votes, he instead courted the right-wing MHP party, who regularly won around 10 per cent of the vote. Historically these secular Turkish nationalists with fascist sympathies abhorred Islamists, but Erdoğan won them round by toughening his policies on the Kurds. The tactic worked and Erdoğan scraped a victory in the referendum and then again in the subsequent election that confirmed him as Turkey's powerful new president. Internationally, packing the army with loyalists and having the MHP on side allowed Erdoğan to be more assertive in Syria against the PKK's allies, the PYD. There were four military interventions into Syria from 2016, aimed at securing the borderlands and keeping the PYD out. These included apparent ethnic cleansing in the Syrian town of Afrin in 2018, where many of the Kurdish population were displaced and replaced by Turkey's Syrian Arab allies.[22] The same pattern occurred in 2019, when a new operation captured a strip of land near Tal Abyad. Such brutal treatment once again confirmed to Turkey's Kurds that whatever Erdoğan's promises early on in his rule, he ultimately differed little from Ataturk and his Kemalist successors in his attitude to Kurdish rights.

War and Opportunity in Syria

Syria's civil war proved something of an awakening for its Kurdish population. Historically they had been the least well politically organised of the Kurds living in the four countries, but the collapse of central authority that occurred after 2011 (see chapter 1) presented an opportunity. Changes were already under way the previous decade. The advent of satellite television, followed by mobile phones and the internet, gave Syrian Kurds access to Kurdish-language, culture and communication with Kurds in other countries they had previously lacked, helping to strengthen Kurdish identity.[23] Tensions caused by the war in neighbouring Iraq led to the first serious Kurdish–Arab clashes in 2004, while Kurdish political parties had also begun to solidify. The most significant was the PYD, which formed in 2003. Officially it claimed to not be the PKK's Syrian arm, but it openly followed Ocalan's leftist ideology and many of its leaders had fought for the PKK in Turkey. Crucially, it appeared to be bankrolled by the PKK and, when it formed fighting militias, the spine of the fighters were veterans from the war in eastern Turkey.[24]

Despite years of discrimination from the Syrian government, many Kurdish political groups were reluctant to join the opposition when protests against President Bashar al-Assad broke out in 2011, even though some youths did join demonstrations. Kurdish leaders distrusted the Islamists and Arab nationalists that dominated the opposition, especially since many were backed by Turkey. Eventually ten groups formed an anti-Assad coalition known as the Kurdish National Council (KNC), with the support of the KRG's president, Masoud Barzani, who already sponsored many Syrian Kurdish politicians. However, the PYD refused to join, wary of Barzani's involvement given his closeness to Turkey, but also opposing the mostly conservative ideology of the KNC. The PYD took a more ambiguous position towards Assad, recalling the PKK's historically close ties to Assad's father, Hafez, and not openly calling for his overthrow. Moreover, as would be seen, the PYD were by far the best-armed and -trained of the Kurdish groups and had little to gain by joining the hastily put together KNC. In mid-2012 Assad opted to remove all troops from Kurdish-dominated areas, to focus on the more populated western Syrian heartlands. Almost immediately, vacated government positions were filled by PYD fighters, leading their opponents to insist they must have collaborated with Assad – a plausible charge.[25] While the KNC protested and insisted they co-rule the Kurdish regions together, the PYD refused, leading to brief clashes that ultimately saw the KNC outmuscled and its leadership fleeing to Iraq. The PYD now effectively ruled over almost all of Syria's Kurdish areas, which in 2013 they named 'Rojava', meaning 'west' in Kurdish, implying this was the western region of Kurdistan.

Ocalan's ideas were put into practice for the first time in Rojava, which had been revised away from Marxist authoritarianism to a progressive 'democratic confederalism' while he was in prison.[26] Local councils were elected to rule Rojava's provinces, with a strong emphasis on gender equality – one of Ocalan's core values – and a male and female co-chair every time. Supporters among the Kurds and Western admirers lauded this experiment in local progressive governance, but critics argued the PYD was imposing its will on often quite conservative societies and permitted little opposition.[27]

However, the experiment was nearly strangled at birth as Islamic State stormed westward from Iraq. The PYD's brave stand in Kobani halted the advance and allowed Rojava to live another day, but also persuaded the United States that it could prove a reliable partner to fight Islamic State. The problem for Washington, however, was that it had designated the PKK a terrorist group in the 1990s at the request of its ally, Turkey. It therefore stuck to the PYD's questionable line that the two groups were totally different but, even so, insisted the Kurdish group join forces with non-Kurdish fighters. The 'Syrian Democratic Forces' were thus created, allowing the US to fund, train, and arm 50,000 fighters to take on Islamic State. However, the PYD's militia, including its separate female units, were by far the strongest and dominated the coalition, fighting in the vanguard of all the major battles.

When Islamic State was eventually defeated, this left the PYD's leadership in effective control of a huge area of eastern Syria, having moved far beyond the Kurdish-dominated areas along the Turkish border. The United States had, in effect, facilitated the creation of a semi-independent Kurdish enclave. The PYD made efforts to be more inclusive. The name Rojava was dropped, while elected councils had representatives of all ethnic and religious communities in the area. Sunni Arabs and Assyrian Christians, for example, were given prominent positions. However, most privately acknowledged that the PYD were the real force in the area, and it was their philosophy that guided governance – prompting quiet resentment in some quarters.

But this experiment in autonomy was built on shaky ground. Turkey never accepted the PYD as anything other than the PKK – in its view a terrorist entity worse than Islamic State. When Rojava was armed by its American allies, Ankara was furious with Washington, causing a significant rupture in their relationship. A spurned Erdoğan instead courted Washington's rival, Russia, which had intervened to help Assad in 2015, and gained permission for Turkey to occupy parts of northern Syria to keep the PYD away. First Turkey moved against Islamic State in al-Bab in 2016, stopping the PYD from capturing the border town. It then moved directly against the Kurdish militia in Afrin two years later: a major blow to the PYD, which had a deep footprint in the city long before the civil war. Ankara then oversaw the demographic transformation of the city, shifting its Kurdish population from 85 per cent to barely 20 per cent in two years.[28] For all the PYD's military successes, it was suddenly clear that their fate might be determined by outside powers.

This was underlined in 2019 when US president Donald Trump suddenly announced he would be withdrawing the 2000 or so US troops from eastern Syria, abandoning the PYD. At the same time, he appeared to greenlight another Turkish invasion of PYD-held territory near Tal Abyad. Pentagon officials eventually persuaded Trump to reverse course and keep some US forces on the ground, including vital air support, but it was too late to save Tal Abyad and its environs. The episode raised serious doubts among the PYD leadership about America's reliability. Two years earlier, in Iraq, the US had done nothing to prevent Iraqi forces from retaking Kirkuk, despite Washington's close alliance with the KRG. Fears of abandonment were further increased when Trump's successor, Joe Biden, withdrew from Afghanistan in 2021, leading to the swift collapse of its allies there. With Turkey lurking like a sword of Damocles to the north, older PYD leaders suggested reconciliation with Assad. Many had close ties with Russia, having trained in the Soviet Union, and military commanders had turned to Russia, not the US, for protection against Turkey in 2019. The younger generation, who had come of age during the Syrian civil war, were more fearful of Assad, believing he would give them nothing close to autonomy if his forces returned, and held out hope for an indefinite American presence. However, all were aware of how precarious their position was, and that their futures would likely be determined in Washington, Ankara, or Moscow.

Iraq: Autonomy at a Price

By far the most successful among Kurdish nationalists were those in Iraq who, after the horrors of the 1980s, experienced not just autonomy but significant prosperity. However, after securing this long craved for freedom, the leaders proved corrupt and hubristic in office. An early sign of this came in the 1990s, when the Kurdish region of Iraq enjoyed de facto autonomy after Saddam Hussein was excluded by the no-fly zone imposed by a US-led international coalition. The first democratic elections held in 1992 saw the region split between Barzani's KDP and its main rival, the Patriotic Union of Kurdistan (PUK), led by Jalal Talabani. Though the parties had different ideologies, the KDP's conservative traditionalism contrasting with the PUK's leftist progressiveness, they also exposed wider fault lines based on geographical regions and linguistic differences. Incredibly, Barzani and Talabani opted to ignore the formal election results, which gave the KDP a narrow lead, and instead opted to share government positions equally between them.[29] It was an inauspicious start to the democratic experiment, but one that set the tone.

Thereafter the two parties monopolised power and shared out offices. While traditional tribalism had faded in the 1970s, a 'neo-tribalism' emerged, where membership of a party was essential for advancement. The coalition was fragile though, and both parties sought to outmanoeuvre each other. This erupted into violence in 1994, beginning three years of fighting, with both seeking outside help to survive. Barzani welcomed support from Saddam Hussein, prompting Talabani to get assistance from Iran. To both Baghdad and Tehran's frustration though, it was the US that was now the dominant force in the region and ultimately mediated the dispute. One positive was that this meant that the Kurds had already worked through some of their differences when Saddam was toppled in 2003, while Iraq's Arabs were consumed by violence.

After the 2003 invasion of Iraq (see chapter 5), the relative consensus among the Kurdish parties meant they were able to unite in negotiations over a post-Saddam government. Barzani and Talabani proved shrewd operators and outmanoeuvred both the US administrators and the newly formed Arab Iraqi political parties. Despite Baghdad's new political class wanting a strong centralised government, something also favoured by Washington, the Kurdish leaders were able to secure the formal autonomy of the KRG. This included the right for the KDP and PUK's fighters, the Peshmerga, to retain their arms and prohibited the Iraqi military from entering the region without the Kurdish parliament's approval. It also gave the KRG considerable autonomy on exports from its oil and gas fields.

This latter point proved key as it allowed the KRG to boom while the rest of Iraq succumbed to sectarian violence. International companies were deterred from investing heavily in southern Iraq, while political corruption, incompetence, and instability meant that it took years for Baghdad's oil exports to reach pre-2003 levels. But foreign businesses were much more comfortable in the comparatively stable KRG. Production levels rocketed and the big oil companies soon arrived: ExxonMobil in 2011, followed by Total and Chevron.[30] Turkey also became a surprising but vital economic partner. Despite Ankara retaining its hostility to any form of Kurdish independence, Erdoğan seemed happy enough with KRG autonomy, provided it didn't evolve into anything more. It helped that the region's leader was Barzani, who had cut a deal that gave Talabani the presidency of Iraq in exchange for Barzani taking the presidency of the Kurdish region. While Talabani's PUK had historically been sympathetic to the PKK, the conservative KDP had frequently clashed with Ocalan's Marxists, and granted Turkey the right to pursue militants into northern Iraq.

The economic relationship proved symbiotic. Turkey lacked energy resources and so eagerly consumed the KRG's oil and gas. In a sign of growing independence from Baghdad, Erbil built a new oil pipeline direct to Turkey so that it didn't have rely on the existing one controlled by the Iraqi government.[31] In turn, the KRG spent much of their new oil wealth on Turkish goods and services. As Erbil was transformed with shiny new buildings and malls, much of the construction was done by Turkish companies, while the KRG imported substantial food and manufactured goods from its northern neighbour. By 2010 Iraq was Turkey's second biggest trading partner, 70 per cent of that trade being with the KRG.[32] All this contrasted sharply with events in the south. A decade after Saddam's fall, the standard of living in the Kurdish region was for the first time higher than that of Arab Iraq. This increased resentment from Baghdad, which already felt the KRG was taking more than its fair share of oil revenue.

The economy was booming, and a new generation was coming of age without any memory of the past horrors. Kurdish youths were heading to the many new universities that popped up across the KRG, often not even learning to speak Arabic as they seemed more and more detached from the rest of Iraq. But three crises stopped progress in its tracks – two of which were own goals from the KRG's leaders. The first was an economic downturn after 2013. Global oil prices dropped, but the Kurdish government had racked up huge debts without keeping proper accounts of income and expenses. Corruption at the top was rife, with Barzani himself accused of having accumulated over $2 billion worth of assets.[33] It wasn't a sovereign state so had limited options to borrow, while its disputes with Baghdad meant the Iraqi central government was no longer sending it a share of the federal budget. The result was a prolonged period of economic stagnation, leading to business closures, economic migration, and unpaid salaries.

This was the backdrop for the second crisis: the rise of Islamic State. As the Jihadists expanded their 'Caliphate' they reached within 30 miles of Erbil and humiliated the KRG's fighters when the Peshmerga fled from Sinjar leaving 5,000 Yazidis to be massacred and another 5,000 to be enslaved. This humiliation was compounded when their rivals, the Syrian PYD, fought their way across the border to provide a safe route for the survivors to escape. However, the KRG eventually turned this disaster around, cooperating with the United States and Iran, separately, to defeat the Jihadists and expand the territory under its control to include the contested oil-rich city of Kirkuk. The third crisis emerged from this when Barzani, hubristic after the military success, called a referendum on KRG independence from Iraq in 2017. Despite pleas from Turkey, the US, and Iran not to proceed, the vote went ahead and was won by 93 per cent, with a turnout of 72 per cent.[34] However, the referendum was not legally binding and provoked fury from all of Erbil's neighbours.

Iran immediately conducted military manoeuvres on the KRG's borders, as did Turkey, who also cancelled all flights into the region and cut ties with Barzani. The Iraqi military and its militia allies, many of whom were employed by Iran, marched on Kirkuk, which the Peshmerga surrendered without a fight. The KRG, already in economic dire straits, was now cut off, deprived of Kirkuk's oil, and desperate. A humiliated Barzani was forced to acknowledge that the referendum was illegal in order for Baghdad to agree to a financial bailout, and subsequently resigned as KRG president, to be succeeded by his nephew. Eventually Iran and Turkey reestablished ties, but the Kurdish nationalists had been cut down to size. Any question of imminent independence now seemed off the table.

Little Progress in Iran

In a reversal of the situation in Iraq, Iran's Kurds made the least progress in improving their situation in the early twenty-first century. The Kurdish region of Iran remains the least developed part of the country, with one of the highest levels of unemployment.[35] Kurdish political parties remain banned while the population in general face sporadic repression. Tehran's attitude to its Kurds has varied from government to government. The reformist president Muhammad

Khatami (1997–2005) eased the heavy military presence that had been present since the Iran–Iraq war and permitted greater cultural freedom. His successor Mahmoud Ahmadinejad (2005–13), in contrast, oversaw a harsher approach, with executions of political prisoners, including Kurdish activists, increasing during his rule. The next president, Hassan Rouhani (2013–21) was another moderate, and attempted dialogue, including appointing a Sunni Kurd to his cabinet, although he also deployed the military to Kurdish cities in 2017 after the KRG's independence referendum as a show of force. The pendulum swung rightward again when Ebrahim Raisi became president in 2021. When nationwide protests broke out over women's rights the following year, the Kurdish region was the epicentre of the revolt and crackdowns were particularly hard.

In the face of repression, militant groups continued to launch sporadic attacks on government forces. Historically the two strongest players were the Kurdish Democratic Party of Iran (not to be confused with Iraq's KDP, despite having similar origins), and the Marxist Komala group, but both faded in importance after violent campaigns against the Islamic Republic during the 1980s. In the 1990s, their place was usurped by a new group, the Kurdistan Free Life Party (PJAK), the Iranian affiliate of the PKK, which became the most effective guerrilla movement in the 2000s. However, none of these ever came close to replicating the organisation or support enjoyed by the PKK in Turkey, the KDP or PUK in Iraq, or (after 2011) the PYD in Syria. While proving an irritant to Tehran, they looked unlikely to force the Islamic Republic into granting anything resembling autonomy.

For that reason, perhaps, Iran's Kurdish region was the least influenced by foreign forces. Israel (see chapter 4) had a covert presence just over the border from Iran, in the KRG, having forged undeclared ties with Barzani, but this was primarily a listening post for Iranian activity and was not known to have extended its influence to Iran's Kurdish community. In fact, the greatest foreign leverage came from other Kurdish groups, not rival governments. The PJAK was influenced by the PKK and Iraq's PUK, and was persuaded by both to suspend attacks on Tehran's forces in 2012, given Iran's support for Assad in the Syrian civil war and Iran's sympathetic view of the PYD. The KDPI also has close ties with the PUK, often retreating to its territory in Iraq, prompting Iran to launch occasional air raids or drone attacks across the border.

Tehran itself has cynically made use of Kurdish groups abroad, shifting positions regularly to suit changing goals and strategies, all while cracking down on similar militants at home. In the 1980s it happily funded and trained Kurdish Islamists to form Hizbullah in Turkey, despite them being Sunni, hoping to undermine Turkey's secular Kemalists, who were allies of the West.[36] In the 2000s, in contrast, it signed a security pact with Erdoğan against the PKK and PJAK, each side agreeing to hand over captured Kurdish fighters from the respective groups. It regularly sent support to Kurds in Iraq, whether to the PUK in its fight with Barzani in the 1990s, or to help the KRG's Peshmerga fight Islamic State two decades later. Similarly, it did little to stop Iranian Kurds leaving Iran to join the PYD to fight Islamic State, and Iran welcomed the presence of the PYD given its role in weakening Assad's enemies. In short, Tehran, perhaps more than any other government save the USA, proved able to make use of Kurdish fighters when this suited its aims, while minimising the blowback at home. For its own Kurds, however, there appeared little hope of a breakthrough.

Freedom without Independence?

The likelihood of an independent Kurdistan emerging looks as forlorn as ever. It has thus far failed to come into being for three main reasons. First, the Kurdish national movement started on the wrong foot. It developed later than rival nationalisms in its neighbourhood, ensuring that Kurdish claims for independence were less prominent than those voices. The community was harshly treated by Western governments, which partitioned the Kurds between four states where they formed minority groups. The governments of Turkey, Iran, Syria, and Iraq that ruled over them were equally harsh, each seeking to repress Kurdish culture and force assimilation. This oppression transformed Kurdish identity into a mass nationalism so, ironically, the partition both made Kurdish nationalism possible but also made a united independent Kurdistan unlikely.

Second, once Kurdish nationalism emerged, its leaders and movements made a series of self-defeating errors. The most obvious was internal division. Even within each state, Kurds have been divided by ideological, geographical, and personal factors, meaning they have rarely been able to present a united front against oppressive governments. Rivalries have even emerged across national boundaries, with the most powerful players – Turkey's PKK and Iraq's KDP and PUK – sponsoring rival groups in other parts of Kurdistan, exacerbating divisions further. This has been especially true in Syria, where Kurdish groups have all relied on, and been divided by, external patronage by foreign Kurdish parties. Leaders have made other errors, notably pursuing self-interest over a common Kurdish cause.

Finally, internal divisions have been greatly exacerbated by the machinations of different governments. Syria, Iraq, Iran, and Turkey have all, at times, been crushing Kurdish dissent at home while simultaneously aligned with Kurdish groups abroad. External governments have added to this, with Israel and Russia both having an influence on Kurdistan's fate in recent years. The most consequential outsider, however, has been the US, which helped to bring about the two most successful instances of Kurdish autonomy in Iraq and Syria. Yet, at the same time, Washington has been an unreliable friend, willing to drop its Kurdish allies at different times when it needed to. The Kurds in Iraq, and especially Syria, are right to fear this could happen again.

Despite these hurdles, Iraqi and Syrian Kurds have still managed to claw a path towards some freedom, even if it still eludes their Turkish and Iranian brethren. Though flawed and possibly unsustainable, this is still an achievement given the obstacles in their way. That said, it is a much larger step for either to achieve full independence, as the KRG discovered in 2017. This would require overcoming the deep opposition of the Turkish, Iraqi, Iranian, and Syrian governments and getting significant buy-in from key external players like the US. Yet, for many Kurds, there is no going back to the repression of their identity they experienced in the past. Whatever their political fate, the disruptions of the past few decades have awoken Kurdish culture and identity. Politicians, activists, and others – whether inside the region or in the now extensive diaspora – are pushing for improved rights and conditions across Kurdistan. Even if independence proves elusive, the struggle in the mountains may yet continue in a different form.

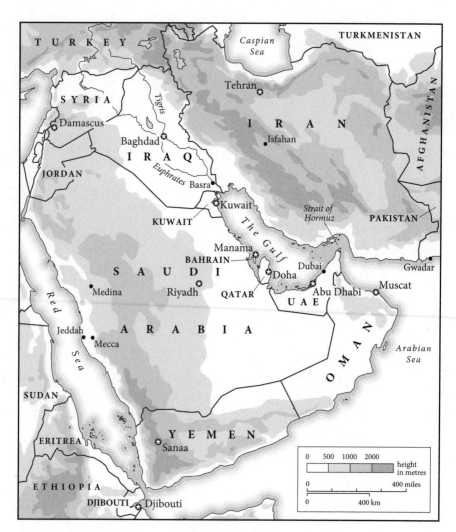

The Gulf states

9

The Gulf
Wealth and Insecurity

The 2022 FIFA Men's World Cup in Qatar was a lavish affair. Some $220 billion was spent preparing a country smaller than Connecticut to host 1.4 million visitors – over half Qatar's population. Seven new stadiums were constructed, as were new highways, hotels, and a metro system to accommodate the throngs of football fans arriving in the tiny Gulf state.[1] The tournament was somewhat marred by the deaths of migrants who built the new infrastructure and the questionable safety of LGBT football fans in a country where homosexuality is illegal. Even so, Qatar's leaders ignored the censure to bask in being the first Muslim and Middle Eastern state to host a World Cup. It nearly didn't happen. A little under two years before the first ball was kicked, Qatar was facing blockade by its neighbours. Its former allies Saudi Arabia, the United Arab Emirates, and Bahrain, alongside Egypt, had closed Qatar's only land border, demanding radical changes to Doha's foreign policy. With food and other supplies only available via convoluted air and sea routes, the prospect of hosting the World Cup looked fraught. Yet not only was the blockade dropped before the global event, but one of its initiators, Saudi Crown Prince Mohammed Bin Salman, sat draped in a 'Qatar 2022' scarf as a guest of honour in the royal box with Qatar's emir at the World Cup opening ceremony.

The World Cup and the events that preceded it in many ways point to the three central characteristics of the Gulf's position in Middle Eastern geopolitics today. First, wealth. The fact that a tiny country with only one city was able to win and host a global tournament was the result of the vast fossil fuel wealth emanating from the region. Qatar is the wealthiest per capita country in the world, but its Gulf neighbours – Saudi Arabia, the UAE, Kuwait, Bahrain and, to a lesser extent, Oman – similarly hold oil and gas reserves that have transformed their capitals from quiet desert settlements to towering metropolises. Second, insecurity. The Qatar blockade was just the latest in a series of destabilising events to befall the region. The importance of oil and gas to the world economy, and the desire of larger regional powers like Iran and Iraq to dominate those producing it, has made the Gulf a deeply insecure region. This is similarly illustrated by the 60,000 US troops housed in bases along the coast and the purchase of extensive weaponry by regional leaders.

Finally, power. Qatar's hosting of the World Cup was in defiance of both its regional rivals and considerable Western criticism. It even broke a promise to allow alcohol in stadiums on the eve of the tournament, a decision ultimately accepted by FIFA and its sponsors.[2] Rather like the audacity shown by its neighbours in starting the blockade, tiny Qatar behaving this way was symptomatic of a new confidence in international affairs. Where once they were timid, as regional and global rivalries played out around them, their recent wealth has bought some Gulf states, notably Saudi Arabia, the UAE, and Qatar, the ability to be major players themselves. Indeed, the blockade itself was primarily over Qatar's policies in the wider Middle East, not just the Gulf, as Doha, like Abu Dhabi and Riyadh, had become a significant actor in regional politics. While the Gulf region continues to be an arena for regional and global rivalries, it is also home to three emerging powers that have growing local and international heft.

From Pearling to Petro-states

Eight states sit around the part of the Indian Ocean known as the 'Persian' or 'Arabian' Gulf. Of these, Iraq and Iran (see chapter 5) are often considered separate from the others, with whom they have shared recent enmity. Saudi Arabia, Qatar, the UAE, Kuwait, Bahrain, and Oman are all conservative monarchies, rentier states that depend on hydrocarbons, and members of the Gulf Cooperation Council (GCC), which they formed in 1981, partly to defend against Iraq and Iran. Bordering the inhospitable deserts of the Arabian Peninsula, the region was sparsely populated before the discovery of oil and gas, with local tribal sheikhs dominating the modest port towns that relied on trade and pearl-diving. Recognising the region's strategic value in protecting the route to India, Britain took an increased interest from the eighteenth century. Gradually its presence deepened and agreements were formed with the ruling sheikhs on the Arabian side of the Gulf to complement its earlier ties on the Persian (Iranian) side. They became British Protected States, which gave London control over the sheikhs' external affairs but, theoretically, left them to their own devices at home. Yet British backing changed the nature of the territories, empowering families that would go on to become the ruling monarchs of independent states. When Britain eventually departed in 1971, Kuwait, Bahrain, Qatar, and the UAE arguably owed their separate existence to London's long presence. The exceptions were Saudi Arabia and Oman. Oman had a long history as a powerful maritime state, expanding its influence over the Indian Ocean as far off as Zanzibar, before declining and looking to Britain for protection. Saudi Arabia, meanwhile, was formed in 1932 after a war of conquest with British backing but remained outside of London's formal orbit.

Saudi Arabia is by far the largest of the GCC states, with a population of 34 million that dwarfs that of its nearest rival, the UAE (9 million). It also has the largest oil reserves, the second-largest in the world behind Venezuela, allowing it to dominate the GCC. The ruling Al-Saud family, which united the disparate Arabian territories, used religion to bind the tribal and nomadic peoples of the peninsula together, relying heavily on a conservative form of Islam, known as Wahhabism. As a result, Riyadh has historically wanted to preserve the regional status quo, fearful of ideological threats like Arab nationalism or political Islam that might encourage its population to overthrow the Al-Sauds.[3] Qatar, based on a tiny peninsula attached to Saudi Arabia, also formally follows Wahhabi Islam, but enforces it less rigidly. Its monarchs, the Al-Thani family, have ruled since the eighteenth century, but not especially securely. The first two emirs after independence were both deposed in coups, led by their cousin and son respectively. While blessed with modest oil reserves, it wasn't a major fossil fuel exporter until the 1990s, when its huge natural gas reserves were tapped to transform Qatar into one of the wealthiest states in the world.

The UAE is unique within the Gulf as it is a federation of seven emirates, each controlled by different families. The most important are Abu Dhabi and Dubai. Abu Dhabi possesses 94 per cent of the UAE's oil and, as a result, dominates the federation politically. By convention, Abu Dhabi's ruling family, the Al-Nahyan, have always held the powerful presidency since independence, an agreement accepted by the other emirates given its superior wealth. The vice presidency is held by the Al-Maktoum family that rules Dubai, which, despite having little oil wealth itself, has established itself as a regional (and now global) hub for trade, finance, tourism, and services. Abu Dhabi and Dubai have both thrived in recent years, attracting workers from developed and developing countries, pushing the population from 3.3 million in 2000 to over 9 million today. Bahrain, in contrast, has very modest oil reserves, meaning the ruling Al-Khalifa family have diversified the island's economy to focus on finance. This has been partly successful but has not allowed Bahrain anywhere near the international freedom of other Gulf states, leaving it often reliant on neighbouring Saudi Arabia. This reliance on Riyadh is amplified by religious demographics. The Al-Khalifas are Sunni Muslims, but most of their subjects are Shia. Bahrain's leaders fear the Shia could revolt against them, a sentiment shared by the Al-Sauds, whose Shia minority live in the most oil-rich parts of Saudi Arabia.[4]

While the Gulf states are mostly autocracies, the partial exception is Kuwait. Kuwait has a functioning parliament, though the ruling Al-Sabah family is rarely criticised, and an historical merchant class that continued to be influential even after oil was discovered. As a result, Kuwait is the only Gulf state to regularly be labelled 'partly free' by think tank Freedom House, unlike the others which are all deemed 'not free'.[5] This, and its historic fears of invasion by larger neighbours, have made Kuwait often adopt neutral or mediating positions in the Gulf, eschewing the activism of Riyadh, Abu Dhabi, and Doha. Oman likewise favours neutrality. It enjoys closer ties with Iran than most Gulf states, partially the result of the two states' much longer history of cooperation across the Gulf dating back centuries. The ruling Al-Busaidi are also wary of too much foreign adventurism. They experienced a long civil war in the 1960s and 1970s and have only modest oil reserves so cannot placate their population with the kind of luxuries enjoyed in Qatar or the UAE.

All six Gulf states have a deep relationship with the United States that has greatly shaped their development and geopolitical position. American companies found oil in Saudi Arabia in 1938, but the current partnership didn't emerge until seven years later, when Washington agreed to guarantee Riyadh's security in exchange for access to affordable energy supplies. When Britain withdrew from the region in 1971, the US gradually took over its role as protector. Two years later Saudi Arabia led an oil boycott against the US and other Western states to protest their support for Israel in the Yom Kippur/October war, almost quadrupling oil prices and pushing the US economy into recession. This highlighted to Washington just how much its economy depended on Gulf oil and the importance of securing it. Fears of losing access were amplified when another oil-producing ally, the Shah of Iran, was replaced by the hostile Islamic Republic in 1979, before it was engulfed in an eight-year war with Iraq – another key oil state – threatening the supply. The White House first declared the 'Carter Doctrine' in 1980, stating it would use military force if necessary to protect its interests in the Gulf. Under Jimmy Carter's successor, Ronald Reagan, the US then encouraged the five smaller Gulf states and Saudi Arabia to band together to form the GCC in 1981, committing to common security. Thereafter Washington gradually ramped up its own military presence in the region, offering naval protection to Kuwaiti and Saudi tankers, under threat from Iranian attacks for their financial support of Iraq in the Iran–Iraq war. When Iraq then invaded Kuwait in 1990 after concluding its war with Iran, Saudi Arabia, nervous it would be next, naturally looked to Washington for help.

Operations Desert Shield, to defend Saudi Arabia from Iraqi attack, and Desert Storm, to push Saddam Hussein out of Kuwait, brought 700,000 US troops to the Gulf in 1990–1. With the end of the Cold War ushering in an era of global US dominance, the Gulf War, as it became known, also solidified Washington's unquestionable primacy in the region. While most US troops left after Saddam's defeat, the White House concluded agreements with all six GCC states in the early 1990s to secure a permanent military presence. They retain these bases today, except for in Saudi Arabia, which asked the US military to leave in 2003, conscious their presence was provoking religious opposition. This tied the GCC firmly to US primacy, with Washington using the Gulf as a platform to dominate the Middle East, including carrying out punitive raids on Saddam's Iraq, and enforcing sanctions on Iran.

Tensions emerged the following decade, however. The 9/11 attacks had been precipitated by Al-Qaeda terrorists, mostly hailing from Gulf states – 15 of the 19 being from Saudi Arabia, and 2 from the UAE – indicating that not all Gulf citizens welcomed what they saw as an 'imperial' presence. Indeed, one of Al-Qaeda's core concerns was the presence of non-Muslim US troops on the sacred Arabian Peninsula. The US response, the invasion of Iraq in 2003, raised concerns among GCC leaders, especially Saudi Arabia. While Saddam was unloved by the Gulf states he had formerly invaded and threatened, Riyadh correctly feared that his removal would unleash sectarian and Jihadist violence that could spill into the Gulf. It might also empower Iran, whose Islamic revolution the Gulf states had long feared could inspire their own populations to overthrow their autocratic regimes. GCC leaders were therefore frustrated when the White House ignored their warnings and the predicted chaos in Iraq came to pass. They were further irked when President George W. Bush, in order to justify his invasion retrospectively, pushed them to embrace democracy and improve human rights – something no previous US leader had insisted on. While these proved wrinkles rather than vicissitudes in the relationships with the US, they set the scene for greater tensions to follow and moves by GCC leaders to diversify their international ties in order to ease their reliance on Washington.

The Arab Uprisings

The popular uprisings of 2011 rocked the Gulf. Most GCC leaders, with one exception, initially viewed the protests with consternation, determined to prevent similar unrest from threatening their own regimes. Once that early threat was contained, violently in the case of Bahrain, the new regional dynamics that the uprisings ushered in prompted a shift in the foreign policies of several GCC states. The Gulf was not immune from the unrest. When Tunisian protesters forced the resignation of their autocratic president, who fled to Saudi Arabia, and Egyptian demonstrators followed suit, youthful activists across the Arab world flooded onto the streets. In Oman, protesters demanded improved living standards, more jobs, and less corruption, but were largely placated by budget increases, minor reforms, and the sacking of some ministers. In Saudi Arabia, unrest also broke out, especially in the Shia-dominated eastern province. Riyadh swiftly promised $130 billion for new welfare measures, but also arrested handfuls of protesters and oppositionists, particularly cracking down on Shia-dominated areas. Kuwait and the UAE also experienced minor unrest.[6]

The most dramatic events occurred in Bahrain, however. In February and March, prompted by the fall of Egypt's president, hundreds of thousands gathered to demand political reform in public places centred on the capital Manama's Pearl Roundabout. Though only a handful were against the monarchy, most called for improved political rights, more power to the toothless parliament, and the resignation of the long-standing prime minister, the king's uncle. While there were few religious demands, most protesters were from the country's Shia majority, a point not lost on either the king or his neighbours.[7] Saudi Arabia and the UAE were particularly worried that a Shia-led revolution could transform Bahrain into a pro-Iranian satellite on its doorstep and even claimed, erroneously, that the protesters were encouraged by Tehran. After a month of failing to deter the protesters with minor concessions and police crackdowns, the king called on his GCC neighbours for help. In response, 2,000 troops, 1,000 from Saudi Arabia, 500 from the UAE, a handful from Qatar, but none from Kuwait or Oman, crossed over the bridge from Saudi Arabia to help the regime squash the unrest. Thousands of protesters were arrested, over 150 were killed, while many were later dismissed from their government jobs, stripped of citizenship, or expelled from university. The Pearl Roundabout, meanwhile, was bulldozed to the ground, to 'boost traffic flow'.[8]

The conservative autocrats of the GCC, especially the UAE and Saudi Arabia, were shocked at the sudden fall of fellow autocrats in Egypt and Tunisia and astounded that their own populations would be inspired to try the same. They were furious, moreover, with the United States. US President Barack Obama had facilitated the overthrow of Egyptian President Hosni Mubarak (see chapter 6), angering Riyadh and Abu Dhabi, which believed Washington should stand by its partners and, privately, feared the White House might similarly desert them in the future. As a result, neither Saudi Arabia nor the UAE informed Washington of their intention to send forces into Bahrain, despite the US Fifth Fleet being based there.[9] The abandonment of Mubarak, coming on the back of a decade of tension with Washington and a specific dislike of Obama, whom the Saudis struggled to warm to, prompted both Riyadh and Abu Dhabi to conclude that they could no longer rely on the US. They would need to increase their own involvement in regional affairs. Though conservative, Riyadh and Abu Dhabi, did not uniformly oppose the overthrow of the region's autocrats in the instability that followed 2011. They both supported the rebellion in Libya, while Riyadh also backed the opposition in Syria (see chapter 1). However, they shared a deep opposition to the Muslim Brotherhood and sought to prevent their coming to power in both theatres, while conspiring (with Kuwait) to fund the military coup against an elected Brotherhood president in Egypt in 2013. They also collaborated in Yemen, brokering the departure of the long-reigning autocrat and then intervening militarily in 2015 when his replacement was overthrown by pro-Iranian forces (see chapter 3). While Riyadh and Abu Dhabi were historically reluctant to get involved, the events of 2011 shook them into action as they attempted to roll back the popular uprising, and the increased power of the Muslim Brotherhood and Iran that they feared would come about as a result.

In contrast, Qatar largely welcomed the uprisings. Al Jazeera, the Arabic news station established in Doha with Qatari backing, was instrumental in spreading the protests across the Arab world. At the same time, Doha was the most vocal supporter of the rebels in Libya (see chapter 2) and, for a time, Syria too. In contrast to Saudi Arabia and the UAE, it had close ties to the Muslim Brotherhood, whose spokesmen and allies were given regular airtime on Al Jazeera. As the dust settled after 2011, it soon became clear that in Egypt, Syria, and Libya, Doha was backing the opponents of its GCC allies, and pushing for different outcomes in the conflicts. The exceptions, however, were Bahrain and Yemen. In the former, Al Jazeera was notably quiet on the protests, in contrast to the wall-to-wall coverage it offered of the revolutions outside of the Gulf. It similarly showed little of the protests in Oman or Saudi Arabia. In Yemen, Doha joined the Saudi–UAE-led coalition a few months after the initial intervention. Despite its differences with allies elsewhere in the Middle East, Qatar signalled that on matters in the Gulf's neighbourhood, GCC solidarity still held – for now.

Between Washington and Beijing?

The vast natural resources of the Gulf have long attracted foreign interest, but its geography makes it even more strategically important. Most oil and gas is shipped in tankers that must pass through the narrow Strait of Hormuz, barely 40 km wide. With Iran controlling one side and Oman and the UAE controlling the other, the oil-producing states and their customers have long feared that Tehran might deliberately close access, disrupting global fuel supplies and hiking prices. Indeed, this is a 'weapon' Iran keeps up its sleeve to deploy should it ever be attacked. Keeping the straits open has been a key goal of the US and one of the reasons for its large post-Cold War deployment to the region to deter Iran. This geographical feature adds to the Gulf's already strategically useful location at a key point on the Indian Ocean, close to the Suez Canal, and on the major shipping lanes between Europe, Africa, India, China, and East Asia.

The United States remains by far the most powerful and important foreign player, though China has enhanced its position in recent years. Washington is the only foreign country with multiple bases, and the only one to guarantee the security of all six GCC states. Both the US and the Gulf states describe this as a 'security umbrella', meaning Washington would be expected to defend the GCC if any of them were attacked. But the dynamics of the relationship have changed. The US no longer relies on Gulf oil in the way it once did. The 'Shale Revolution' that massively increased the domestic oil supply of the US, as well as the growth of imports from Canada, mean the US now imports little oil from GCC states.[10] It remains important for Washington for energy supplies to flow, though, to keep global oil prices reasonable and to ensure the key allies and trade partners of the US maintain access. This also, at times, serves Washington's strategic purposes elsewhere. An example was in 2022 when the White House urged the GCC to increase oil and gas production to help its European allies cope with the loss of Russian energy after Moscow invaded Ukraine. But the original reasons for America's close ties to the Gulf, the 'affordable energy supplies' of the agreement with Saudi Arabia in 1945, no longer have the same weight they once did.

However, the US has shown no inclination to abandon the Gulf. Different White House administrations have had different foreign policy priorities, but all eventually underlined the importance of Washington's continued commitment. George W. Bush needed the buy-in of the Gulf states to legitimise his 'war on terror', despite their reservations, and access to US bases from which to attack Iraq and Afghanistan. Barack Obama, despite his instinctive hostility to the autocratic monarchs, sought their support, with mixed success, in various Middle Eastern arenas after the 2011 uprisings, and then again courted their approval for his 2015 nuclear deal with Iran. Donald Trump was far friendlier to Gulf leaders than his predecessor, following Saudi (and Israeli) advice to abrogate Obama's deal and reintroduce sanctions on Iran. This also followed Trump's preference for transactional foreign relations, coming after Riyadh had agreed to buy $100 billion worth of US weapons.[11] Joe Biden, like Obama, was initially hostile to Gulf leaders, especially Saudi Crown Prince Mohammed Bin Salman. However, he U-turned when he sought (unsuccessfully) to increase energy production in 2022 to compensate

Western allies for the loss of Russian oil and gas after Moscow was sanctioned for the Ukraine war. Alongside these specific needs, Washington policy makers have noted anxiously that China's role in the region has deepened. As well as the various advantages of remaining in the Gulf, many in DC now argue that, at the minimum, the US needs to stay to keep China from taking its place.

But China is not the only foreign power to increase its footprint. In 2009 France agreed to open a new military base in Abu Dhabi, hosting 650 personnel, while in 2014 the UK established a permanent presence in the region for the first time since 1971 by opening a naval base for 500 troops in Bahrain. In 2015, meanwhile, Turkey agreed to build a military base in Qatar, with an eventual capacity for 5,000 Turkish troops.[12] These bases benefit both sides. The foreign governments were rewarded domestically with the prestige of new overseas military bases, though fully aware they were dwarfed by Washington's presence. The GCC states gained further security guarantees from the US's allies to guard against any reluctance from Washington to come to their aid in a crisis – something that was particularly pertinent for Doha after 2017. These European states took advantage of a perceived cooling of GCC–US ties to increase their foothold and boosted their trade and diplomatic ties. However, Washington was not concerned by these moves, and some in DC wanted their allies to share the burden of ensuring Gulf security. This was not the case, however, with China.

Beijing's global rise has brought with it an increased interest in the Middle East. China played a notable diplomatic role in the Syria crisis, joining Russia in vetoing numerous UN resolutions against President Bashar al-Assad, and has deepened its investments in Israel, Jordan, Iraq, Turkey, Iran, and Egypt.[13] But by far the most important relationships have been with the GCC, expanding its economic, military, and cultural presence. After the Communist Revolution of 1949, China at first showed little interest in the Gulf, seeing its states as far-off, US-aligned enemies. When it did eventually engage, it was to sponsor leftist rebels in the Omani civil war in the 1960s. This changed as Chinese–Western ties warmed after Nixon's détente with Beijing, and with the rise to power of Deng Xiaoping (1978–89), who favoured a 'low-profile' approach to foreign affairs. Improved ties with the Gulf states, focused on trade, soon followed. Gradually this morphed into an interdependent relationship in the 1990s and 2000s, as Gulf energy fuelled China's roaring economy. By 2014, GCC states provided a quarter of China's liquefied natural gas (LNG), second only to Australia, and a third of its crude oil.[14]

But changes inside and outside China would bring closer ties. The 2008 financial crash and its aftermath saw Western economies weaken while China grew. Already some in China's elite had begun to question Deng's 'low profile'. Beijing became more activist in global affairs, using its new wealth to carve out areas where its influence surpassed that of the US, notably sub-Saharan Africa and southeast Asia. China's influence expanded after 2012, when Xi Jinping became head of the Communist Party and, shortly afterwards, China's new president. Xi outmanoeuvred his domestic rivals to become the most powerful Chinese leader since Chairman Mao. He discarded Deng's philosophy and promoted a more assertive foreign policy. Donald Trump helped by initiating a trade war with Beijing that galvanised Chinese nationalism, but even before that Xi was flexing his muscles in the South China Sea. Xi's centrepiece was the 'Belt and Road Initiative' (BRI), launched in September 2013. This massive $4 trillion–$8 trillion project envisaged new infrastructure links across Asia, Africa, and Europe to construct a land 'belt' and a maritime 'road' to China. The Middle East was designated a 'neighbour' region for the BRI: a top geostrategic priority, with China recognising, as Washington once did, that its prosperity was heavily dependent on Gulf energy. By 2022, 140 countries had signed up to the BRI, including all the GCC states, Iraq, and Iran. Although progress stalled somewhat and many of the infrastructure projects promised by the BRI were slow to take off, the programme still represented a statement of intent from Beijing.

China's interests in the Gulf were primarily economic. The GCC is China's eighth-largest source of imports and exports.[15] Saudi Arabia is China's biggest trade partner, being a key market for Chinese construction firms as well as the single largest source of Beijing's oil. Riyadh values its ties with China so highly that it accepts Beijing's extensive ties with its rival, Iran, also a key BRI partner. As Prince Turki al Faisal, once Saudi Arabia's ambassador to the US, has said, 'China is not necessarily a better friend than the United States, but it is a less complicated friend.'[16] UAE–China relations are also well developed. Alongside energy supplies, China makes great use of Dubai's role as the world's third-largest re-export hub. Over 4,000 Chinese companies are based in the UAE to facilitate vital trade running through the port, while the UAE is also a major destination for Chinese tourists.[17] In Qatar, China is a key customer for LNG, while Chinese construction firms played a major role in preparations for the 2022 World Cup, including building the 89,000-seater Lusail Stadium that hosted the final.[18] Most Gulf states have national infrastructure plans to diversify their economies away from oil and gas, such as New Kuwait 2035 and Saudi Vision 2030, and Chinese investment and construction is seen as key to achieving these goals.

Beyond economics, China's interests are primarily military and cultural. Chinese weaponry is historically less popular among the Gulf states than American, European, and Russian arms, though Saudi Arabia has made some major purchases in the past and China is looking to expand its share of the market. More important has been gaining access to strategically important ports. In 2010 the UAE became the first Gulf state to host the Chinese navy, and became a regular port of call thereafter, as did Oman.[19] Contrary to Washington's fears, China has thus far shown no interest in replacing the US as the primary military power in the region, building bases and permanent outposts. However, in 2015 a Chinese company signed a forty-three-year lease for the port of Gwadar in Pakistan – an early signatory to the BRI – 600 miles east of the Strait of Hormuz, opening the possibility that eventually the Chinese navy may have a base not far from the region. Culture is also a feature of the relationship, particularly Islam. Islamic banks based in the UAE are seen as important facilitators for China in the Muslim-majority states of Central Asia that have joined the BRI. Closer to home, China has a sizeable Muslim minority and utilises Saudi Arabia to help manage it. The Hui Muslims of Ningxia province are tolerated, and Beijing uses its ties with Riyadh to underline this tolerance, such as securing pilgrimage spots to Mecca and Medina. In contrast, the Uighur Muslims of Xinjiang province have been harshly repressed in recent years, and Beijing appreciates Riyadh and the Saudi religious establishment staying relatively quiet on the matter.[20]

It is understandable for Washington to be frustrated at China's increased presence in the Gulf, but perhaps it should not be alarmed. China has taken advantage of the relative security that the US gives the GCC to maximise its benefits. However, it has not had to provide any security itself. Some in Washington, including Trump when he was president, accused China of 'free-riding' on the US presence, but at the same time the White House wouldn't want Beijing to increase its military footprint. This clearly benefits both China and the Gulf states, who mutually benefit without having to pay the security costs. This leaves Washington facing a dilemma though: it neither wants to leave the Gulf, in case it destabilises, nor does it want China to have a bigger military presence, thus the US is forced to stay, but with diminishing returns.

The Qatar Crisis

The continued importance of the US would be seen in both the outbreak and eventual resolution of the Qatar crisis that rocked the Gulf from 2017 to 2021. Tensions had been brewing between Doha, Riyadh, and Abu Dhabi for some time. Historically, after independence Qatar had subordinated its foreign policy to Saudi Arabia's, like Bahrain. However, the massive increase in its wealth after the 1990s, coupled with the coming to power of an ambitious new emir, Hamad, prompted Doha to break free. It pursued increasingly independent regional policies, such as mediating in Lebanon, Palestine, and Yemen, often disregarding Saudi Arabia's agenda, while Al Jazeera frequently criticised Riyadh and other GCC governments.[21] Qatar's sponsorship of rival factions across the region after 2011, often aligned with the Muslim Brotherhood, heightened Riyadh's (and Abu Dhabi's) frustration with its neighbour.

Tensions had bubbled up first in 2014. A year earlier Hamad had voluntarily stepped down in favour of his son, Tamim, whom Saudi Arabia and the UAE believed to be more weak and pliable. In 2014 they sought to force Tamim to abandon his father's foreign policies by withdrawing their ambassadors, alongside Bahrain, severing relations over Qatar's continued support for the Brotherhood. After eight months ties were restored once Qatar had ejected some Brotherhood members and there was a temporary reconciliation, with all GCC states campaigning against Islamic State in Iraq and all bar Oman joining the anti-Houthi coalition in Yemen.[22] However, after 2015 the new de facto leader of Saudi Arabia, Mohammed Bin Salman (MBS) was eager to pursue a more activist foreign policy, prompting impulsive moves like the intervention in Yemen and detaining Lebanon's prime minister (see chapter 7). He was also heavily influenced by his counterpart in the UAE, Mohammed Bin Zayad (MBZ). MBZ was fundamentally opposed to the Brotherhood and was convinced that Qatar's continued sponsorship risked inspiring Emirati Islamists to challenge his rule at home.[23] Crucially, both were spurred on by the election of Donald Trump, who made Saudi Arabia one of his first foreign visits and seemed to acquiesce to MBS and MBZ's stance on Qatar.

Two weeks after Trump's visit in summer 2017, the blockade began. The trigger was a piece of 'fake news'. Hackers posted comments on the Qatar News Agency allegedly from Tamim that praised Hamas, Hezbollah, and Iran. Qatar immediately insisted these weren't genuine, but they were widely redistributed on Saudi- and Emirati-owned media. No evidence suggests these hackers were agents of either Abu Dhabi or Riyadh, but both governments and their allies Bahrain and Egypt, used the incident to cut ties.[24] Saudi Arabia closed Qatar's only land border and forbade Qatar Airways from using its airspace. The four blockading governments ceased all economic activity with Qatar, Qatari citizens were expelled, while citizens of UAE and Bahrain were forbidden to express any support for Qatar on social media. The quartet soon issued a list of thirteen demands. These included: closing Al Jazeera; ejecting Turkey's new base; ceasing diplomatic contact with Iran; severing all links with the Muslim Brotherhood, Hamas, and Hezbollah – labelled 'terrorists' by the blockaders; stopping alleged interference in the quartet's domestic affairs; and fully aligning Qatar's diplomacy with the other GCC states. To comply would end Qatar's independence internationally and reduce it to being a vassal of Riyadh and Abu Dhabi. Tamim refused, and instead sought ways to overcome the boycott, reaching deals with Iran, Turkey, and East Asian states to provide essential goods by air and sea. If the quartet had intended the blockade to weaken Qatar's resolve, it failed. Doha used its vast wealth, via its $300 billion sovereign wealth fund, to pay inflated prices to keep food and goods flowing, and the besieged population rallied around the young emir, strengthening his position.[25]

The blockade shattered the perceived stability of the GCC. During the Arab Uprisings the Gulf states insisted that their autocratic monarchies enjoyed calm not found elsewhere in the region, conveniently glossing over the disruption in Bahrain. Now, four members that were theoretically committed to mutual security had turned on one another. Kuwait and Oman, meanwhile, remained neutral and tried in vain to mediate. Both were concerned that, should the quartet succeed in reducing Qatar's independence, they might be next – especially Oman, which also enjoyed good ties with Iran. The echoes of the rupture were felt across the region. Divided Libya's two governments backed different sides, while in the Horn of Africa different Somali factions, backed respectively by Qatar and the UAE, weighed in behind their Gulf allies (see chapter 10). Iran and, especially, Turkey, supported Qatar and protested the blockade, while small distant players like Mauritania and Djibouti joined the boycott to curry favour with the UAE and Saudi Arabia. However, many regional states remained neutral. Syria and Yemen were distracted by civil war, while Lebanon, Iraq, Tunisia, Algeria, and Morocco hedged their bets given the financial clout of both sides. Even Jordan, a key Saudi ally and dependent on grants from Riyadh, tried to tread a middle path. International powers were similarly loath to strongly back one side. China and the EU were key Qatari customers for LNG and Qatar was a source of investment in their economies, but they also traded extensively with Riyadh and Abu Dhabi. They therefore urged reconciliation but were wary of putting real pressure on either side to relent.

The one state that arguably had the influence to do this was the United States, but the Trump administration's haphazard approach to diplomacy proved an obstacle. When the crisis broke out, Trump's Defense Secretary and Secretary of State urged calm and reconciliation, aware that Qatar housed 10,000 US airmen on its Al-Udeid air base. Trump, however, being close to MBS, tweeted within days that Qatar might be funding groups subscribing to a radical ideology.[26] While this wasn't an explicit endorsement of the blockade, it was likely interpreted as one by Riyadh and Abu Dhabi, given that it echoed their line about Doha sponsoring terrorists. Moreover, Trump then did little to de-escalate the crisis or use his leverage to pressure MBS in the years that followed. Trump reportedly only started trying to end the boycott when he realised Qatar was paying Iran $100 million a year to use its airspace, giving Tehran an income at a time when the White House was trying to cripple its economy with sanctions.[27]

However, Trump's envoys proved ineffectual until, ironically, he lost his re-election bid in November 2020. Joe Biden was more hostile to Saudi Arabia, having condemned the violence in Yemen and MBS's alleged role in the murder of a Saudi dissident, Jamal Khashoggi, in 2021.[28] Riyadh therefore was keen to resolve the dispute before Biden took office – perhaps as a last reward for Trump or to garner goodwill from the incoming administration. In early January 2021, a fortnight before Biden's inauguration, Trump officials and Kuwait jointly brokered an end to the blockade. Qatar made next to no concessions and the action was widely seen as a failure. Tamim immediately travelled to Saudi Arabia for a GCC summit, where the leaders all embraced – the club apparently restored. However, the episode had damaged GCC credibility.

The Global Gulf

A key reason for the blockade's failure was the extent of Qatar's integration into the world economy. European, Chinese, and American leaders weren't just concerned about losing vital LNG supplies, Qatar was also a key source of investment. In London alone, Doha owns such landmark assets as Harrods department store, the Shard skyscraper, the Savoy hotel, as well as 50 per cent of Canary Wharf, 20 per cent of Heathrow Airport and 14 per cent of Sainsbury's supermarket. Investing in Western and Asian economies has been a deliberate tactic by all the GCC governments, especially the wealthiest trio of Saudi Arabia, the UAE, and Qatar. As economist Adam Hanieh notes, many well-known international firms like Credit Suisse, Deutsche Bank, Barclays, Volkswagen, Glencore, P&O, British Airways, and Twitter now count Gulf investors as major shareholders or controlling owners. Meanwhile, three top European football teams, Manchester City, Newcastle United, and Paris St Germain, are owned by the UAE, Saudi Arabia, and Qatar, respectively, while Barcelona, Bayern Munich, Chelsea, and Arsenal have all been sponsored by Gulf airlines. These investments have dual purposes. On the one hand, they make economic sense, adding more assets to growing sovereign wealth funds – utilised expertly by Qatar to survive the blockade. But they also serve geopolitical goals. Making foreign economies reliant on Gulf largesse will make foreign governments more likely to support the incumbent regimes in the event of a domestic or international threat, as happened with Qatar in 2017–21 and Bahrain in 2011.

Gulf states have also invested widely in the developing world, especially sub-Saharan Africa, purchasing extensive farmland to ensure 'food security': a guaranteed supply of food for their mostly desert kingdoms.[29] They have also inserted their own economies into the heart of globalisation. Heavy investment in aviation has seen Gulf state airlines – Qatar Airways, Emirates Airways (Dubai's carrier), and Etihad (Abu Dhabi's) – become world leaders, with the Gulf becoming the top stopover destination. Indeed, in 2015 Dubai International surpassed Heathrow as the world's busiest airport for international passengers. Similarly, Dubai's Jebel Ali is now the world's fourth-largest container port. Such is the growing importance of the Gulf, the BRICS (Brazil, Russia, India, China, and South Africa) group of the world's leading emerging economies invited Saudi Arabia and the UAE, along with four others, to join them in 2023.[30]

Perhaps one reason economists were previously reluctant to include GCC in such company is the dominant position fossil fuels continue to play. For all their investments elsewhere, were oil and gas to collapse in value, many forecast that the Gulf's global importance and influence would evaporate. All GCC governments are hyperconscious of this and have launched grand plans to diversify their economies. Saudi Vision 2030, for example, was launched in 2016 with the ambitious goal of diversifying away from oil by embracing other sources of investment like tourism, entertainment, and sports. The UAE, similarly, launched various '2030' strategy documents for Abu Dhabi and Dubai, making similar claims of diversification. However, this is not a new challenge, and Gulf leaders have been trying to diversify, unsuccessfully, for decades. Oman's 'Vision 2020', launched in 1995, has already passed its target date with only modest results. Five years into Saudi Vision 2030, Riyadh was still relying on oil exports for 70 per cent of its budget.[31] This is especially problematic for Saudi Arabia, as it has a much larger population than the other Gulf states, most of whom seem to tolerate autocratic rule provided the Al-Sauds continue to hand out subsidies, jobs, and services. A sudden and prolonged collapse in global energy prices would challenge this bargain, as Riyadh would rapidly run out of funds, despite its considerable wealth. Qatar and the UAE, with smaller populations, would be better placed to use their sovereign wealth funds to cushion the blow, though they too might eventually have to find alternative incomes or consider opening up their political systems.

This latter option seems unlikely, with most of the GCC states becoming more autocratic after 2011, especially Bahrain, Saudi Arabia, and the UAE. Since coming to power in 2015, MBS has given with one hand, but taken with the other. He has reduced the authority of the 'religious police', which once roamed Saudi streets enforcing conservative behaviour and Islamic observance. He has also improved women's rights, notably permitting women to drive for the first time. But he also brooks less dissent than his predecessors, handing out long sentences for relatively minor opposition, for example to human rights and women's rights activists. In 2022, a mother of two in her mid-thirties was sentenced to thirty-four years in prison, apparently just for following and retweeting dissidents and activists on Twitter.[32] Close monitoring of social media is particularly prevalent in Saudi Arabia and elsewhere in the Gulf. On the one hand, given the Arab Uprisings were initially spread by Facebook, there is a determination to crack down on any whisper of a repeat. At the same time though, there is a conscious effort by these regimes to use digital media to their advantage. This includes agents hiring Western PR agencies to place positive stories in Western news outlets and using 'bots' and fake Twitter accounts to promote certain narratives online. These are targeted at both domestic and international audiences.[33] At home, the leaders wish to weed out criticism and inculcate a positive image, while abroad there is an effort to improve foreign, especially Western views of the region. This everyday image building comes alongside marquee events like the UAE's hosting the COP28 United Nations climate change conference in 2023 – despite being a significant emitter – Qatar hosting the World Cup, or Riyadh's heavy investment in global sport – derided as 'green washing' and 'sports washing' by critics.

Castles in the Sand?

Ostensibly, Gulf leaders might look back on recent decades with a degree of pride. The historically vulnerable states have navigated a potentially perilous path since gaining independence, preventing domination by more powerful neighbours in Iraq and Iran, and largely avoiding the internal fissures that rocked many Middle Eastern states after 2011. They are now well integrated into the global economy, investing their wealth to secure support from Western and Asian powers, adding to their already important role as a global supplier of energy. Moreover, they have successfully diversified their international ties, getting closer to China and other states, without seriously damaging the key security relationship with the United States. This has allowed for greater international independence, seen after the outbreak of the Russia–Ukraine war in 2022 when leading Gulf states declined to join Western sanctions on Moscow. Instead they became a safe haven for fleeing Russian oligarchs, as well as declining to produce more oil to help energy-starved struggling Western economies.

It has also seen the Gulf states, especially Saudi Arabia, the UAE, and Qatar, become increasingly active in the region, transforming the dynamics of the Middle East whereby traditionally powerful states like Egypt, Syria, and Iraq are now fought over by others, including the historically weaker Gulf players. However, they have not proved especially successful in this regard. Qatar's involvement in Libya, Syria, and Egypt has not reaped rewards, while Saudi Arabia's intervention in Yemen and the Qatar blockade largely failed.

The UAE has proven cannier, successfully getting its way in Egypt, with Saudi Arabia, and gaining more than Riyadh from its limited involvement in Yemen, though it too failed with Qatar blockade. Whether these relative failures will deter further activism in the future is unclear. All three states are led by relatively new leaders of a different generation to the one that founded the GCC in the 1980s. This may have contributed to some of their impulsive policies and they could mellow over time. Yet at the same time, the leaders of Saudi Arabia and the UAE have also shown themselves to be far more autocratic than their predecessors, so this may be down to character rather than inexperience.

Either way, despite foreign policy failures, Gulf leaders can still feel relatively secure for now, but face the same challenge moving forward. All their success, power, influence, and external support stems from their wealth, which remains intrinsically tied to fossil fuels. Should prices permanently collapse, following a global shift away from the combustion engine to electric vehicles, for instance, the Gulf's significance could diminish. All must therefore rapidly find ways to diversify their economies, while keeping their subsidised populations on board. Achieving this while maintaining autocratic systems of rule will be hard. Meanwhile, Western (and Asian) governments will continue to support them and turn a blind eye to human rights abuses and repressive politics for as long as the wealth continues to flow. Were it dry up though, the Gulf may find itself on its own.

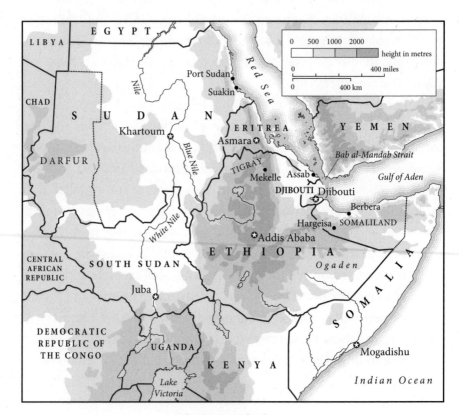

The Horn of Africa

10

The Horn of Africa
A New Arena

The Horn of Africa is one of the most beautiful and most violent regions in the world. It boasts stunning landscapes and rich culture: Ethiopia's lush highlands and ancient churches; Somalia's golden beaches and medieval ports; Eritrea's rolling green hills and the forgotten Art Deco buildings of its capital, Asmara. Yet it has also been home to state collapse, famine, ethnic cleansing, mass migration, maritime piracy, and some of the longest and most lethal wars in recent history. Jutting out from the African continent where the Red Sea meets the Indian Ocean, the region has long held strategic importance for outsiders. The Bab al-Mandab Strait, with Eritrea and Djibouti on one side and Yemen on the other, controls access to the Red Sea and the flow of goods through the Suez Canal. The Gulf of Aden, flanked by Somaliland on the African side, still formally part of Somalia, is also narrow, allowing predators to pick off vessels if the beaches are controlled by unfriendly forces.

In the late nineteenth and early twentieth centuries, it was European imperialists who tried to influence the region, either to protect and promote their trade, or to capture territory as part of a wider carve-up of the African continent. During the Cold War, the USA and USSR courted clients. After the collapse of the Soviet Union,

Washington took particular interest, first in trying to stabilise Somalia, without success, and then, after 9/11, seeing the Horn as a battleground in the 'war on terror'. Curiously, despite its proximity, particularly to the Arabian Peninsula and Egypt, Middle Eastern powers have historically taken only limited interest in modern times. This has changed, however. The UAE, Qatar, Saudi Arabia, Iran, Israel, and Turkey have all increased their involvement. While not being in the Middle East itself, the Horn has become a new arena of competition for that region's battling powers, with some now viewing it as a key part of their 'neighbourhood'.

However, the Horn is complex, and the governments and peoples are far from passive proxies. The region is dominated by an African superpower, Ethiopia, which has the continent's largest army, second-largest population, and has itself interfered in its neighbours' affairs for years, something that has been reciprocated. The Horn likewise boasts strong national identities born of years of fighting and colonial partition, and determined leaders who, if willing to accept outside help, are rarely controlled by it. Moreover, the Middle Eastern players are far from the only outsiders pushing their agenda. The US arguably remains the most significant power, despite a recent retreat, while France has long had an influence from its base in Djibouti. Italy and the UK, both of which once had colonial bases in the Horn, retain a presence, and now so does China. The entry of several Middle Eastern actors into this arena therefore has the potential to be explosive, adding more competition to a region that really could do without it. Yet, at the same time, it also may have the potential to pacify, as Middle Eastern countries' involvement has at times been more reconciling than their destabilising interventions elsewhere.

A History of Violence

The Horn of Africa today consists of four states: Ethiopia, Eritrea, Somalia, and Djibouti, though a fifth territory, Somaliland, claims an independence from Somalia that is not recognised internationally. Sudan is just outside the Horn, but competition for influence, including access to its Red Sea coast, has drawn in Middle Eastern rivals, and so will also be briefly discussed here. The Horn is dominated by Ethiopia, which claims roughly 120 million of the 140 million inhabitants of the Horn region and is by far the largest economic and military power.[1] But Ethiopia is landlocked, blocked from the sea by the three (or four) smaller countries, shaping interactions that have frequently been hostile. These have also been greatly impacted by demographic, economic, and cultural differences. Ethiopia, with its plateaued highlands, has a long history of settled agriculture, allowing it to develop surpluses, wealth, and governmental organisation that enabled it to dominate its lowland, pastoralist neighbours. Ethiopia is approximately two-thirds Christian, adopting Eastern Orthodoxy in the fourth century, while Somalia, Somaliland, and Djibouti are mostly Muslim, having been early converts in the seventh century. Eritrea is roughly half Muslim, half Christian. While religious difference is not the only regional fault line, it did inform some past hostilities, long before European imperialists arrived.[2]

Unlike all other states in Africa, Ethiopia was not colonised. Italy tried in the late nineteenth century, when the rest of the continent was being brutally carved up by other Europeans, but was humiliated. Ethiopia then mimicked the Europeans by joining the scramble for Africa, expanding beyond its traditional highlands to build an empire that encompassed Somali and other peoples to create an ethnically diverse state.[3] Ethiopian independence also informed European engagement with the Horn. Recognising they couldn't conquer the highlands, the Europeans instead created colonies in the coastal lowlands that became four smaller states. Italy took what became Eritrea and Somalia to build maritime trade and box in the audacious Ethiopians. France similarly developed an outpost in Djibouti to boost its trade but worked with Addis Ababa to build a rail link that made the French colony Ethiopia's main port. Britain, meanwhile, created a colony in Somaliland, primarily to support its naval base in South Yemen. The fascist regime of Benito Mussolini eventually did capture Ethiopia in 1936, but early in the Second World War British troops from Sudan and Kenya forced the Italians out and restored the Ethiopian emperor Hailie Selassie.

These colonial and indigenous legacies had dramatic consequences during the Cold War years. Selassie leveraged his status as a victim of fascism to forge a close alliance with first Britain, then the United States, using both to persuade the United Nations to integrate Eritrea into Ethiopia after the war. An important part of this negotiation was a communications base near Asmara that Selassie awarded to Washington soon afterwards.[4] But Selassie oversaw an increasingly autocratic and centralising state, frustrating the Eritreans. Armed resistance to Ethiopian rule began in 1961, eventually exploding into a full-blown war of independence that lasted thirty years. Meanwhile a popular revolution broke out in Addis Ababa in 1974, inspired by the leftist ideologies of the day. Selassie was deposed and, after considerable bloodletting, replaced by a Marxist military dictatorship, known as the Derg.

Somalia also found itself under military rule. Britain and a now democratic Italy retained control over Somaliland and Somalia respectively after the Second World War, before granting both independence in 1960, whereupon the two united. This came amid a nationalist fervour to unite all 'Somali' territory to the new state, especially the Somali lands previously captured by Ethiopia. Believing Ethiopia distracted by its revolution and war with the Eritrean separatists, Mogadishu launched an opportunistic invasion in 1977. The Cold War played a role in both this attack and its outcome. Somalia's own Marxist military dictators, in power since 1969, had been emboldened by the military hardware sent by their Soviet allies. They believed Ethiopia, in contrast, to have been weakened by its American ally's limited military aid since the toppling of Selassie. Yet Mogadishu miscalculated. Not only was Ethiopia's army able to rally, but when the

Derg appealed to Moscow for help, the USSR saw the value in peeling the Horn's largest state away from its American rival and switched sides. Addis Ababa repelled the invasion, shattering Somalian nationalist dreams and paving the way for the collapse of Mogadishu in 1991.[5] The invasion also prompted France to finally grant Djibouti formal independence in 1977, but with a permanent French military garrison to warn off any Somali military designs.

The year 1991 proved a pivotal one for the Horn. In May, the Eritrean war finally ended when the separatists, who had frequently looked on the brink of defeat, marched into Asmara. Military defeat contributed to the fall of the Derg back in Ethiopia. The brutal Marxist regime was increasingly unpopular, not helped by disastrous economic policies that contributed to the infamous famine of 1984. Military opposition increased, especially in the north where a movement based around the ethnic Tigray community launched an insurgency. With the Ethiopian military demoralised and defeated by the collapse in Eritrea, this movement, the Tigray People's Liberation Front (TPLF) marched almost unopposed into Addis Ababa and toppled the Derg. Unlike the centralised governments of Selassie and the Derg, this new government opted for federalism, giving considerable autonomy to Ethiopia's various ethnic communities. This was no democracy and the TPLF and its allies still dominated, but it opened the way for both economic development and a reconciliation with the West.[6]

The Somali state, in contrast, collapsed in 1991. As in Ethiopia, Somalia's dictatorship had been harsh and autocratic, prompting armed opposition, particularly in the north. Unlike in Ethiopia or Eritrea, most Somalis shared the same ethnicity, but belonged to different clans. When the great nationalist dream of uniting all Somalis into a single state evaporated, clan differences reasserted themselves. The clan that dominated the north, roughly the area of the old British colony of Somaliland, felt neglected by Mogadishu and launched a rebellion in the early 1980s, backed, of course, by Ethiopia.

245

The conflict culminated in a vicious crackdown by the Somali government, which oversaw a bombing campaign that killed over 60,000 people and virtually destroyed the regional capital, Hargeisa. The devastation hardened the north's determination to separate from Somalia and, when the dictatorship was toppled three years later, Somaliland announced its independence.[7] With Mogadishu in chaos and never again recovering the ability to reconquer the province, Somaliland has remained de facto independent ever since.

In Mogadishu, the regime was toppled by another rival clan, forcing the dictator to flee. But, unlike in either Ethiopia or Somaliland, these armed groups did not come with a political programme to establish a new government. Instead they ransacked the capital, leaving it in a state of anarchy, unable to extend its rule over the rest of the country. Instead, the power vacuum was filled by various local clan-based warlords. International players then made the situation worse by offering aid to the various warring bosses, in the hope of re-establishing order. Instead, Somalia became dependent on foreign aid and factions would fight for access to external funds. A brief effort was made by the US to stabilise the situation, leading a UN task force deployed to Mogadishu from 1992 to 1993. But this did not return order beyond parts of the capital and, as Washington lost interest and withdrew, fighting resumed. Until the mid-2000s, outsiders largely left Somalia's factions to fight among themselves, while sponsoring various fruitless peace conferences.

Peace between Eritrea and Ethiopia, meanwhile, proved fleeting. Though the new government in Addis Ababa had approved Eritrean independence as one of its first acts, a new war broke out in 1998. Disputes over a relatively minor piece of territory provoked horrendous fighting for two years, costing over 100,000 lives – more than died in Eritrea's thirty-year independence struggle.[8] After Ethiopia triumphed militarily, a ceasefire was agreed, but the conflict remained unresolved, and the borders closed. While Eritrea turned in on itself, resentful of Ethiopia and its allies, especially the African Union and the United States, Ethiopia continued to thrive despite the frozen conflict. It especially benefited from 9/11 and Washington's renewed interest in the Horn. Addis Ababa was quick to sign up as a partner in the 'war on terror', granting it access to yet more high-end military equipment denied to its neighbours.

Washington renewed its engagement in the Horn in 2002 when it launched Operation Enduring Freedom – Horn of Africa and moved a permanent force into a new base in Djibouti a year later, focusing on Islamic militants, particularly in Somalia.[9] Islamists had been gaining ground amid the anarchy, and some had links to Al-Qaeda, having initially fought in Afghanistan during the 1980s. However, at first they were overshadowed by clan-based militants. This changed in 2006 when a coalition of Islamists, the Islamic Courts Union, captured Mogadishu and extended their authority over most of southern Somalia. For the first time in over a decade, a degree of order and safety was restored. However, as well as Islamists, they took on the mantle of Somali nationalists and once again threatened to invade Ethiopia's Somali lands, prompting Addis Ababa to launch a massive pre-emptive strike, with US approval. But Washington warned Ethiopia against what followed, a march into Mogadishu itself.[10] The Islamic Courts were swiftly destroyed as Ethiopia established an occupying administration, which it later transferred to the oversight of the African Union. Not only did this shatter Somalia's brief era of order, prompting a return to internal fighting, but youthful supporters of the Islamic Courts would go onto to form Al-Shabab, a far more extremist Islamist Somali force – the very Jihadists the US had hoped to prevent emerging.

The UAE and its Horn Rivals

Proximity and cultural links, particularly Sunni Islam, Orthodox Christianity, and Arab identity – in the case of Arab League members Somalia and Djibouti – ensured that the Horn of Africa maintained connections with the Middle East throughout these traumas. However, until the twenty-first century few Middle Eastern governments took more than a passing interest. Israel was a notable exception, partnering with Selassie's government in the 1960s, aiding his war against Eritrea, and continuing covert links to the Derg after he was toppled. These ties helped the famous operation to evacuate 10,000 Ethiopian Jews during the 1984 famine and resettle them in Israel. In the 2000s, Israel took a renewed interest in the region, increasing its naval and covert presence, this time to counter Iranian activity in the Red Sea.[11] Iran built links with Sudan and Eritrea, which Israel had initially established cordial ties with, and used both to smuggle weapons to its Palestinian allies in Gaza (see chapter 4). Iranian ships would dock in Assab to unload the weapons, which were then taken overland via Sudan and smuggled through Egypt into Gaza.

Iran's presence on the Red Sea similarly alarmed Saudi Arabia, especially after it had launched its war in Yemen in 2015 (see chapter 3). This prompted Riyadh to up its engagement in the Horn, particularly in Djibouti and Eritrea. Saudi Arabia was also reacting to increased activity from Qatar and Turkey that Riyadh was keen to counter. Qatar had ties to Somalia dating back to the Islamic Courts Union, while Turkey increased its economic and military investment there after 2011. Ankara also stepped up its engagement with Sudan. As elsewhere, the entry of one Middle Eastern power into the region created something of a domino effect, drawing others in to counter their rivals.

Of all the Middle Eastern governments newly engaged in the Horn, the UAE was arguably the most prominent. As in Libya, Egypt, and Yemen, Abu Dhabi's entry stemmed from a shift in international policy following the 2011 Arab Uprisings (see chapter 9). Much of this shift derived from the beliefs and approach of its leader, Mohammed Bin Zayed (MBZ). On the death of his half-brother in 2022, MBZ became ruler of Abu Dhabi and president of the UAE, but he wielded considerable power as crown prince from 2004. He consolidated his rule by placing key allies, notably his full brothers, into prominent government positions. He also benefited from the other leading emirate in the UAE, Dubai, requiring a $20 billion bailout from Abu Dhabi after the financial crash of 2008/9, in exchange for which MBZ demanded greater control over security and foreign policy.[12] When the Arab Uprisings broke out in 2011, MBZ was in a commanding position at home to lead the UAE's response abroad.

As the regional landscape shifted, MBZ's UAE had no strategic masterplan, but rather a loose set of priorities. Decision making was limited to a small circle of MBZ's confidants, allowing for rapid, often opportunistic, shifts in approach. MBZ had two primary defensive concerns. First, to contain Iran. Abu Dhabi had long feared either invasion or being forced into subservience should the UAE's powerful neighbour Tehran dominate the Gulf or the wider Middle East. Second, a fear of the Muslim Brotherhood. From an early age MBZ had developed a deep opposition to Islamism in general and the Muslim Brotherhood in particular, seeing little difference between its relatively moderate ideology and the more extreme Jihadism of Al-Qaeda or Islamic State. While personally religious, MBZ believed religion should stay out of politics and feared the Muslim Brotherhood could overthrow his own and fellow autocratic regimes. Indeed, he reportedly warned Barack Obama against supporting the ouster of Hosni Mubarak in 2011 (see chapter 6), warning that the Muslim Brotherhood would take over Egypt followed by up to eight other Arab countries.[13]

Other factors motivated UAE foreign policy. One was commerce. Abu Dhabi made economic openness and international trade central to its efforts to diversify away from hydrocarbons. This led to investment not only in its own trade and travel hubs, but those across its neighbourhood, thus positioning itself as the keystone to increased regional trade.[14] Another, related priority was prestige. MBZ tried to build a positive global image for the UAE to attract tourism, investment, and diplomatic clout. This included investing in popular enterprises abroad, such as Manchester City Football Club, and a concerted effort to be more visible in international affairs, aided by a dedicated and skilled team of diplomats.[15] Finally, MBZ was very conscious of shifting regional and global power dynamics. While the UAE remained close to the US, Washington's actions in the Middle East after 2011 suggested it was retrenching and could no longer be relied on to support Abu Dhabi's interests. MBZ consequently became closer to neighbouring Saudi Arabia, particularly the new de facto ruler Mohammed Bin Salman, given their shared interests in containing Iran, opposing the Muslim Brotherhood, and sustaining autocratic monarchy. He also developed more open diplomacy, accompanying his open economic outlook, courting non-Western powers, including China, Russia, and India.

These priorities all contributed to draw the UAE to the Horn. Its involvement in the Yemen War, partly to get closer to Riyadh and partly to limit Iran's foothold there, prompted its engagement with Eritrea and Somaliland. Its fears of the Muslim Brotherhood generated a hostility to Turkey and Qatar, provoking it to try to outflank them in both Sudan and Somalia. Its desire for diplomatic prestige saw it try to broker peace between Ethiopia and Eritrea, while its focus on commerce has seen it invest in port facilities in Eritrea, Djibouti, and Somaliland. This was also tied to China's growing presence in Africa, with the hope that UAE facilities in the Horn can partner Beijing's Belt and Road Initiative developments. However, despite its flurry of activity, the UAE remained only one player of several and, like its rivals, it would find that its impact on and leverage in the Horn's complex politics was limited.

Somalia and Somaliland

Somalia and the breakaway state of Somaliland became surprising arenas for Middle Eastern competition in the mid-2010s, particularly between Qatar, Turkey, and the UAE, which joined a host of other international and regional powers already vying for influence. Ethiopia's capture of Mogadishu in late 2006 had been ostensibly in support of a transitional Somali government formed in one of the many international peace conferences but controlling only limited territory.[16] With the Islamic Courts Union defeated, Addis Ababa installed the transitional government in the capital. A federal system was established, granting considerable autonomy to regions headed by clan leaders, and an indirect voting system was put in place that led to a series of successful presidential elections. However, the security situation remained unstable, and the new government struggled either to rebuild a functioning state or extend its authority across the whole country. Moreover, the electoral system was deeply corrupt, allowing foreign governments to deliver huge bribes for their favoured candidates to buy votes.[17]

Despite the state's limited reach, foreign governments pursued numerous interests in Somalia and wanted Mogadishu on-side. The collapse of law and order alongside a related weakening of the economy prompted a significant rise in piracy. Somalia's strategic location near major international shipping lanes presented lots of juicy targets, and the international community was alarmed when tankers were frequently hijacked. The continued presence of Al-Shabab, which was affiliated with Al-Qaeda, also attracted outside concern. Its capture of large chunks of southern and central Somalia, at different times, triggered further Western, especially American, involvement, as fears increased that the whole country could become a Jihadist outpost. The US upped its presence after 2006, including deploying 500 troops and taking over a former Soviet base in 2017. The UK similarly sent a handful of special forces, while the EU deployed a mission to train Somalia's military. At sea, the US established a thirty-three-state Combined Maritime Forces naval partnership to counter both terrorism and piracy, while the EU established Operation Atalanta in 2008 to combat Somali piracy.[18] But alongside containing threats, outsiders saw opportunities. Several states coveted military bases and/

or access to commercial ports. With aid still pouring in, along with remittances from Somalia's now extensive diaspora (after years of emigration), there were further economic openings in areas such as telecoms. The environmentally damaging charcoal trade attracted outsiders too, as did thriving smuggling operations. Engaging Somalia also provided an opportunity to build international prestige, through states sending infrastructure investment, undertaking personnel training, and offering considerable humanitarian aid, especially after a horrendous famine killed over 250,000 in 2011.

Ethiopia has been arguably the most consequential outside player, acting as an informal guarantor of the government it helped to install. It maintains thousands of troops in Somalia's south-western provinces, officially part of the African Union force supporting the government. Addis Ababa has deployed further troops at will, as it did in 2022, sending 2,000 soldiers to push Al-Shabab's forces from its border.[19] It further maintains a network of agents and allies within Somali politics aimed at preventing hostile forces from regaining power in Mogadishu. However, despite this outlay, its influence remains limited, as was seen in 2017 when a populist anti-Ethiopian Somali nationalist was elected president. This episode further illustrated the role of other foreign backers in Somali politics. Mohamed Abdullahi Mohamed, known as Farmaajo, surprisingly defeated the incumbent, Hassan Sheikh Mohamud, in a contest heavily influenced by foreign money. The same had been true in 2012 when Hassan Sheikh had been elected. The president is selected by members of parliament, who themselves are selected by clan leaders rather than universal suffrage, with many MPs selling their votes for hefty bribes. In 2012 Hassan Sheikh had received considerable sums from Qatar, which had ties with the moderate Somali Islamists who were backing him for the presidency, and Doha provided much of the funding that helped sway the election.[20]

By 2017, even more money came from abroad, with MPs reportedly demanding $50,000–$100,000 for their vote, despite the average

Somali income being $2 a day.[21] After five years in power, Hassan Sheikh was expected to gain re-election easily. He had forged close ties with Turkey, which had expanded its presence in Somalia. Ankara sent considerable famine relief and became Somalia's fifth-biggest source of imports. It built new hospitals, schools, and roads via aid programmes, and won contracts for Turkish companies to upgrade and run Mogadishu's port and airport. Later in 2017 Ankara also built a new military training facility to help strengthen Somalia's elite forces. But Turkey remained neutral in the election. In contrast, the UAE, Somalia's largest trading partner and a rival to Turkey, saw an opportunity. Having also invested in Somalia, deploying considerable humanitarian aid and anti-terrorism assistance, including a training base for the Somalia military, Abu Dhabi used these connections and its considerable wealth to back a rival to Hassan Sheikh. The hope was to topple what they saw as Qatar's and Turkey's man.

However, while Turkey remained neutral, Qatar's priorities had changed. Doha felt Hassan Sheikh had sidelined their Somali Islamist allies and so instead quietly backed Farmaajo.[22] Hassan Sheikh still had the most money, and enjoyed important support from Ethiopia, the US, and the UK. However, he was unpopular on the street, whereas Farmaajo's anti-Ethiopian campaign speeches won popular approval. While Hassan Sheikh mismanaged his war chest, Farmaajo made careful use of his Qatari funds, winning power. The Ethiopians soon came to terms with the new leader, especially after a change of leader in Addis Ababa, and Turkey retained its good relations with the new government, but ties with the UAE ruptured. In a clear sign of Gulf rivalries spilling over into the Horn, Farmaajo remained neutral during the 2017 Qatar blockade, infuriating Abu Dhabi. The UAE pulled out of its Somali military base, ending all security cooperation and, to the anger of Mogadishu, instead engaged Somaliland about deploying Emirati forces there. UAE diplomats would later concede this may have been an over-reaction that handed the advantage to Qatar.[23]

The 2022 election, in contrast, saw a less zero-sum approach by Middle Eastern players. The resolution of the Qatar blockade in early 2021 helped, as did a related thawing of ties between the UAE and Turkey. The election remained deeply corrupt, with the price of an MP's vote now up to $100,000–$300,000, and most money came from the Gulf.[24] However, though Qatar continued to fund Farmaajo, it did so more cautiously. In the preceding years, Farmaajo had attempted to expand his authority, violently clashing with oppositionists in Mogadishu and elsewhere, prompting fears of a return to civil war. This election was also influenced by external players. In the dying days of his administration, Donald Trump had withdrawn the 450 US troops embedded in the Somali military, who would likely have been able to prevent Farmaajo's military aggression.[25] Although Farmaajo stepped back after this clash, Doha and other supporters distanced themselves from the president. Farmaajo's other key foreign supporter, Ethiopia's new prime minister, was distracted by his own civil war in Tigray that broke out in late 2020. Meanwhile, in a twist, the UAE decided to sponsor Hassan Sheikh's bid to return to power, despite his former closeness to Qatar. Farmaajo's limited backing, Hassan Shekih's Emirati funds, and his popular slogan of 'no enemies' at home and abroad, in contrast to his rival's recent violence, turned the contest in his favour and he returned to the presidency. Days afterwards, the US's new president, Joe Biden, returned the 450 withdrawn troops.[26] The relatively peaceful transfer of power, despite fears of renewed conflict, hinted at the reconciliatory role outsider powers like Qatar and the UAE could play when they weren't using Somalia as a battleground.

Foreign influence in Somali politics was not limited to Mogadishu but was also present in the breakaway state of Somaliland. Uniquely for the Horn, Somaliland developed a successful stable democratic government after it declared independence from Somalia. The system, formalised in a 2001 constitution, built on clan relationships and collaborative negotiation, and was developed internally rather than imposed from the outside, as in Mogadishu in 2006. Somaliland remains unrecognised internationally, partially because the African Union will not accept the breakaway republic without Mogadishu's agreement, which it flatly refuses.[27] Even so, Hargeisa has developed important foreign relations. Partly this is down to Somaliland's strategic location, partly its extensive diaspora, and partly its influential business community, which played a key role in pushing for independence and maintaining its democratic structures. Its hostility to Mogadishu has contributed to its close ties since 1991 with Ethiopia, which welcomes Somalia's balkanisation.

In 2016 Addis Ababa controversially lobbied the UAE to develop Somaliland's Berbera port. The agreement, which granted the Dubai-based company DP World a thirty-year concession to develop the port and a 51 per cent stake, also gave 30 per cent to Somaliland and 19 per cent to Ethiopia. Though Mogadishu was formally outraged, it still rubber stamped the agreement, reportedly receiving payments from Abu Dhabi and under pressure from Addis Ababa.[28] The deal furthered Somaliland's informal secession by granting it powerful external protectors. This was compounded by the $400 million construction of a road linking Berbera to the Ethiopian border, funded by the UAE and UK, granting Addis Ababa access to another port, and boosting Somaliland's ability to survive without Mogadishu. As discussed, the UAE was able to leverage these commercial ties to increase its military connections. The DP World deal included an option to build an Emirati military and naval base in Berbera, while Abu Dhabi stepped up its military cooperation when it fell out with Mogadishu in 2017, helping to train the Somaliland coastguard, police, and security services.[29]

However, the increased ties with the outside world have impacted Somaliland's democracy. In 2022 scheduled presidential elections were postponed because of disputes over the electoral process, and government and opposition forces clashed, killing five. The influx of outside trade, particularly the development of Berbera and foreign governments' increased interest in courting Somaliland – especially after it declared an anti-China position by forging ties with Taiwan – raised the electoral stakes. With more to gain and lose, factions hardened, and the collaborative approach weakened, especially as a new generation came of age with little memory of the violence of the 1980s.[30] While Somaliland remains a democratic outlier on the Horn, as it grows in importance to outsiders it is not immune from the kind of damaging external interference seen in Mogadishu.

Ethiopia and Eritrea

Middle Eastern influence in Ethiopia and Eritrea also grew from the 2010s onwards, though its impact was less significant than in neighbouring Somalia. One of the most consequential interventions came from the UAE in 2018 when it successfully mediated a peace in the long-running Ethiopia–Eritrea conflict. Much of this was driven, however, by internal changes in Ethiopia. Since 1991, Ethiopia had enjoyed a degree of political, if autocratic, stability under the leadership of Miles Zenawi, the TPLF guerrilla who designed the post-Derg federal system. Though power passed peacefully to a successor after he died in 2012, tensions remained under the surface and bubbled up in 2016. After several years of popular protests, especially over the government's human rights abuses, Zenawi's successor resigned, to be replaced by 42-year-old Abiy Ahmed. Abiy promised domestic reform on assuming office, and immediately released thousands of political prisoners. He also promised peace with Eritrea, opening the way to UAE mediation. This was partly enabled by the manner of Abiy's rise to power. The coalition of parties that Zenawi had established to dominate post-1991 Ethiopia fractured when selecting Abiy, with Zenawi's TPLF refusing to back the new prime minister. Abiy responded by dissolving the twenty-eight-year-old coalition in 2019, and forming a new one, 'the Prosperity Party', that excluded the TPLF. This aided peace with Eritrea as much of the animosity was between the TPLF and the ruling party of Eritrea, former allies against the Derg in the 1980s that then fell out bitterly.[31]

This shift in Addis Ababa suited the UAE, which had recently forged closer ties with the historically isolated Eritrean government. To grease the wheels, Abu Dhabi injected $3 billion into Ethiopia's economy in June 2018, and soon an agreement was reached between the two sides.[32] The dispute that launched the 1998 war was resolved, the front lines demilitarised and relations between the two states re-established. Abiy's warming to Eritrea and the Gulf mediators indicated a more open approach to foreign affairs. He dropped his predecessors' hostility to Somalia, prompting a closer relationship with then-Somali president, Farmaajo. More significantly, he ended decades of suspicion about working with Arab Middle Eastern governments, dating back to the Cold War, when some had supported Muslim groups among the Eritrean separatists. This opened the way for more investment from both the UAE and Saudi Arabia. But Ethiopia was too big and powerful to be swayed by Middle Eastern rivalries and strengthened its ties with Abu Dhabi and Riyadh's rivals Turkey, Qatar, and Iran as well, with the latter reportedly sending weapons to Addis Ababa when civil war again erupted in 2020.[33] Despite this proliferation of international friendships, the US remained an important security partner, though its limited military presence dating from the 'war on terror' years had ended by 2018. Such was Abiy's growing clout that he was awarded the 2019 Nobel Peace Prize for his reconciliation with Asmara.

However, acclaim for Abiy was soon tempered by the outbreak of the Tigray war in 2020. The TPLF, excluded from power, returned to fighting for ethnic Tigray rights in the northern Tigray region, protesting Abiy's efforts to re-centralise control. The TPLF and federal Ethiopian forces both escalated their military activities, raising tensions. This culminated in November 2020 when the TPLF launched an insurrection against federal forces based in Tigray, prompting a massive counter-attack by Addis Ababa. A major conflict followed, killing up to 600,000 within two years. War crimes were committed on both sides, including civilian massacres and wide-spread rape.[34] Abiy's new partners in Eritrea joined the fight, attacking Tigray from the north. Though the Tigray federal capital Mekelle changed hands several times, Abiy ultimately triumphed and the TPLF, facing a siege that triggered famine across Tigray, sued for peace. An African Union-brokered ceasefire was agreed in November 2022, which saw the TPLF agree to disarm and restore federal control to Tigray. However, the war had highlighted future problems, as other Ethiopian regions also protested Addis Abba's centralisation. For Western allies, the war left a bitter taste after they heralded Abiy as a man of peace. The UAE and other Middle Eastern states were less critical. But Abu Dhabi had very little say on the war and discovered that largesse bought only limited influence. This was also seen when Ethiopia gave little ground on its controversial Grand Ethiopia Renaissance Dam, which threatened to reduce the Nile water running into Sudan and Egypt – both UAE allies – and Abu Dhabi's attempts to mediate made little headway (see chapter 6). That said, Ethiopia's invitation alongside Egypt, Saudi Arabia, and the UAE to join the BRICS group in 2023 might give all four actors more opportunities (and incentive) for future compromises.

Middle Eastern states' impact on Eritrea was more pronounced, helping it break out of decades-long international isolation, even if that ultimately meant little for the lives of its long-oppressed people. After independence, the victorious separatists, the Eritrean People's Liberation Front (EPLF) formed a nationalist, some would say totalitarian, regime. Its autocratic president, Isaias Afwerki, the former head of the EPLF, has remained in power unopposed since 1991. The Isaias regime attempted to recreate the disciplined militarism of the EPLF's military struggle against Ethiopia by enforcing national service for all Eritrean adults from school until the age of 40 for women and 50 for men. Some serve in the military, but many end up in labour battalions working on public infrastructure projects or for companies owned by party bosses. Flight from this modern slavery has made Eritrea one of the highest producers of refugees per capita in the world.[35]

Internationally, Isaias's instincts were isolationist. He received little support in the independence struggle, save for some supplies from Sudan, while Ethiopia was backed by both Cold War superpowers. After the 1998–2000 war, Ethiopia used its international clout, notably hosting the African Union permanently in Addis Ababa, to isolate Eritrea further. The UN Security Council was persuaded to impose arms embargoes and other sanctions for human rights abuses, despite similar crimes going unpunished elsewhere, and Eritrea lacked external champions to stop this. Asmara didn't help itself by opportunistically backing the enemies of its enemies, such as Somalia's Islamists, prompting Washington's ire. Similarly, in 2008 it allowed Iran to use the port of Assab, generating further hostility from the US, Saudi Arabia, and Israel.

The UAE and Saudi Arabia's war in Yemen offered Eritrea a partial route out of this diplomatic wilderness. As well as wanting Iran out of Assab, both Abu Dhabi and Riyadh were looking for military bases to launch attacks on the Houthis. DP World had recently been ejected from neighbouring Djibouti, prompting the UAE to seek alternative Red Sea ports. Riyadh and Abu Dhabi approached Isaias offering much-needed economic support and international reintegration in exchange for kicking Iran out of Assab and offering it to them.[36] Eritrea accepted and joined the international coalition against the Houthis. Abu Dhabi acted quickly and used the facility to launch attacks on Yemen and ship Sudanese mercenaries to the front. The UAE followed up on its promise of breaking Eritrea's isolation by mediating a peace with Ethiopia in 2018. It then lobbied successfully to have several UN sanctions dropped, though not the arms embargo.[37] Isaias embraced the spirit of reconciliation, resuming ties with Somalia, forming a tripartite agreement with Abiy and Farmaajo, and agreeing to settle long-running boundary disputes with Djibouti. However, his eager engagement in the Tigray war and Eritrea's alleged involvement in war crimes provoked the same international distaste as for Abiy. Moreover, despite hopes at home that peace with Ethiopia might improve the domestic situation, no opening came. While the Gulf states, in pursuing their own strategic and commercial interests, helped to resolve a long-running Horn of Africa conflict, this seemingly opened the way for a new one in Tigray, and there has been no obvious improvement in the lives of civilians.

Djibouti and Sudan

Djibouti has historically been something of an exception in the Horn, mostly avoiding the violence and instability that troubled its neighbours. Much of this was down to outside protection. It remained under French control until 1977 and continued to host a sizeable French garrison after independence. Ethiopia has also been a staunch defender. The most populous land-locked country in the world has relied heavily on Djibouti's port for international trade, especially during the long years of estrangement with Eritrea. Indeed, congestion in Djibouti's port and the hunt for new outlets to the sea informed both Addis Ababa's reconciliation with Asmara and its support for developing Berbera port in Somaliland.[38] The hosting of further international military bases, from 2001, adds another layer of external protection. Djibouti is a relative minnow compared to other Horn states, with a population of under 1 million. The majority live in Djibouti city, after which 'French Somaliland' was named on independence. Though united by religion, namely Sunni Islam, Djibouti is ethnically divided between the Somali majority, roughly 60 per cent of the population, and the Afar minority of roughly 25 per cent, plus smaller groups of Arab, Ethiopian, or European origin. Since independence, politics has been dominated by ethnic Somalis, most of whom belong to the Issa clan, producing Djibouti's only two presidents. The current leader, Ismaïl Omar Guelleh, has been in power since 1999, after being handpicked by his uncle and predecessor to succeed him. Re-elected five times, his rule is designated 'not free', by think tank Freedom House, with authoritarian means used to retain power, opposition severely constrained, human rights abuses frequent, and severe limits placed on the press.[39]

However, Djibouti's prime location as an island of stability on the Horn has provided its leadership with essential foreign support and funds. France's base is the oldest and largest, with 1,450 troops stationed there, alongside Mirage fighter jets, and, at times, nuclear submarines. The French also host Spanish and German military personnel and support staff for the EU's Operation Atalanta anti-piracy force. In 2001, Djibouti agreed to lease a new base, Camp Lemonnier, to the US, which was keen to establish a presence in the Horn as part of its 'war on terror'. Significantly expanded in 2013, it now hosts 1,000 troops and is the only permanent US base in Africa. It forms the centrepiece in Washington's network of drone and surveillance bases in the region, particularly focused on targeting Al-Shabab in Somalia and Al-Qaeda in the Arabian Peninsula in Yemen (see chapter 3). Significantly though, Djibouti views itself more as a land-lord than a US ally and arranged similar deals with other powers. In 2011, it agreed to host a Japanese base and an Italian one two years later. Russia has reportedly been exploring the possibility of a base, as has India, but neither has been granted one thus far. In contrast, China was permitted to open a base in 2017. Beijing had been using Djibouti port since 2008 as part of its anti-piracy operations and as a hub for its commercial expansion into Africa. The US was alarmed at the presence of its rival so close to Camp Lemonnier, but Djibouti insisted the two could coexist. The construction of Beijing's first overseas naval base was part of a wider Chinese expansion in the region, with Djibouti playing a key role in its Belt and Road Initiative. China helped to build key infrastructure, such as upgrading the Ethiopia–Djibouti Railway, the Ethiopia–Djibouti Water Pipeline, and Djibouti port.[40]

Given the heavy external presence, Middle Eastern powers have struggled for influence, which explains their willingness to look elsewhere in the Horn. The UAE and Saudi Arabia made the most effort. The UAE's DP World operated Djibouti port from 2006, but relations soured in 2015 when Djibouti rescinded the agreement, claiming the Dubai-based company was deliberately underusing its terminal. The dispute provoked a rupture in UAE–Djibouti relations, with Guelleh ordering the handful of UAE (and Saudi) troops based in the African state to leave. Saudi Arabia eventually reached an agreement with Djibouti in 2016 to host a new Saudi base, though it remains unconstructed.[41] Ironically, Djibouti's quarrel with Abu Dhabi may have unforeseen damaging effects for Guelleh. The affair catalysed the UAE's closer ties with Eritrea and Somaliland as it searched for bases and ports. Were Assab, Berbera, or others to become economic successes, they would challenge Djibouti's monopoly on Ethiopian trade, lessening Addis Ababa's incentive to protect its tiny neighbour. It is also unclear whether its 'landlord' approach to foreign bases is sustainable. It certainly won't be if Washington and Beijing's growing rivalry ever turns hot. Further complicating this is an increased economic dependency on China. New infrastructure projects saw Djibouti's public debt nearly double between 2016 and 2018, leaving it heavily indebted to Beijing – a position other states, like Sri Lanka, have found can be perilous.[42] Djibouti's value for outsiders lies in its stability, and Guelleh and future leaders will be wary that foreign entanglements don't threaten that.

Sudan's history differed from those of its neighbours in that one of its colonial rulers was a Middle Eastern state, Egypt, and another was a European one, Britain. In the early nineteenth century Egypt's ruler, Muhammad Ali (see chapter 6) conquered most of Sudan and his successors ruled there even after Egypt had been absorbed into the British empire in 1882. Sudanese rebellions were violently crushed by British forces, leading the region to be co-administered by Cairo and London, but in reality the latter dominated. After Egypt's 1952 revolution, it abandoned its claims and pushed for Sudan's independence, thereby ejecting Britain from its southern flank. This came in

1956, but Egypt retained a considerable interest, not least because its southern neighbour was upstream on the vital River Nile.

Following what had proved to be a pattern for the region, independent Sudan suffered under several autocratic leaders, most significantly its leader from 1989 to 2019, Omar al-Bashir. Like the government of Eritrea, the regime in Sudan faced international condemnation and isolation for much of this period. Internally, Bashir waged two bloody wars: with the Christian-majority south that eventually seceded from the Muslim-majority north in 2012, and against the Darfuri people in western Sudan from 2003, resulting in mass killing, famines, and alleged genocide. Externally, Bashir allied with Al-Qaeda in the early 1990s, granting them a safe haven, and with Iran and Hamas in the 2000s, allowing Tehran a supply line to Gaza. As a result, Khartoum was subject to a range of economic and military sanctions. However, this began to shift in the 2010s, partly aided by some moderation in Bashir's policies, including the peaceful end of the war with the south, some dialling down in Darfur, and the severing of all ties with Al-Qaeda. Also as in Eritrea, the UAE and Saudi Arabia used financial incentives and the offer of international rehabilitation to coax Sudan away from Iran. Sudan severed its ties with Tehran and joined the Saudi-led coalition in Yemen, sending one of the largest contingents of foreign troops in the early years.[43] But they were not alone in courting Sudan, with Turkey agreeing in 2017 to redevelop the ruined former Ottoman Red Sea city of Suakin as a tourism destination, amid claims they may also build a military facility there. With Egypt and the UAE at loggerheads with Turkey at that time, rumours swirled that Cairo, which continued to see Sudan as within its sphere of influence, would send troops to the Emirati base in Assab to counter this Turkish expansionism. Ankara defused the station in 2018 by insisting it had no military designs on Suakin, though the possibility remained.[44]

External influence further complicated Sudan's political landscape after Bashir was overthrown in 2019. Echoing scenes in Egypt and Tunisia eight years earlier, popular protests prompted Bashir's security chiefs to overthrow the president in a coup. The new leadership was dominated by the army, led by General Abdel Fattah al-Burhan, and the Rapid Support Forces (RSF), a paramilitary wing established by Bashir to fight in Darfur that had become his praetorian guard.[45] Both Burhan and the RSF's leader, General Mohamed 'Hemedti' Hamdan Dagalo, had fought together in Yemen, building close ties to Saudi Arabia and the UAE. Riyadh and Abu Dhabi used this influence, under some pressure from the United States, to persuade the generals to accept some civilian rule after Bashir's ouster. Abu Dhabi was especially keen to keep Turkey, Qatar, and their allies the Muslim Brotherhood, out of post-Bashir Sudan, which was largely achieved. However, after two years of joint military–civilian rule, marred by regular protests, the military launched another coup in 2021. Many, especially Sudan's frustrated civilian oppositionists, believed that continued Emirati and Saudi support emboldened them to act. However, to the military's surprise, the UAE and Saudi Arabia were not enthusiastic about the power grab, believing the previous arrangement gave them sufficient influence without the instability that accompanied the coup.[46] In contrast, Egypt, now ruled by its own military dictator, Abdel Fattah El-Sisi, was supportive, especially of Burhan, whom Sisi saw as a potential protégé.

Foreign hands further impacted the chaos that followed. Protesters soon returned to the street while the US and EU froze development programmes and the African Union suspended Sudan's membership. After more than a year of disrupted rule, the military junta agreed to a compromise deal in late 2022, heavily influenced by external pressure from the US, Saudi Arabia, and the UAE. However, tensions grew between the army and RSF. The army command was dominated by Sudan's elite and viewed Hemedti and the RSF as upstarts from poorer tribal regions. Hemedti made no secret of his desire to ultimately rule Sudan, worrying Burhan, who was nominally head of the military government. They also disagreed over the 2021 coup, with Hemedti urging greater cooperation with civilians to outflank

Burhan who was opposed to this. In April 2023 fighting broke out between the two factions and soon escalated into a major conflict.

Fighting raged in the capital, Khartoum, as well as in Darfur, the RSF's stronghold, provoking panic. Over a million were displaced while large parts of Khartoum were destroyed. The rivalry was not driven by outsiders, but they facilitated it. The UAE was close to the RSF, as was Russia, whose Wagner Group had a small operation in Sudan and reportedly supplied the paramilitaries with weapons.[47] Saudi Arabia, meanwhile, was closer to the army, as was Egypt, which seemed most eager for Burhan to overcome his rival, seeing this as a way to reassert Egyptian influence in a state where it had recently been marginalised by Egypt's Gulf allies. While efforts were made to broker ceasefires, notably by the US and Saudi Arabia in Jeddah, they made little headway as Sudan seemed to be slipping into civil war. Also, there was little consensus among the key external players, Saudi Arabia, the UAE, Egypt, and the US, despite all nominally being allies, while a rival peace process led by the African Union proved equally unsuccessful. With a history of ethnic conflict, the potential existed for Sudan to become the region's latest failed state, another new arena for Middle Eastern rivalry, as well as the instability spilling over to combustible neighbours like Chad, South Sudan, and Libya.[48]

Disrupter or Stabiliser?

In evaluating the entry of Middle Eastern powers into the Horn of Africa in the last decade or so, it is important to recall that the region had a history of violence long before these new outsiders arrived. European imperialism and Cold War rivalries all played a role, but much stemmed from the circumstances of the region's dynamics, especially the presence of a regional superpower, Ethiopia, surrounded by weaker neighbours that it sought to influence. Before Middle Eastern states began engaging in the 2000s, two of the Horn's four states were locked in a cold conflict, while a third had essentially disintegrated. Did Middle Eastern involvement make matters worse? The rivalry between Qatar, the UAE, and Turkey in Somali politics was unhelpful, corrupting the electoral process further and exacerbating tensions. Similarly, the UAE's courting of Somaliland has deepened Hargeisa's estrangement from Mogadishu and, indirectly, contributed to challenges for its democracy. However, many such tensions already existed, and it is hard to lay the blame squarely at the feet of the outsiders. Moreover, the most destabilising recent developments in the Horn have largely originated from within. Ethiopia's invasion of Somalia in 2006, the outbreak of war in Tigray in 2020, the growth of Al-Shabab, and Farmaajo's failed power grab in Mogadishu, while influenced by foreigners, including Middle Easterners, came from the Horn's local and regional politics.

On the other hand, some Middle Eastern involvement has been positive. The growth of aid and infrastructure construction, whether from Turkey and the UAE in Somalia, or the construction of new port facilities in Eritrea and Somaliland, all have the potential to stabilise economics and, possibly, politics. Perhaps the greatest recent achievement by Middle Easterners is the UAE brokering Eritrea and Ethiopia's peace agreement in 2018, leveraging its deep pockets to aid the deal. But once again local factors were more important: Abiy's push to resolve the conflict and Isaias's desire to end his isolation. Abu Dhabi facilitated the talks but did not initiate them, and another mediator could have brought about a similar outcome. On balance then, Middle Eastern powers have increased their presence, but had only limited influence. This is perhaps unsurprising, given they entered a region already very used to outside influence, with governments experienced at extracting as much from foreign patrons as they can for limited concessions. Indeed, for all their enthusiasm, Middle Easterners are competing and/or collaborating with major global actors, notably the US, EU, and China. While the same outside powers are also present in the Middle East, there regional powers like the UAE, Saudi Arabia, Iran, and Turkey have a local legitimacy and existing network absent in the Horn of Africa. As such, it is not surprising that their efforts to influence are often limited. While the Horn of Africa is a new arena for Middle Eastern competition, unless a dramatic transformation takes place, it seems unlikely it will ever be dominated by these regional players in the way parts of the Middle East are.

Conclusion

Aleppo, the second city of Syria, where we began, and Mogadishu, the capital of Somalia on the Horn of Africa, where we ended, are 2,500 miles apart. Even so, they share some similarities. Both were ancient trading cities, with a rich heritage still evident from the medieval buildings now pock-marked by bullet holes. Both experienced vicious recent civil wars, gutting large parts of the once-prosperous settlements. And the fate of both has been greatly influenced by outsiders in recent years. The foreign governments involved are not identical. Russia, Iran, and Israel, key players in Syria, took little interest in Somalia, despite having interests elsewhere in the Horn. The United Arab Emirates, despite some post-conflict engagement with Syria, was not a major actor in its civil war but was very active in Somalia. Yet the other major foreign powers involved in the two conflicts: Qatar, Turkey, Saudi Arabia, the United States, and to a lesser extent China and the EU; are the same. And Aleppo and Mogadishu are far from unique. In the lands in between them the same foreign governments can be found interfering in conflicts across the Middle East, whether it is in Libya's and Yemen's civil wars, or in the contentious politics of Iraq, Lebanon, Palestine, Kurdistan, Egypt, or the Gulf. Such is the region's insecurity it seems that any domestic fault line is liable to be exploited by an outside power and, when this happens, rivals soon pile in to gain the upper hand.

Complex Competition

This book has sought to introduce readers to the geopolitics of the Middle East by examining how and why this regional and international rivalry occurs. In doing so, it has made several arguments. The first, and most simple, is to underline the complexity of international relations in the region known as 'the Middle East'. The ten examples discussed underline that simplified explanations for conflict and instability such as religion, oil, or imperialism are inadequate and unhelpful. Rather these factors feed into a wider, more nuanced, multi-faceted set of causes and explanations.

The second argument was to emphasise the interaction between domestic and external players in driving conflict, in contrast to those who prioritise one over the other. This is true both historically and contemporaneously. European imperialism, for example, bequeathed several Middle Eastern states political orders that proved destabilising. France's empowering of Maronite Christians in Lebanon and its divide-and-rule tactics in Syria laid the groundwork for the destructive identity politics that followed, as did Britain in establishing the primacy of Sunni Muslims in Iraq and Jews in Palestine. Elsewhere, Europeans shaped the region by creating new statelets in the Gulf and a belt of unstable states around Ethiopia in the Horn of Africa, and vetoing an independent Kurdistan after the First World War. However, these externally imposed policies interacted with domestic players who embraced the new structures that rewarded them. When independence came, ruling elites mostly maintained the colonially created systems and often exacerbated divisions as a means of control, as seen in Iraq, Syria, Lebanon, Palestine, Libya, Yemen, and Egypt. Once again, these divisive regimes interacted with outside powers to shore up their rule, whether Cold War superpowers or the regional giants of the day like Nasser's Egypt.

The constant interaction between internal and external players continues today. Conflicts like those in Syria, Libya, and Yemen may be casually characterised as 'proxy wars', but domestic players are far from puppets. Bashar al-Assad in Syria, Ali Abdullah Saleh in Yemen, or Khalifa Haftar in Libya repeatedly found ways to leverage foreign interest to maximise their own goals, even if constrained by some external parameters. Likewise Lebanese, Kurdish, Iraqi, and Horn of Africa politicians proved remarkably obstinate in the face of outside pressure. Indeed, this has forced some regional powers to create their own local allies from scratch, such as Iran's Shia militia in Iraq and Syria or Turkey's pro-Ankara Syrian rebel fighters. Russia and the UAE have had to deploy mercenaries in Syria, Libya, and Yemen, such was their lack of faith in local allies. It is therefore a bit of a redundant argument, despite its popularity, to seek primacy in either domestic or external factors. States rarely exist in a vacuum and leaders and their opponents are constantly aware of and informed by how their actions will be received by the outside world. At the same time, try as they might, outsiders can rarely control actions inside a foreign state. Even if they have cultivated one set of allies, those allies' interactions with other domestic players throw out unpredictable outcomes that are responded to at a local level. The internal and external, in short, have historically been and continue to be in constant interaction to inform outcomes on the ground.

A third argument centred on why there was a marked increase in Middle Eastern conflict in the twenty-first century, suggesting that the United States' recent approach was an important factor. In the 1990s and 2000s Washington inserted itself into the Middle East and its neighbourhood as the dominant power, or hegemon. It built bases in the Gulf, took charge of the Israeli-Palestinian peace process, poured anti-terror funds and weaponry into allies like Yemen and Ethiopia, and pushed Lebanon, Egypt, and Saudi Arabia to reform, all the while excluding and punishing those that resisted: Iran, Syria, Libya, and Iraq. While this was far from successful, it created the expectation among Washington's allies and enemies that its dominance would continue. But the disastrous invasion of Iraq in 2003 followed by a shift in the global balance of power cowed the US, and successive presidents, Obama, Trump, and Biden, all wanted to step back from the Middle East, leading to confusion and opportunism. While the US remains a powerful player in the Middle East, intervening against Islamic State and maintaining important security and economic alliances, it is no longer the undisputed hegemon. But its thirty-year dalliance with dominance has imbalanced the region, and many of the recent conflicts have been influenced by that imbalance.

This relates to the final argument, that the vacuum left by Washington's retreat has led to a range of regional and other international powers intervening in arenas that once would have been dominated by the US. Unlike China in East Asia, the US in North America or, indeed, Ethiopia in the Horn of Africa, there is no obvious regional hegemon in the Middle East, but rather a series of middle-sized powers. While the US dominated none could rival it, but now Washington has stepped back those regional powers are not intimidated by a single powerful local giant. Instead, Turkey, Iran, Israel, and Saudi Arabia have all been willing to enter new arenas in their rivalries with one another, while the UAE and Qatar, though smaller, have used their vast wealth to join in. This regional competition is complicated by the entry of new international powers, seeking to take advantage of Washington's retreat, in the case of Russia and China, or continuing a largely fruitless engagement, in the case of the EU. What made this situation particularly destabilising in the Middle East after 2011, compared to other regions, is the sheer number of intervening powers involved, often pursuing their own independent interests. It was particularly unfortunate for the region that the 2011 Arab Uprisings occurred against the backdrop of this shift in global and regional power. It created several destabilised arenas in which competition could be played out, just when the number of players in the game increased. The result has catalysed and widened regional instability, mostly at the expense of the civilians living in the countries being fought over.

Few Winners

Has it been worth it for the intervening governments? On balance, probably not. A decade after the Arab Uprisings and twenty years after the Iraq war, few of the ten intervening powers profiled in this book could claim to be in a stronger regional or global position than before because of their engagement in Middle Eastern conflicts. The US is worse off. The invasion of Iraq destabilised the Middle East, empowering Iran and creating a Jihadist threat that did not previously exist, while demoralising a US public now less willing to support foreign wars. The fallout from Iraq cast a shadow over Washington's engagement with the region after the 2011 Uprisings, limiting it to modest goals like the containment of Tehran and combatting Jihadism, with mixed results. The EU is similarly in a weaker position, having a more unstable region on its doorstep than before its American ally's push for dominance, that periodically spills out mass migration or Jihadist attacks.

Russia temporarily benefited from its Middle East interventions, especially after forays into Syria and Libya, but events elsewhere, notably its 2022 invasion of Ukraine, have undone some of those gains. While it retains influence that it lacked prior to 2011, its shortcomings in Eastern Europe have pierced the commanding reputation it won after its Syria intervention and any perceived defeat in Ukraine could weaken its regional position further. China is arguably in the most improved position among the international powers, but it has had only limited engagement with the region, restricted to economic and diplomatic advances, with military deployment only in the Horn of Africa. This might point to an advantage in having a mostly economic focus, but it's a position built on the relative stability in the Gulf brought by America's security presence. Such 'free-riding' would not continue if the US withdrew from the Gulf or if Beijing and Washington's rivalry became violent. In such circumstances China might have to reconsider its aversion to a military presence in the Middle East.

For the regional powers, all have gained in some ways but lost in others. The most successful have been Israel and the UAE. Israel has managed to retain its grip on the Occupied Palestinian Territories, while building new ties via the Abraham Accords and containing the advance of Iran. That said, its continued shift to the right and oppression of the Palestinians has damaged its global reputation, making some Western voters, if not yet politicians, question the continued alliance. The UAE, meanwhile, has greatly expanded its regional influence, intervening widely, boosting its regional and global diplomatic clout, but criticism over some of its interventions, notably in Yemen, has also negatively raised its profile in the West and will make it a target for some. Qatar and Iran, in contrast, had periods of success, followed by a fall. Qatar was hyperactive immediately before and after the Arab Uprisings, but saw its influence in Syria, Egypt, Libya, and the Gulf curtailed when its GCC allies turned on it. While far from defeated, Doha is likely to be more modest regionally and internationally in the coming years. Iran also successfully expanded its influence in Iraq, Lebanon, Syria, and Yemen to unprecedented levels in the 2000s and 2010s, but this also provoked an international and regional backlash and sanctions. Domestic troubles, in the form of new protest movements, partly influenced by the economic impact of sanctions as well as opposition to the ruling elite's brutality, may further limit Tehran's future regional ambitions.

Saudi Arabia and Turkey, meanwhile, have both had mixed results. Saudi Arabia has ambitiously stepped into several conflicts in Syria, Qatar, Egypt, and the Horn, achieving little but without having disastrous consequences for Riyadh. Its biggest intervention though, in Yemen, has been a different matter, with Saudi Arabia damaging its international reputation at significant financial cost, with very little to show for it other than a decimated southern neighbour. That said, these moves have all helped to solidify the domestic position of Mohammed Bin Salman, and whether that will prove to be a positive or negative development in the long term is yet to be seen. Turkey has also attempted several interventions in Syria, Libya, Iraq, Egypt, Kurdistan, and the Horn, with similarly mixed outcomes. The moves have also helped Recep Tayyip Erdoğan consolidate control but, unlike in Saudi Arabia, he is an old hand and Turkey could yet be destabilised when he eventually departs the scene, likely altering Ankara's regional outlook.

No Going Back

For readers of a certain outlook, it might be easy to conclude that the key to regional stability in the Middle East is therefore a return to US dominance. After all, though it was imperfect, the period from 1990 to 2003 was comparatively secure, so perhaps this could be replicated once again? But this is the wrong approach. First, the same conditions do not exist to rebuild this era, with shifts in the global, regional, and local environments such that Washington would not be able to rebuild this hegemony, even if it wanted to. Second, US dominance was damaging to the region, creating power imbalances, and raising expectations. Moreover, it was unsustainable. The US imploded its own dominance with the disastrous Iraq invasion, but other events would likely have prompted a US withdrawal in the end, precipitating the same scramble in the vacuum described in this book. The fault, then, was arguably not the US's decision to withdraw, but its stepping into the region so fully in the first place.

For Western policy makers today, however, that leaves some unpalatable choices. They could advocate another attempt at dominance, but this will be even harder than before and will still be unsustainable in the long term. The alternative is to accept the region may be unstable for some years while the regional and global players reach a new balance of power. This could be a bloody and violent process, and arguably this is what has been occurring since 2011. It need not be though. In 1967, in the Sudanese capital, Khartoum, a previous generation of Middle Eastern leaders agreed, after defeat by Israel in the Six Day War, that they would stop interfering in each other's affairs, a compact that largely held for a decade before old habits resurfaced. Such mature statesmanship began to infiltrate regional politics in the early 2020s, with former rivals Turkey, Qatar, UAE, and Saudi Arabia burying the hatchet and re-establishing cordial ties. Riyadh even re-opened relations with its arch-rival Tehran in 2023, in a deal, notably, brokered by China, hinting that the decade of competition between them may be relegated to the past. This detente was seemingly strengthened further in mid 2023 when both Saudi Arabia and Iran were invited by China and the other members of the BRICS group to join. Whether high-level agreements between rival governments translate into a reduction in tensions in the countries they competed over, remains to be seen. The aftermath of the Saudi-Iranian deal saw Syria's Assad readmitted to the Arab League and suggestions of a breakthrough in peace talks in Yemen, indicating there might be a corresponding easing of regional conflict. That said, at the same time the escalation of violence in Sudan and Gaza, influenced but not determined by outsider rivalries, illustrated that there remained many corners of instability.

Moreover, what regional rivalry remains may no longer be restricted to the Middle East. Competition in the Horn of Africa is the most extensive example, but recent years have seen rivalries play out elsewhere. Russia and Turkey backed different sides in the 2020 war between Armenia and Azerbaijan, while Israel, Egypt, and the UAE have weighed in against Turkey in disputes over gas exploration in Cyprus. Middle Eastern powers have expanded their reach far beyond the region, as can be seen in Turkey's links to Central Asia, Saudi Arabia's ties to Pakistan, or the UAE's growing relationship with India. Iran, similarly, has growing links to Shia communities in West Africa via Hezbollah. On the one hand, this might lessen tensions in the Middle East, as regional powers look in different directions to one another to expand their influence. On the other hand, their involvement also raises the risk that, should domestic dynamics in these distant areas provoke conflict, Middle Eastern rivalries could once again influence matters.

It may be an uncomfortable watch for Western leaders and commentators to leave the region be, used as they are to their governments intervening, often informed by simplistic explanations of the region's problems. However, ultimately these organic, regional, and local solutions and accommodations, hopefully based on an understanding of the true complexity of the factors at play, will have more long-term success than those imposed by outsiders. Barack Obama controversially stated in 2016 that Middle Eastern leaders needed to, 'find an effective way to share the neighbourhood'.[1] Given the dramatic levels of conflict and instability in the previous decade or so, as they, alongside international powers, opted to fight over the region instead, he may have been right.

Acknowledgements

I am indebted to so many for their help and guidance, without which this book would not have happened. Heather McCallum, my editor at Yale University Press, has been encouraging from the beginning and helped to refine the project's argument and scope. I would also like to sincerely thank Yale's Sophie Richmond and Rachael Lonsdale for their thorough editorial work. David Lesch kindly read through an early draft, offering valuable suggestions and recommendations, as did another anonymous reviewer, for which I'm incredibly grateful. Sincere thanks are also due to Kristian Coates Ulrichsen, May Darwich, Tim Eaton, Jacob Eriksson, Jef Feltman, Laleh Khalili, Thomas McGee, Peter Salisbury and Bassel Salloukh, who all looked through individual draft chapters and offered me their expert advice. I am also indebted to my former Head of School at Queen Mary University of London, David Williams, who was deeply supportive of my efforts, including granting extended research leave in which to write up the manuscript.

This project was the culmination of over a decade's research on the international relations of the Middle East. It draws indirectly on countless interviews and fieldwork conducted for previous projects and, while not cited in the text, I'd like to thank everyone that I've engaged with over the years from within the Middle East who have enhanced and deepened my understanding of its geopolitics. Similarly, given that this book mostly draws from secondary sources for its data, I must thank the many excellent writers and analysts who have gone before me in producing a rich seam of scholarship for me to mine. In particular I must credit Tim Marshall's excellent *Prisoners of Geography* (London: Elliot and Thompson, 2015). While the content is obviously different, I have consciously emulated Marshall's excellent structure of breaking down my analysis into manageable interconnected but separate chapters with the goal of producing a book that, I hope, presents complex geopolitics in an accessible form. I must also thank my wonderful students at Queen Mary who, over the years, have posed many of the questions I sought to answer in this book and helped develop my thoughts on the subject.

Thanks are also due to the members of the two main scholarly networks I have belonged to during the course of my research. The Project on Middle East Political Science (POMEPS) run by Marc Lynch, and the Sectarianism, Proxies and De-sectarianisation network run by Simon Mabon and Edward Wastnidge have offered me the opportunity to exchange ideas with some of the world's leading scholars and experts on Middle Eastern geopolitics, shaping this work throughout.

Finally, I must thank my friends and family for all their love and support. My wife, Lindsay, and daughters, Margot and Beatrice, have been a welcome source of distraction and joy throughout the long research and writing process. I cannot begin to say how blessed I feel and how grateful I am to all of you.

Queen Mary University of London, 2023

Abbreviations

AKP	Justice and Development Party (in Turkey)
AQAP	Al-Qaeda in the Arabian Peninsula
BRI	Belt and Road Initiative
EPLF	Eritrean People's Liberation Front
EU	European Union
GCC	Gulf Cooperation Council
GNA	Government of National Accord
IMF	International Monetary Fund
IRGC	Islamic Revolutionary Guard Corps
KDP	Kurdistan Democratic Party
KDPI	Kurdish Democratic Party of Iran
KNC	Kurdish National Council
KRG	Kurdistan Regional Government
LAAF	Libyan Arab Armed Forces
LNG	liquified natural gas
MBS	Mohammed Bin Salman (deputy crown prince and, from 2017, crown prince, Saudi Arabia)
MBZ	Mohammed Bin Zayed (crown prince and, from 2022, president, UAE)
NTC	National Transition Council

PA	Palestinian Authority
PJAK	Kurdistan Free Life Party
PKK	Kurdistan Workers' Party
PLC	Presidential Leadership Council
PLO	Palestinian Liberation Organization
PMU	Popular Mobilisation Units
PUK	Patriotic Union of Kurdistan
PYD	Democratic Union Party (Kurdish)
SCAF	Supreme Council of the Armed Forces
SDF	Syrian Democratc Forces
STC	Southern Transitional Council
TPLF	Tigray People's Liberation Front
UAE	United Arab Emirates
UN	United Nations
WMD	weapons of mass destruction

Notes

Introduction

1. There are multiple examples of this approach: by politicians such as Barack Obama stating that difference between Sunnis and Shias is the biggest cause of conflict in the Middle East, see Patrick Temple-West, 'Obama cites Sunni, Shia Islamic conflicts', *Politico*, 28 Sept. 2014, https://www.politico.com/blogs/politico-now/2014/09/obama-cites-sunni-shia-islamic-conflicts-196210 (accessed 10 March 2023); and by journalists such as Thomas Friedman discussing how US politics has been 'infected' by Middle Eastern tribalism, see Thomas Friedman, 'Have we reshaped Middle East politics or started to mimic it?', *New York Times*, 14 Sept. 2021, https://www.nytimes.com/2021/09/14/opinion/america-democracy-middle-east-tribalism.html (accessed 10 March 2023); or in popular culture, for example *The Daily Show* declaring that the arbitrary drawing of borders by European imperialists is the cause of the Middle East's instability, see Nick Danforth, 'Stop blaming colonial borders for the Middle East's Problems', *The Atlantic*, 11 Sept. 2013, https://www.theatlantic.com/international/archive/2013/09/stop-blaming-colonial-borders-for-the-middle-easts-problems/279561/ (accessed 10 March 2023).
2. Ariel I. Ahram, *War and Conflict in the Middle East and North Africa* (London: John Wiley & Sons, 2020), p. 48.
3. Fred Halliday, *The Middle East in International Relations* (Cambridge: Cambridge University Press, 2005), pp. 1–18.
4. Christopher Phillips, *The Battle for Syria: International Rivalry in the New Middle East* (New Haven, CT and London: Yale University Press, 2016; 3rd edn 2020), pp. 1–9.
5. For an interesting discussion of how to define the Middle East see Brian Whitaker, 'Middle of where?', *Guardian*, 4 June 2008, https://www.theguardian.com/commentisfree/2008/jun/04/middleeast; see also 'Where is the Middle East?' (https://mideast.unc.edu/where/) at the University of North Carolina

Center of Middle East and Islamic Studies, for a series of maps illustrating how perceptions of where the region is have changed over time.

6. Christopher Phillips, *Everyday Arab Identity: The Daily Reproduction of the Arab World* (London: Routledge, 2013), pp. 8–39.

7. Marc Lynch, 'The end of the Middle East: How an old map distorts a new reality', *Foreign Affairs*, 101 (2022), https://www.foreignaffairs.com/africa/middle-east-map-new-reality (accessed 10 April 2023).

8. To avoid overloading the reader with academic jargon, I have opted not to name these theories of international relations in the main text. However, for those want to learn more about them, I will offer more detail here. For discussions of the importance of domestic state structure look to scholars of 'Historical Sociology'; while for those emphasising the decision-making elites either at home or abroad, look to 'Neo-Classical Realism'. For a focus on identity, such as religion or ideology, look for 'Constructivist' scholarship. For those looking at international structure and the balance of power, look for 'Neo-Realists'. For discussions of race, both 'Critical Race Theory' and 'Decolonisation' are good places to start, while 'Feminist' and 'Queer' theories are useful introductions to exploring gender and sexuality. 'Green' theories have also recently emerged in the discipline to focus more on environmental issues. For a summary of these theories and a general introduction to the discipline of international relations see John Baylis, Patricia Owens, and Steve Smith (eds), *The Globalization of World Politics: An Introduction to International Relations* (Oxford: Oxford University Press, 2022). For a Middle East-focused discussion of these theories, see Marc Lynch, Jillian Schwedler, and Sean Yom (eds), *The Political Science of the Middle East: Theory and Research since the Arab Uprisings* (Oxford: Oxford University Press, 2022).

9. Curtis Ryan, 'Shifting alliances and shifting theories in the Middle East', memo in *POMEPS Studies* 34: *Shifting Global Politics and the Middle East* (2019), pp. 7–13.

10. Edward Said, *Culture and Imperialism* (New York: Vintage, 1993), pp. xi–xxviii.

11. Halliday, *The Middle East in International Relations*, p. 6.

12. Steven Simon and Jonathan Stevenson, 'The end of Pax Americana: Why Washington's Middle East pullback makes sense', *Foreign Affairs*, 94:6 (2015), pp. 2–10.

13. Micah Zenko, 'What Obama really meant by "No boots on the ground"', *The Atlantic*, 3 Dec. 2015, https://www.theatlantic.com/international/archive/2015/12/obama-boots-on-the-ground/418635/ (accessed 10 Feb. 2023).

14. There are various names used to describe Islamic State in the West, including Daesh (a pejorative term used by some in the Middle East) and ISIS (based on the acronym for the organisation's name from 2013–14, Islamic State in Iraq and Sham [Greater Syria]). In this book, for the period after 2014, the organisation will be referred to as Islamic State.

15. Christopher Layne, 'This time it's real: The end of unipolarity and the Pax Americana', *International Studies Quarterly*, 56 (2012), pp. 203–13.

16. Christopher Phillips, 'The international system and the Syrian civil war', *International Relations*, 36:3 (2022), pp. 358–81.

17. Ibid.

18. Bassel F. Salloukh, 'Overlapping contests and Middle East international relations: The return of the weak Arab state', *Political Science and Politics*, 50:3 (2017), pp. 660–63.
19. Martin Chulov and Michael Safi, 'Did Jordan's closest allies plot to unseat its king?', *Guardian*, 26 May 2021, https://www.theguardian.com/world/2021/may/26/did-jordans-closest-allies-plot-to-unseat-its-king (accessed 10 May 2023).
20. May Darwich, 'Foreign policy analysis and armed non-state actors in world politics: Lessons from the Middle East', *Foreign Policy Analysis*, 17:4 (2021), pp. 1–11.

1 Syria

1. *New York Times*, 'The 31 places to go in 2010', 7 Jan. 2010, https://www.nytimes.com/2010/01/10/travel/10places.html (accessed 1 June 2023).
2. Phillips, *The Battle for Syria*, p. 1.
3. James Barr, *A Line in the Sand: Britain, France and the Struggle that Shaped the Middle East* (London: Simon & Schuster, 2011).
4. Haian Dukhan, *States and Tribes in Syria: Informal Alliances and Conflict Patterns* (London: Routledge, 2018), pp. 26–49.
5. Ben White, *The Emergence of Minorities in the Middle East: The Politics of Community in French Mandate Syria* (Edinburgh: Edinburgh University Press, 2011), p. 1.
6. Phillips, *Everyday Arab Identity*.
7. David Lesch, *The New Lion of Damascus: Bashar al-Assad and Modern Syria* (New Haven, CT and London: Yale University Press, 2005), p. 1.
8. Bassam Haddad, 'The Syrian regime's business backbone', *Middle East Report* 262 (2012).
9. Geneive Abdo, *The New Sectarianism: The Arab Uprisings and the Rebirth of the Shia–Sunni Divide* (Washington, DC: Saban Center for Middle East Policy at Brookings, 10 April 2013).
10. 'Interview with Syrian President Bashar al-Assad', *Wall Street Journal*, 31 Jan. 2011.
11. 'Syrians commemorate graffiti that "kickstarted" the Syrian revolution', *The New Arab*, 17 Feb. 2022, https://www.newarab.com/news/syrians-remember-anniversary-iconic-revolution-graffiti (accessed 1 June 2023).
12. Al Jazeera, 'Profile: Bashar al-Assad', *Al Jazeera* 17 April 2018, https://www.aljazeera.com/news/2018/4/17/profile-bashar-al-assad (accessed 2 June 2023).
13. Phillips, *The Battle for Syria*, pp. 50–53.
14. Rania Abouzeid, 'Meet the Islamist militants fighting alongside Syria's rebels', *Time*, 26 July 2012.
15. Dexter Filkins, 'The shadow commander', *New Yorker*, 30 Sept. 2013.
16. Ibid.
17. Henri J. Barkey, 'Erdoğan's foreign policy is in ruins', *Foreign Policy*, 4 Feb. 2016.
18. Ibid.
19. Khaled Yacoub Oweis, 'Insight: Saudi Arabia boosts Salafist rivals to al Qaeda in Syria', *Reuters*, 1 Oct. 2013, http://www.reuters.com/article/2013/10/01/

us-syria-crisis-jihadists-insight-idUSBRE9900RO20131001 (accessed 13 Oct. 2015).

20. Phillips, *The Battle for Syria*, p. 130.
21. Elizabeth Dickinson, 'Follow the money: How Syrian Salafis are funded from the Gulf', *Diwan* (Carnegie Endowment for International Peace), 23 Dec. 2013, http://carnegieendowment.org/syriaincrisis/?fa=54011 (accessed 17 March 2014). Unless stated otherwise, all $ symbols in this book will be US dollars.
22. Mark Mazzetti, Adam Goldman, and Michael S. Schmidt, 'Behind the sudden death of a $1 billion secret C.I.A. war in Syria', *New York Times*, 2 Aug. 2017, https://www.nytimes.com/2017/08/02/world/middleeast/cia-syria-rebel-arm-train-trump.html (accessed 10 May 2023).
23. Phillips, *The Battle for Syria*, p. 80.
24. Thomas McGee, 'Mapping action and identity in the Kobani crisis response', *Kurdish Studies Journal*, 4:1 (2016), pp. 51–77.
25. Dimitri Trenin, 'Putin's Syria gambit aims at something bigger than Syria', *The Tablet*, 13 Oct. 2015, http://www.tabletmag.com/jewish-news-and-politics/194109/putin-syria-trenin (accessed 24 Feb. 2016).
26. Steven Lee Myers and Anne Barnard, 'Bashar al-Assad finds chilly embrace in Moscow trip', *New York Times*, 21 Oct. 2015, https://www.nytimes.com/2015/10/22/us/politics/assad-finds-chilly-embrace-in-moscow-trip.html (accessed 10 May 2023).
27. Phillips, 'The international system and the Syrian civil war'.
28. Charles Lister, *The Syrian Jihad: Al-Qaeda, the Islamic State and the Evolution of an Insurgency* (London: Hurst, 2016), p. 338.
29. Haid Haid, 'Did Turkey abandon Aleppo to fight Syrian Kurds?', *Now*, 4 Oct. 2016, https://now.mmedia.me/lb/en/commentaryanalysis/567401-did-turkey-abandon-aleppo-to- fight-the-syrian-kurds (accessed 10 Aug. 2017).
30. Lewis Sanders and Khaled Salameh, 'Syrian mercenaries sustain Turkey's foreign policy', *DW*, 30 Sept. 2020, https://www.dw.com/en/turkey-syrian-mercenaries-foreign-policy/a-55098604 (accessed 12 April 2023).
31. Ehud Eilam, 'Israel and the Russian presence in Syria', in *Israeli Strategies in the Middle East: The Case of Iran* (Cham: Springer International Publishing, 2022) pp. 125–36.
32. Andrew England and Laura Pitel, 'Syria: What is Turkey's grand plan?', *Financial Times*, 27 July 2022, https://www.ft.com/content/a14241de-8dbf-4a69-b064-2991f5992503 (accessed 22 May 2023).

2 Libya

1. Statista, 'Oil production in Libya from 1998 to 2021', *Statista*, 2 March 2023, https://www.statista.com/statistics/265194/oil-production-in-libya-in-barrels-per-day/#:~:text=Lybia's%20oil%20production%20amounted%20to,thousand%20barrels%20of%20oil%20daily. (accessed 24 May 2023).
2. Dirk Vandewalle, *A History of Modern Libya* (Cambridge: Cambridge University Press, 2012), pp. 30–31.
3. Ulf Laessing, *Understanding Libya since Gaddafi* (London: Hurst, 2020): Kindle edn, l. 866.
4. Vandewalle, *A History of Modern Libya*, p. 190.

5. Mark Tran, 'Libya undecided on future of African investments', *Guardian*, 27 Jan. 2012, https://www.theguardian.com/global-development/2012/jan/27/libya-undecided-future-african-investments (accessed 10 Jan. 2023).
6. Laessing, *Understanding Libya*, Kindle edn, l. 483.
7. Al Jazeera, 'Former French President Sarkozy charged over Libyan financing', *Al Jazeera* 16 Oct. 2020, https://www.aljazeera.com/news/2020/10/16/former-french-president-sarkozy-charged-over-libyan-financing (accessed 20 Feb. 2023).
8. Simon Denyer, 'Gaddafi's son: We will deal with terrorists first and then talk reform', *Washington Post*, 17 April 2011, https://www.washingtonpost.com/world/gaddafis-son-we-will-deal-with-terrorists-first-then-we-will-talk-reform/2011/04/17/AFbTpHvD_story.html (accessed 23 April 2023).
9. Laessing, *Understanding Libya*, Kindle edn, l. 1958.
10. Ibid., l. 1984.
11. Laessing, *Understanding Libya*, Kindle edn, l. 837.
12. Missy Ryan, 'Libyan force was lesson in limits of U.S. power', *Washington Post*, 5 Aug. 2015, https://www.washingtonpost.com/world/national-security/a-security-force-for-libya-becomes-a-lesson-in-failure/2015/08/05/70a3ba90-1b76-11e5-bd7f-4611a60dd8e5_story.html (accessed 10 March 2023).
13. Jeff Goldberg, 'The Obama doctrine', *The Atlantic*, April 2016, https://www.theatlantic.com/magazine/archive/2016/04/the-obama-doctrine/471525/ (accessed 10 March 2023).
14. Wolfram Lacher, *Libya's Fragmentation: Structure and Process in Violent Conflict* (London: I.B. Tauris, 2020), p. 66.
15. Kristian Coates Ulrichsen, *Qatar and the Arab Spring* (London: Hurst, 2014), p. 112.
16. Andreas Krieg, 'Qatar: From activism to pragmatism', Sadeq Institute, 17 March 2021.
17. Tarek Megerisi, 'Libya's global civil war', Policy Brief, European Council on Foreign Relations, June 2019, https://ecfr.eu/publication/libyas_global_civil_war1/ (accessed 3 April 2022).
18. Lacher, *Libya's Fragmentation*, p. 70.
19. Tim Eaton, *The Libyan Arab Armed Forces*, Research Paper (London: Chatham House, June 2021).
20. Laessing, *Understanding Libya*, Kindle edn, l. 1263.
21. Ibid., l. 1125.
22. Frederic M. Wehrey, *The Burning Shores* (London: Farrar, Straus and Giroux, 2018), pp. 202–20.
23. Megerisi, 'Libya's global civil war'.
24. Wehrey, *The Burning Shores*, p. 210.
25. Nadja Berghoff and Anas al-Gomati (eds), *The Great Game* (Tripoli: Sadeq Institute, 22 Feb. 2021).
26. Lacher, *Libya's Fragmentation*, p. 285.
27. Ibid., p. 107.
28. Laessing, *Understanding Libya*, Kindle edn, l. 2309.
29. Ibid., l. 3177.
30. Laessing, *Understanding Libya*, Kindle edn, l. 3312.

31. Eaton, *The Libyan Arab Armed Forces*.
32. Samer Al-Atush and Laura Pitel, 'Russia reduces number of Syrian and Wagner troops in Libya', *Financial Times*, 28 April 2022, https://www.ft.com/content/88ab3d20-8a10-4ae2-a4c5-122acd6a8067 (accessed 10 June 2023).
33. Ibid.
34. Ahmet S. Yahya, 'Erdoğan's Libya adventure: Turkey, Russia, gas pipelines and missiles', *The Investigative Journal*, January 2020, https://www.researchgate.net/publication/338555807_Erdoğan%27s_Libyan_Adventure_Turkey_Russia_Gas_Pipelines_and_Missiles (accessed 2 March 2023).

3 Yemen

1. Helen Lackner, *Yemen in Crisis: Road to War* (London: Verso, 2019), p. 34.
2. Fred Halliday, *Revolution and Foreign Policy: The Case of South Yemen, 1967–1987* (Cambridge: Cambridge University Press, 2002), pp. 1–8.
3. Lackner, *Yemen in Crisis*, p. 108.
4. Halliday, *Revolution and Foreign Policy*, pp. 41–3.
5. Lackner, *Yemen in Crisis*, p. 120.
6. Isa Blumi, *Destroying Yemen* (Oakland, CA: University of California Press, 2018), p. 155.
7. Lackner, *Yemen in Crisis*, p. 219.
8. Ibid.
9. Ibid., p. 239.
10. Ibid., p. 41.
11. Ibid., p. 291.
12. Ginny Hill, *Yemen Endures: Civil War, Saudi Adventurism and the Future of Arabia* (London: Oxford University Press, 2017), p. 263.
13. Noel Brehony and Saud Sarhan (eds), *Rebuilding Yemen: Political, Economic and Social Challenges* (Berlin: Gerlach, 2015), p. 2.
14. Gregory Johnson, 'Seven Yemens: How Yemen fractured and collapsed and what comes next', The Arab Gulf States Institute in Washington, Oct. 2021 https://agsiw.org/wp-content/uploads/2021/10/Johnsen_Yemen_ONLINE.pdf (accessed 24 Jan. 2022)
15. Ibid.
16. Lackner, *Yemen in Crisis*, p. 72
17. Madawi Al-Rasheed, 'King Salman and his son: Winning the US losing the rest', LSE Middle East Centre Paper Series (2017), https://eprints.lse.ac.uk/84283/ (accessed 21 Sept. 2023).
18. Hill, *Yemen Endures*, p. 238.
19. Thomas Juneau, 'Iran's policy towards the Houthis in Yemen: A limited return on a modest investment', *International Affairs*, 92:3 (2016), pp. 647–63.
20. Sam Perlo-Freeman, Aude Fleurant, Pieter Wezeman and Siemon Wezeman, 'Trends in world military expenditure 2015', SIPRI Fact Sheet, April 2016, https://www.sipri.org/sites/default/files/EMBARGO%20FS1604%20Milex%202015.pdf (accessed 21 Sept. 2023).
21. Johnson, 'Seven Yemens'.
22. Borzou Daragahi, 'Yemen has become a Vietnam-like quagmire for Saudi Arabia – with no simple solution to end the war', *Independent*, 10 Oct. 2021,

https://www.independent.co.uk/independentpremium/voices/yemen-saudi-arabia-houthis-b1935664.html (accessed 21 Dec. 2022).

23. Peter Salisbury, *Risk Perception and Appetite in UAE Foreign and National Security Policy*, Research Paper (London: Chatham House, July 2020), https://www.chathamhouse.org/sites/default/files/2020-07-01-risk-in-uae-salisbury.pdf (accessed 2 March 2023).

24. Elisabeth Kendall, *Iran's Fingerprints in Yemen*, Issue Brief (Washington, DC: Atlantic Council, October 2017).

25. Ibid.

26. Juneau, 'Iran's policy towards the Houthis'.

27. Johnson, 'Seven Yemens'.

28. International Crisis Group, *Rethinking Peace in Yemen*, Middle East Report 216 (Brussels: International Crisis Group, 2 July 2020).

29. Lackner, *Yemen in Crisis*, p. 86.

30. Ibid., p. 57.

31. Johnson, 'Seven Yemens'.

32. BBC, 'Yemen: UK to resume Saudi arms sales after humanitarian review', *BBC News*, 7 July 2020, https://www.bbc.co.uk/news/uk-politics-53324251 (accessed 3 April 2023).

33. Johnson, 'Seven Yemens'.

4 Palestine

1. Anshel Pfeffer, 'The Israel–Palestine conflict is not just about land. It's a bitter religious war', *Guardian*, 20 Nov. 2014, https://www.theguardian.com/commentisfree/2014/nov/20/israel-palestine-conflict-religious-war (accessed 20 Jan. 2023).

2. Massoud Hayoun, *When We Were Arabs: A Jewish Family's Forgotten History* (London: The New Press, 2019).

3. Joel Beinin and Lisa Hajjar, 'Palestine, Israel and the Arab-Israeli conflict: A primer', Middle East Research and Information Project (2014).

4. Ibid.

5. Rashid Khalidi, *The Hundred Years' War on Palestine: A History of Settler Colonial Conquest and Resistance* (London: Macmillan, 2020), p. 8.

6. Ibid., p. 25.

7. Zena Al-Tahhan, 'More than a century on: The Balfour Declaration explained', *Al Jazeera*, 2 Nov. 2018, https://www.aljazeera.com/features/2018/11/2/more-than-a-century-on-the-balfour-declaration-explained (accessed 4 Feb. 2023).

8. Khalidi, *The Hundred Years' War*, p. 25.

9. Beinin and Hajjar, 'Palestine, Israel and the Arab-Israeli conflict'.

10. Ibid.

11. C.R. Jonathan and Glenn Frankel, 'Iron fist policy protested in Israel', *Washington Post*, 24 Jan. 1988, https://www.washingtonpost.com/archive/politics/1988/01/24/iron-fist-policy-protested-in-israel/3235bc64-60f0-4462-9b88-c273c49cc6c2/ (accessed 10 Nov. 2022).

12. Avi Shlaim, 'The rise and fall of the Oslo Peace Process', in Louise Fawcett (ed.), *International Relations of the Middle East* (Oxford: Oxford University Press, 2016), p. 285.

13. Khalidi, *The Hundred Years' War*, p. 203.
14. Orna Ben-Naftali, Michael Sfard, and Hedi Viterbo, *The ABC of the OPT: A Legal Lexicon of the Israeli Control over the Occupied Palestinian Territory* (Cambridge: Cambridge University Press, 2018).
15. Saleh Hijazi and Hugh Lovatt, 'Europe and the Palestinian Authority's authoritarian drift', European Council on Foreign Relations, 20 April 2017, https://ecfr.eu/article/commentary_europe_and_the_palestinian_authoritys_author-itarian_drift_7274/ (accessed 10 April 2023).
16. David Ignatius, 'The Mideast deal that could have been', *Washington Post*, 26 Oct. 2011, https://www.washingtonpost.com/opinions/the-mideast-deal-that-could-have-been/2011/10/25/gIQAxaREKM_story.html (accessed 10 Nov. 2022).
17. Mairav Zonszein and Daniel Levy, 'Israel's winning coalition: Culmination of a long rightward shift', International Crisis Group Q&A, 8 Nov. 2022, https://www.crisisgroup.org/middle-east-north-africa/east-mediterranean-mena/israelpalestine/israels-winning-coalition (accessed 10 Dec. 2022).
18. Khalidi, *The Hundred Years' War*, p. 248.
19. Mehul Srivastava, 'Netanyahu ratchets up anti-Arab rhetoric ahead of knife-edge vote', *Financial Times*, 29 March 2019, https://www.ft.com/content/169dcc74-4a9e-11e9-bbc9-6917dce3dc62 (accessed 12 Dec. 2022).
20. For a detailed breakdown of the Oslo system of government see Ben-Naftali et al., *The ABC of the OPT*.
21. Zonszein and Levy, 'Israel's winning coalition'.
22. UN, 'Israeli occupation of Palestinian territory in facts and figures', United Nations: The Question of Palestine https://www.un.org/unispal/in-facts-and-figures/ (accessed 10 May 2023).
23. Adi Cohen, 'Go West Bank: Israel is using the housing crisis to lure Israelis into becoming settlers', *Haaretz*, 15 Feb. 2023, https://www.haaretz.com/israel-news/2023-02-15/ty-article-magazine/.premium/go-west-bank-israels-housing-crisis-plan-turns-even-more-israelis-into-settlers/00000186-545c-de95-a1fe-f65f212f0000 (accessed 25 April 2023).
24. Khalidi, *The Hundred Years' War*, p. 209.
25. Ibid., p. 217.
26. John Mearsheimer and Stephen Walt. 'The Israel lobby', *London Review of Books*, 28:6 (2006), pp. 3–12.
27. Nasuh Uslu and İbrahim Karataş. 'Evaluating Hamas' struggle in Palestine', *Insight Turkey*, 22:1 (2020), pp. 109–24.
28. B'Tselem, 'Fatalities', B'Tselem Statistics, https://www.btselem.org/statistics/fatalities/after-2009-01-19/by-date-of-death (accessed 10 May 2023).
29. Khalidi, *The Hundred Years' War*, p. 224.
30. Ibid. pp. 209–10.
31. Shlomo Roiter Jesner, 'Qatar is using the Palestinians to assert its regional influence', *Foreign Policy*, 26 Jan. 2021, https://foreignpolicy.com/2021/01/26/qatar-is-using-the-palestinians-to-assert-its-regional-influence/ (accessed 2 May 2023).
32. Palestinian Central Bureau of Statistics, 'On the occasion of International Population Day', 11 July 2022, https://pcbs.gov.ps/post.aspx?lang=en&ItemID=4279 (accessed 12 March 2023).

33. Zonszein and Levy, 'Israel's winning coalition'.
34. Ibid.
35. Michael Barnett, Nathan Brown, Marc Lynch, and Shibley Telhami, 'Israel's one-state reality: It's time to give up on the two-state solution', *Foreign Affairs*, 102 (2023).
36. Khalidi, *The Hundred Years' War*, p. 253.

5 Iraq

1. Ali A. Allawi, *Faisal I of Iraq* (New Haven, CT and London: Yale University Press, 2014), pp. 410–32.
2. Zaid Al-Ali, *The Struggle for Iraq's Future: How Corruption, Incompetence and Sectarianism have Undermined Democracy* (New Haven, CT and London: Yale University Press, 2014), Kindle edn, l. 405.
3. Ibid., l. 466.
4. Harvey Sicherman, 'Saddam Hussein: Stalin on the Tigris', Foreign Policy Research Institute, 7 Feb. 2007, https://www.fpri.org/article/2007/02/saddam-hussein-stalin-tigris/ (accessed 2 Feb. 2023).
5. Fanar Haddad, *Sectarianism in Iraq: Antagonistic Visions of Unity* (London: Hurst, 2014), pp. 65–9.
6. Al-Ali, *The Struggle for Iraq's Future*, Kindle edn, l. 677.
7. Elana Schor, 'Saddam Hussein had no direct ties to al-Qaida, says Pentagon study', *Guardian*, 13 March 2008, https://www.theguardian.com/world/2008/mar/13/iraq.usa (accessed 10 Jan. 2023).
8. BBC, 'Chilcot Report: Findings at a glance', *BBC News*, 6 July 2016, https://www.bbc.co.uk/news/uk-politics-36721645 (accessed 10 April 2023).
9. Al-Ali, *The Struggle for Iraq's Future*, Kindle edn, l. 841.
10. Ibid., Kindle edn, l. 1265.
11. Garrett M. Graff, 'Orders of disorder: Who disbanded Iraq's army and de-Baathified its bureaucracy?', *Foreign Affairs*, 5 May 2023, https://www.foreignaffairs.com/middle-east/iraq-united-states-orders-disorder (accessed 24 May 2023).
12. Al-Ali, *The Struggle for Iraq's Future*, Kindle edn, l. 1649.
13. Ibid., Kindle edn, l. 1219.
14. Erica Hunter, 'Changing demography: Christians in Iraq since 1991', in Daniel King (ed.), *The Syriac World* (London: Routledge, 2018), pp. 783–96.
15. Austin Long, 'The Anbar awakening', *Survival*, 50:2 (2008), pp. 67–94.
16. Lister, *The Syrian Jihad*, p. 34.
17. Firas Maksad and Kenneth M. Pollack, 'How Saudi Arabia is stepping up in Iraq', *Foreign Affairs*, 21 Aug. 2017, https://www.foreignaffairs.com/articles/middle-east/2017-08-21/how-saudi-arabia-stepping-iraq (accessed 10 Nov. 2022).
18. Arash Azizi, *The Shadow Commander: Soleimani, the US, and Iran's Global Ambitions* (London: Simon & Schuster, 2020), Kindle edn, l. 3064.
19. Jessica Watkins, *Iran in Iraq: The Limits of 'Smart Power' amidst Public Protest*, LSE Middle East Centre Paper Series 37 (July 2020).
20. Ibid.

21. For further details on the deal, see Kali Robinson, 'What is the Iran nuclear deal?', Backgrounder, Council on Foreign Relations, 20 July 2022, https://www.cfr.org/backgrounder/what-iran-nuclear-deal (accessed 23 April 2023).
22. Guardian, 'Isis captured 2,300 Humvee armoured vehicles from Iraqi forces in Mosul', *Guardian*, 1 June 2015.
23. Janice Dickson, 'Turkey turns blind eye to ISIS fighters using its hospitals: sources', *Ipolitics*, 27 May 2015, http://ipolitics.ca/2015/07/27/turkey-turns-blind-eye-to-isis-fighters-using-its-hospitals-sources/ (accessed 14 Oct. 2015).
24. Fanar Haddad, 'Understanding Iraq's Hashd al-Sha'bi: State and power in post-2014 Iraq', The Century Foundation, 5 March 2018, https://tcf.org/content/report/understanding-iraqs-hashd-al-shabi/ (accessed 10 Nov. 2022).
25. Azizi, *The Shadow Commander*, Kindle edn, l. 4047.
26. David McDowall, *A Modern History of the Kurds* (London: Bloomsbury, 2021), Kindle edn, l. 19048.
27. Ibid., Kindle edn, l. 19661.
28. Haddad, 'Understanding Iraq's Hashd al-Sha'bi'.
29. Ben Hubbard, Palko Karasz, and Stanley Reed, 'Two major Saudi oil installations hit by drone strike, and US blames Iran', *New York Times*, 14 Sept. 2019, https://www.nytimes.com/2019/09/14/world/middleeast/saudi-arabia-refineries-drone-attack.html (accessed 10 April 2023).
30. Alissa J. Rubin and Ronin Bergman, 'Israeli airstrike hits weapons depot in Iraq', *New York Times*, 22 Aug. 2019, https://www.nytimes.com/2019/08/22/world/middleeast/israel-iraq-iran-airstrike.html (accessed 7 May 2023).
31. Azizi, *The Shadow Commander*, Kindle edn, l. 4394.
32. Al-Ali, *The Struggle for Iraq's Future*, Kindle edn, l. 214.
33. Taif Alkhudary, 'From Muhasasa to Mawatana: The election boycott movement and prospects for effective democracy in Iraq', LSE Blogs, 1 Oct. 2021, https://blogs.lse.ac.uk/mec/2021/10/01/from-muhasasa-to-mawatana-the-election-boycott-movement-and-prospects-for-effective-democracy-in-iraq/ (accessed 10 Jan. 2023).
34. In 2022 Transparency International scored Iraq 23/100 in its Corruption Perception Index. It came 157th out of 180 countries in the world. Of the countries in the Middle East, Iraq only did better than war-torn Syria, Libya, and Yemen. See https://www.transparency.org/en/cpi/2022 (accessed 1 May 2023).

6 Egypt

1. Population figures as of November 2022; see Andrew Douglas, '10 largest cities in the world', *World Atlas*, 1 Nov. 2022, https://www.worldatlas.com/cities/10-largest-cities-in-the-world.html (accessed 10 March 2023).
2. Robert Springborg, *Egypt* (London: John Wiley & Sons, 2017), p. 29.
3. For details of Britain's imperial rule in Egypt see Peter Mangold, *What the British Did: Two Centuries in the Middle East* (London: I.B. Tauris, 2016), pp. 109–19.
4. James Jankowski, *Egypt: A Short History* (London: Oneworld, 2000), p. 134.
5. Ibid., p. 167.
6. Yezid Sayigh, *Owners of the Republic: An Anatomy of Egypt's Military Economy* (Beirut: Carnegie Middle East Center, 2019), https://carnegie-mec.org/

2019/11/18/owners-of-republic-anatomy-of-egypt-s-military-economy-pub-80325 (accessed 20 June 2022).

7. Ibid.
8. Springborg, *Egypt*, p. 81.
9. 'Population in Egypt – Egypt: Demographics', Place Explorer, Data Commons, https://datacommons.org/place/country/EGY?category=Demographics (accessed 10 March 2023).
10. Jankowski, *Egypt*, pp. 174–8.
11. Vali Nasr, *The Dispensable Nation* (London: Scribe, 2013), p. 166.
12. Khalil al-Anani, 'Upended path: The rise and fall of Egypt's Muslim Brotherhood', *Middle East Journal*, 69:4 (2015), pp. 527–43.
13. Ibid.
14. Springborg, *Egypt*, p. 62.
15. Ibid., p. 62.
16. Ibid., p. 93.
17. Ibid., pp. 13–18.
18. David Butter, *Egypt and the Gulf: Allies and Rivals*, Research Paper (London: Chatham House, April 2020), www.chathamhouse.org/sites/default/files/CHHJ8102-Egypt-and-Gulf-RP-WEB_0.pdf (accessed 22 Feb. 2023).
19. Ibid.
20. Mark Heartsgaard, 'Secret tapes of the 2013 Egypt coup plot pose a problem for Obama', *Daily Beast*, 5 Oct. 2015, http://www.thedailybeast.com/articles/2015/05/10/secret-tapes-of-the-2013-egypt-coup-plot-pose-a-problem-for-obama.html (accessed 10 Nov. 2015).
21. Butter, *Egypt and the Gulf*.
22. Ibid.
23. Ibid.
24. Jeremy M. Sharp, *Egypt: Background and US Relations*, Congressional Research Service report, 17 July 2022, https://crsreports.congress.gov/product/pdf/RL/RL33003/116 (accessed 10 Dec. 2022).
25. Ibid.
26. Kim Ghattas, *The Secretary: A Journey with Hillary Clinton from Beirut to the Heart of American Power* (London: Macmillan, 2013), Kindle edn, l. 3972.
27. Alan Gresh, 'Barack Obama. "Lackey" of Egypt's Muslim Brotherhood', *Orient XXI*, 13 Sept. 2018, https://orientxxi.info/magazine/barack-obama-lackey-of-egypt-s-muslim-brotherhood,2623 (accessed 3 Nov. 2023).
28. Clark Mindock, '"Where's my favourite dictator?" Trump comment on Egyptian president "met with stunned silence", report says', *Independent*, 13 Sept. 2019, https://www.independent.co.uk/news/world/americas/us-politics/trump-egypt-president-sisi-favorite-dictator-meeting-a9104951.html (accessed 20 Jan. 2023).
29. Sharp, 'Egypt: Background and US relations'.
30. Butter, *Egypt and the Gulf*.
31. Sayigh, *Owners of the Republic*.
32. Springborg, *Egypt*, p. 97.
33. Sharp, 'Egypt: Background and US relations'.
34. Hamza Handawi, 'Egypt has lost more than 3,000 in fight against militants since 2013, says El Sisi', *The National*, 27 April 2022, https://www.thenational-

news.com/mena/2022/04/27/egypt-has-lost-more-than-3000-in-fight-against-militants-since-2013-says-el-sisi/ (accessed 21 September 2023).

35. Al Jazeera, 'Egyptian pound has lost half of its value since March', *Al Jazeera* 1 Jan. 2023, https://www.aljazeera.com/news/2023/1/11/egyptian-pound-has-lost-half-of-its-value-since-march (accessed 10 April 2023).

36. Butter, *Egypt and the Gulf.*

37. Springborg, *Egypt*, p. 188.

7 Lebanon

1. Ussama Makdisi, 'After 1860: Debating religion, reform, and nationalism in the Ottoman Empire', *International Journal of Middle East Studies*, 34:4 (2002), pp. 601–17.

2. Andrew Patrick, *America's Forgotten Middle East Initiative: The King–Crane Commission of 1919* (London: I.B. Tauris, 2015), pp. 130–64.

3. Michael Hudson, 'The Palestinian factor in the Lebanese civil war', *Middle East Journal*, 32:3 (1978), pp. 261–78.

4. Stathis N. Kalyvas, 'The ontology of "political violence": Action and identity in civil wars', *Perspectives on Politics*, 1:3 (2003), pp. 475–94.

5. David Hirst, *Beware of Small States: Lebanon, Battleground of the Middle East* (London: Bold Type Books, 2011), pp. 75–98.

6. Amos Barshad, 'The world's most dangerous census', *The Nation*, 17 Oct. 2019, https://www.thenation.com/article/archive/lebanon-census/ (accessed 21 March 2023).

7. Nicholas Blanford, *Killing Mr Lebanon: The Assassination of Rafik Hariri and its Impact on the Middle East.* (London: I.B. Tauris, 2006), pp. 40–74.

8. Andrew Arsan, *Lebanon: A Country in Fragments* (London: Hurst, 2020), p. 6.

9. Bassel Salloukh, 'Taif and the Lebanese state: The political economy of a very sectarian public sector', *Nationalism and Ethnic Politics*, 25:1 (2019), pp. 43–60.

10. Khaled Abu Toameh, 'Poll: Nasrallah most admired leader in Arab world', *Jerusalem Post*, 16 April 2008, https://www.jpost.com/middle-east/poll-nasrallah-most-admired-leader-in-arab-world (accessed 4 May 2022).

11. Arsan, *Lebanon: A Country in Fragments*, p. 149.

12. Azizi, *The Shadow Commander*, Kindle edn, l. 3100.

13. Ramzy Baroud, '"Balance of terror" drives Israel's approach to Lebanon', *Arab News*, 10 Aug. 2020, https://www.arabnews.com/node/1717476 (accessed 6 Aug. 2022).

14. Lilach Shoval, 'Israel's shadow war with Iran escalates in Syria with attacks, drone interception', *Al-Monitor*, 3 April 2023, https://www.al-monitor.com/originals/2023/04/israels-shadow-war-iran-escalates-syria-attacks-drone-interception#ixzz83x7eTjJx (accessed 20 May 2023).

15. Arsan, *Lebanon: A Country in Fragments*, p. 95.

16. Ibid., p. 422.

17. Liz Sly and Susan Haidamous, 'Trump's sanctions on Iran are hitting Hezbollah and it hurts', *Washington Post*, 18 May 2019, https://www.washingtonpost.com/world/middle_east/trumps-sanctions-on-iran-are-hitting-hezbollah-hard/2019/05/18/970bc656-5d48-11e9-98d4-844088d135f2_story.html (accessed 22 Feb. 2022).

18. Stefan Lehne, *Time to Reset the European Neighbourhood Policy* (Brussels: Carnegie Europe, Feb. 2014), https://carnegieendowment.org/files/time_reset_enp.pdf (accessed 20 Feb. 2023).
19. Mattia Serra, 'The EU's Lebanon policy: No easy way forward', Italian Institute for International Political Studies – ISPI, 13 May 2022, https://www.ispionline.it/en/pubblicazione/eus-lebanon-policy-no-easy-way-forward-35013 (accessed 1 Sept. 2022).
20. International Crisis Group, *Managing Lebanon's Compounding Crises*, Middle East Report 228, 28 Oct. 2021, https://www.crisisgroup.org/middle-east-north-africa/east-mediterranean-mena/lebanon/228-managing-lebanons-compounding-crises (accessed 20 Jan. 2023).
21. Serra, 'The EU's Lebanon policy'.
22. Heiko Wimmen, 'Lebanon's vicious cycles', Op-ed, MENA, International Crisis Group, 13 May 2022, https://www.crisisgroup.org/middle-east-north-africa/east-mediterranean-mena/lebanon/lebanons-vicious-cycles (accessed 15 Aug. 2022).
23. Arsan, *Lebanon: A Country in Fragments*, p. 387.
24. International Crisis Group, *Managing Lebanon's Compounding Crises*.
25. Ibid.
26. Ibid.
27. Ibid.
28. Wimmen, 'Lebanon's vicious cycles'.
29. Ibrahim Halawi, 'Elite resilience in Lebanon at a time of deep crises', Institute for Social Justice and Conflict Resolution (2021), https://pure.royalholloway.ac.uk/ws/portalfiles/portal/42345677/Elite_Resilience_in_Lebanon_at_a_Time_of_Deep_Crises.pdf (accessed 10 May 2022).
30. Ibid.

8 Kurdistan

1. McDowall, *A Modern History of the Kurds*, Kindle edn, l. 1124.
2. Ibid., Kindle edn, l. 1160.
3. Abbas Vali, 'The Kurds and their Others: Fragmented identity and fragmented politics', *Comparative Studies of South Asia, Africa and the Middle East*, 18:2 (1998), pp. 82–95.
4. Djene Rhys Bajalan, 'The First World War, the end of the Ottoman empire, and the question of Kurdish statehood: A "missed" opportunity?', *Ethnopolitics*, 18:1 (2019), pp. 13–28.
5. Raymond Kévorkian, *The Armenian Genocide: A Complete History* (London: I.B. Tauris, 2011), pp. 799–806.
6. McDowall, *A Modern History of the Kurds*, Kindle edn, l. 7333.
7. Ibid., l. 7363.
8. *Guardian*, 'Turkish forces kill 32 Kurdish militants in bloody weekend as conflict escalates', 11 Jan. 2016, https://www.theguardian.com/world/2016/jan/11/turkish-forces-kill-32-kurdish-militants-in-bloody-weekend-as-conflict-escalates (accessed 10 Jan. 2023).
9. Stefanie K. Wichhart, 'A "new deal" for the Kurds: Britain's Kurdish policy in Iraq, 1941–45', *Journal of Imperial and Commonwealth History*, 39:5 (2011), pp. 815–31.

10. McDowall, *A Modern History of the Kurds*, Kindle edn, l. 10808.
11. Human Rights Watch, 'Genocide in Iraq: The Anfal campaign against the Kurds', July 1993, https://www.hrw.org/reports/1993/iraqanfal/ANFALINT.htm (accessed 10 Feb. 2023).
12. Garrett Nada and Caitlin Crahan, 'Iran's troubled provinces: Kurdistan', United States Institute of Peace – USIP, 3 Feb. 2021, https://iranprimer.usip.org/blog/2020/sep/08/iran%E2%80%99s-troubled-provinces-kurdistan (accessed 1 April 2023).
13. Bryan R. Gibson, *Sold Out? US Foreign Policy, Iraq, the Kurds, and the Cold War* (London: Springer, 2016), pp. 163–98.
14. McDowall, *A Modern History of the Kurds*, Kindle edn, l. 8944.
15. Ibid., l. 14822.
16. Michael M. Gunter, 'The Kurdish question in perspective', *World Affairs*, 166 (2003), p. 197.
17. Aliza Marcus, *Blood and Belief: The PKK and the Kurdish Fight for Independence* (London: NYU Press, 2009), pp. 76–88.
18. Şaban Kardaş, 'From zero problems to leading the change: Making sense of transformation in Turkey's regional policy', TEPAV Turkish Policy Brief Series 5 (2012).
19. McDowall, *A Modern History of the Kurds*, Kindle edn, l. 16804.
20. International Crisis Group, 'Turkey's PKK conflict: A visual explainer', updated 1 Feb. 2023, https://www.crisisgroup.org/content/turkeys-pkk-conflict-visual-explainer (accessed 10 April 2023).
21. France 24, 'Turkey marks fifth anniversary of failed coup that prompted sweeping crackdown', 15 July 2021, https://www.france24.com/en/europe/20210715-turkey-marks-fifth-anniversary-of-failed-coup-against-Erdoğan (accessed 10 April 2023).
22. Thomas McGee, '"Nothing is ours anymore" – HLP rights violations in Afrin, Syria', in Hannes Baumann (ed.), *Reclaiming Home: The Struggle for Just Housing, Land and Property Rights in Syria, Iraq and Libya* (London: Friedrich Erbert Stiftung, 2019), pp. 120–141.
23. Harriet Allsopp, *The Kurds of Syria: Political Parties and Identity in the Middle East* (London: I.B. Tauris, 2016), ch. 7.
24. Zeynep Kaya and Robert Lowe, 'The curious question of the PYD–PKK relationship', in Gareth Stansfield and Mohammed Shareef (eds), *The Kurdish Question Revisited* (London: Hurst, 2017).
25. Phillips, *The Battle for Syria*, p. 133.
26. Thomas McGee, '"Rojava": Evolving public discourse of Kurdish identity and governance in Syria', *Middle East Journal of Culture and Communication*, 15:4 (2022), pp. 385–403.
27. Amy Austin Holmes and Wladimir van Wilgenburg, 'Kurds and Arabs in northeast Syria: Power struggle or power sharing?', *The National Interest*, 11 Aug. 2019, https://nationalinterest.org/feature/kurds-and-arabs-northeast-syria-power-struggle-or-power-sharing-72281 (accessed 24 May 2023).
28. McGee, '"Nothing is ours anymore"'.
29. McDowall, *A Modern History of the Kurds*, Kindle edn, l. 11972.
30. Ibid., l. 19117.
31. Ibid., l. 19127.

32. Ibid., l. 19111.
33. Michael Rubin, 'Is Iraqi Kurdistan a good ally?', American Enterprise Institute, Middle Eastern Outlook 1, 7 Jan. 2008, https://www.aei.org/ publication/ is-iraqi-kurdistan-a-good-ally/ (accessed 8 June 2023).
34. International Crisis Group, *After Iraqi Kurdistan's Thwarted Independence Bid*, Middle East Report 199, 27 March 2019, https://www.crisisgroup.org/middle-east-north-africa/gulf-and-arabian-peninsula/iraq/199-after-iraqi-kurdistans-thwarted-independence-bid (accessed 2 April 2023).
35. McDowall, *A Modern History of the Kurds*, Kindle edn, l. 9239.
36. Ibid., l. 12085.

9 The Gulf

1. Zainab Mansour, 'Qatar hosts more than 1.4 million visitors during FIFA World Cup', *Gulf Business*, 19 Dec. 2022, https://gulfbusiness.com/qatar-hosts-more-than-1-4-million-visitors-during-fifa-world-cup/ (accessed 10 April 2023).
2. Sean Ingle, 'Qatar bans beer from World Cup stadiums after 11th-hour U-turn', *Guardian*, 18 Nov. 2022, https://www.theguardian.com/football/2022/nov/18/qatar-bans-beer-from-world-cup-stadiums-fifa-u-turn (accessed 10 April 2023).
3. Adam Hanieh, *Money, Markets, and Monarchies: The Gulf Cooperation Council and the Political Economy of the Contemporary Middle East* (Cambridge: Cambridge University Press, 2018), Kindle edn, l. 769.
4. Ibid., l. 827.
5. Freedom House, 'Kuwait – Freedom in the world 2023', 2022, https://freedomhouse.org/country/kuwait/freedom-world/2023 (accessed 23 May 2023).
6. Christopher Davidson, *After the Sheikhs: The Coming Collapse of the Gulf Oil Monarchies* (London: Hurst, 2012), pp. 214–15; Mehran Kamrava, 'The Arab Spring and the Saudi-led counterrevolution', *Orbis*, 56:1 (2012), pp. 96–104.
7. Jonathan Fulton, *China's Relations with the Gulf Monarchies* (London: Routledge, 2018), p. 75.
8. Ethan Bronner, 'Bahrain tears down monument as protestors seethe', *New York Times*, 18 March 2011, https://www.nytimes.com/2011/03/19/world/middleeast/19bahrain.html (accessed 12 May 2023).
9. Ghattas, *The Secretary: A Journey with Hillary Clinton*, p. 260.
10. Ed Crooks, 'The US shale revolution', *Financial Times*, 24 April 2015, https://www.ft.com/content/2ded7416-e930-11e4-a71a-00144feab7de (accessed 20 Jan. 2023).
11. Fulton, *China's Relations with the Gulf Monarchies*, p. 77.
12. Jane Kinninmont, *The Gulf Divided: The Impact of the Qatar Crisis*, Research Paper (London: Chatham House, May 2019).
13. Phillips, *The Battle for Syria*, pp. 285–88.
14. Hanieh, *Money, Markets, and Monarchies*, Kindle edn, l. 1144.
15. Fulton, *China's Relations with the Gulf Monarchies*, p. 1.
16. Ibid., p. 38.
17. Ibid., p. 1.

18. Zhong Nan, 'CRCC nets contract for Qatar stadium', *China Daily*, 1 Dec. 2016, www.chinadaily.com.cn/business/2016-12/01/content_27535600.htm (accessed 1 Jan. 2023).
19. Fulton, *China's Relations with the Gulf Monarchies*, p. 154.
20. Ibid., p. 99.
21. Kinninmont, *The Gulf Divided*.
22. Ibid.
23. Salisbury, *Risk Perception and Appetite*.
24. Kinninmont, *The Gulf Divided*.
25. Ibid.
26. Ibid.
27. Vivian Yee and Megan Specia, 'Gulf states agree to end isolation of Qatar', *New York Times*, 5 Jan. 2021, https://www.nytimes.com/2021/01/05/world/middleeast/gulf-qatar-blockade.html (accessed 10 Feb. 2023).
28. Ibid.
29. Hanieh, *Money, Markets, and Monarchies*, Kindle edn, l. 965.
30. Ibid., l. 324.
31. Fulton, *China's Relations with the Gulf Monarchies*, p. 101.
32. Stephanie Kirchgaessner, 'Saudi woman given 34-year prison sentence for using Twitter', *Guardian*, 16 Aug. 2022, https://www.theguardian.com/world/2022/aug/16/saudi-woman-given-34-year-prison-sentence-for-using-twitter#:~:text=A%20Saudi%20student%20at%20Leeds,and%20retweeting%20dissidents%20and%20activists (accessed 10 May 2023).
33. Marc Owen Jones, *Digital Authoritarianism in the Middle East: Deception, Disinformation and Social Media* (London: Hurst, 2022) Kindle edn, l. 338.

10 Horn of Africa

1. 'Population in Ethiopia – Ethiopia: Demographics', Data Commons, https://datacommons.org/place/country/ETH/?utm_medium=explore&mprop=count&popt=Person&hl=en (accessed 10 March 2023).
2. Christopher Clapham, *The Horn of Africa: State Formation and Decay* (London: Hurst, 2023), p. 43.
3. Ibid.
4. Ibid., p. 49.
5. Ibid., p. 67.
6. Bekele Bengessa Hirbe, *Intrastate Conflict in the Horn of Africa: Implications for Regional Security (1990–2016)* (London: Lexington, 2021), pp. 147–76.
7. Alex de Waal, *The Real Politics of the Horn of Africa: Money, War and the Business of Power* (London: Polity, 2015), pp. 130–40.
8. Michael Woldemariam, 'The Eritrea–Ethiopia thaw and its regional impact', *Current History*, 118: 808 (2019), pp. 181–7.
9. Neil Melvin, 'The foreign military presence in the Horn of Africa', Stockholm International Peace Research Institute, SIPRI Background Papers, April 2019, https://www.sipri.org/publications/2019/sipri-background-papers/foreign-military-presence-horn-africa-region (accessed 1 May 2023).
10. Clapham, *The Horn of Africa*, p. 156.
11. Melvin, 'The foreign military presence in the Horn of Africa'.

12. Salisbury, *Risk Perception and Appetite*.
13. Matthew Hedges, 'United Arab Emirates: Reversing the revolution', in Berghoff and al-Gomati (eds), *The Great Game*, pp. 76–8.
14. Salisbury, *Risk Perception and Appetite*.
15. Ibid.
16. Clapham, *The Horn of Africa*, p. 148.
17. Abdi Ismail Samatar, 'Somalia's election raises more questions than answers', *The Conversation*, 31 May 2022, https://theconversation.com/somalias-election-raises-more-questions-than-answers-183833 (accessed 1 June 2023).
18. Jessica Larsen and Finn Stepputat, 'Gulf state rivalries in the Horn of Africa: Time for a Red Sea policy?', DIIS Policy Brief, 1 March 2019, https://www.diis.dk/en/research/gulf-state-rivalries-in-the-horn-of-africa-time-a-red-sea-policy (accessed 10 May 2023).
19. Mohamed Dhaysane, 'Ethiopia deploys new troops into neighboring Somalia', VOA, 8 Aug. 2022, https://www.voanews.com/a/ethiopia-deploys-new-troops-into-neighboring-somalia-/6693095.html (accessed 10 March 2023).
20. Samatar, 'Somalia's election raises more questions than answers'.
21. Ibid.
22. Brendon Cannon, 'Foreign state influence and Somalia's 2017 presidential election: An analysis', *Bildhaan: An International Journal of Somali Studies*, 18:1 (2019), pp. 20–49.
23. Salisbury, *Risk Perception and Appetite*.
24. Omar Mahmood, 'A welcome chance for a reset in Somalia', International Crisis Group Q&A, 31 May 2022, https://www.crisisgroup.org/africa/horn-africa/somalia/welcome-chance-reset-somalia (accessed 1 Jan. 2023).
25. Ibid.
26. Ibid.
27. International Crisis Group, 'Overcoming Somaliland's worsening political crisis', Statement, 10 Nov. 2022, https://www.crisisgroup.org/africa/horn-africa/somalia/overcoming-somalilands-worsening-political-crisis (accessed 10 Dec. 2022).
28. Cannon, 'Foreign state influence and Somalia's 2017 presidential election'.
29. Melvin, 'The foreign military presence in the Horn of Africa'.
30. International Crisis Group, 'Overcoming Somaliland's worsening political crisis', Statement, 10 Nov. 2022.
31. For a detailed account of Abiy's rise to power see Jonathan Fisher and Meressa Tsehaye Gebrewahd, '"Game over"? Abiy Ahmed, the Tigrayan People's Liberation Front and Ethiopia's political crisis', *African Affairs*, 118:470 (2019), pp. 194–206.
32. Woldemariam, 'The Eritrea–Ethiopia thaw and its regional impact'.
33. Lynch, 'The end of the Middle East'.
34. Mariel Müller, 'In Ethiopia's Tigray war, rape is used as a weapon', *DW*, 17 March 2023, https://www.dw.com/en/in-ethiopias-tigray-war-rape-is-used-as-a-weapon/a-65022330 (accessed 10 May 2023).
35. Clapham, *The Horn of Africa*, p. 134.
36. Melvin, 'The foreign military presence in the Horn of Africa'.
37. Woldemariam, 'The Eritrea–Ethiopia thaw and its regional impact'.
38. Clapham, *The Horn of Africa*, p. 175.

39. Freedom House, 'Djibouti – Freedom in the world 2023', 2022, https://freedom-house.org/country/djibouti/freedom-world/2023 (accessed 23 May 2023).
40. Melvin, 'The foreign military presence in the Horn of Africa'.
41. Ibid.
42. Ibid.
43. Camille Lons, 'Gulf countries reconsider their involvement in the Horn of Africa', Online analysis, International Institute for Strategic Studies – IISS, 1 June 2021, https://www.iiss.org/blogs/analysis/2021/06/gulf--horn-of-africa (accessed 10 June 2022).
44. Melvin, 'The foreign military presence in the Horn of Africa'.
45. International Crisis Group, 'A race against time to halt Sudan's collapse', Briefing 190/Africa, 22 June 2023, https://www.crisisgroup.org/africa/horn-africa/sudan/b190-race-against-time-halt-sudans-collapse (accessed 1 July 2023).
46. International Crisis Group, 'A critical window to bolster Sudan's next government', Statement/Africa, 23 Jan. 2023, https://www.crisisgroup.org/africa/horn-africa/sudan/critical-window-bolster-sudans-next-government (accessed 10 May 2023).
47. Jason Burke, ' "It is like a virus that spreads": Business as usual for Wagner group's extensive Africa network', *Guardian*, 6 July 2023, https://www.theguardian.com/world/2023/jul/06/putin-wagner-africa-business-yevgeny-prigozhin-kremlin (accessed 8 July 2023).
48. International Crisis Group, 'A race against time to halt Sudan's collapse'.

Conclusion

1. Goldberg, 'The Obama doctrine'.

Further Reading

Introduction

Ahram, Ariel I., *War and Conflict in the Middle East and North Africa* (London: Polity, 2020).

Gause, F. Gregory, *Beyond sectarianism: The new Middle East Cold War*, Brookings Doha Center Analysis Paper 11 (Doha, Qatar: Brookings Doha Center, 2014).

Halliday, Fred, *The Middle East in International Relations: Power Politics and Ideology* (Cambridge: Cambridge University Press, 2005).

Lynch, Marc, 'The end of the Middle East: How an old map distorts a new reality', *Foreign Affairs*, March/April (2022).

Phillips, Christopher, 'The international system and the Syrian civil war', *International Relations*, 36:3 (2022): 358–81.

Simon, Steven and Jonathan Stevenson, 'The end of Pax Americana', *Foreign Affairs*, Nov./Dec. (2015).

1 Syria

Dagher, Sam, *Assad or We Burn the Country: How One Family's Lust for Power Destroyed Syria.* (London: Hachette UK, 2019).

Lesch, David, *Syria: A Modern History* (London: Polity, 2019).

Lister, Charles, *The Syrian Jihad: Al-Qaeda, the Islamic State and the Evolution of an Insurgency* (London: Hurst, 2016).

Phillips, Christopher, *The Battle for Syria: International Rivalry in the New Middle East* (New Haven, CT and London: Yale University Press, 2016, 3rd edn 2020).

Yassin-Kassab, Robin and Leila Al-Shami, *Burning Country: Syrians in Revolution and War* (London: Pluto, 2016).

Yazbek, Samar, *The Crossing: My Journey to the Shattered Heart of Syria* (London: Rider, 2015).

2 Libya

Collombier, Virginie and Wolfram Lacher (eds), *Violence and Social Transformation in Libya* (London: Hurst, 2023).
Eaton, Tim, *The Libyan Arab Armed Forces*, Research Paper (London: Chatham House, June 2021).
Lacher, Wolfram, *Libya's Fragmentation: Structure and Process in Violent Conflict* (London: I.B. Tauris, 2020).
Laessing, Ulf, *Understanding Libya Since Gaddafi* (London: Hurst, 2020).
Pargeter, Alison, *Libya: The Rise and fall of Qaddafi* (New Haven, CT and London: Yale University Press, 2012).
Wehrey, Frederic M., *The Burning Shores* (London: Farrar, Straus and Giroux, 2018).

3 Yemen

Blumi, Isa, *Destroying Yemen* (Oakland, CA: University of California Press, 2018).
Hill, Ginny, *Yemen Endures: Civil War, Saudi Adventurism and the Future of Arabia* (London: Oxford University Press, 2017).
Lackner, Helen, *Yemen in Crisis: Road to War* (London: Verso Books, 2019).
Johnson, Gregory, 'Seven Yemens: How Yemen fractured and collapsed and what comes next', The Arab Gulf States Institute in Washington, October 2021, https://agsiw.org/wp-content/uploads/2021/10/Johnsen_Yemen_ONLINE.pdf (accessed 24 January 2022).
Juneau, Thomas, 'Iran's policy towards the Houthis in Yemen: A limited return on a modest investment', *International Affairs*, 92:3 (2016): 647–63.
Ramani, Samuel, 'Deterrence through diplomacy: Oman's dialogue facilitation initiatives during the Yemeni civil war', *Middle East Journal*, 75:2 (2021): 285–303.

4 Palestine

Beinin, J. and J. Hajjar, 'Palestine, Israel and the Arab-Israeli conflict: A primer', Middle East Research and Information Project, 2014.
Black, Ian, *Enemies and Neighhbours: Arabs and Jews in Palestine and Israel 1917–2017* (London: Penguin, 2018).
Freedman Robert (ed.), *Israel under Netanyahu: Domestic Politics and Foreign Policy* (London: Routledge, 2019).
Khalidi, Rashid, *The Hundred Years' War on Palestine: A History of Settler Colonial Conquest and Resistance* (London: Macmillan, 2020).
Pappé, Ilan, *The Biggest Prison on Earth: A History of the Occupied Territories* (London: Oneworld, 2019).
Shlaim, Avi, *Israel and Palestine: Reappriasals, Revisions and Refutations* (London: Verso, 2010).

5 Iraq

Al-Ali, Zaid, *The Struggle for Iraq's Future: How Corruption, Incompetence and Sectarianism have Undermined Democracy* (New Haven, CT and London: Yale University Press, 2014).

Azizi, Arash, *The Shadow Commander: Soleimani, the US, and Iran's Global Ambitions.* (London: Simon & Schuster, 2020).

Bluemel, James and Renad Mansour, *Once Upon a Time in Iraq: History of a Modern Tragedy* (London: Penguin, 2021).

Calculli, Marina, 'Middle East security: The politics of violence after the 2003 Iraq war', in L. Fawcett (ed.) *International Relations of the Middle East* (Oxford: Oxford University Press, 2019): 226–40.

Dodge, Toby, *Iraq; From War to a New Authoritarianism* (London: Routledge, 2013).

Haddad, Fanar, 'From existential struggle to political banality: The politics of sect in post-2003 Iraq', *Review of Faith & International Affairs*, 18:1 (2020): 70–86.

6 Egypt

Adly, Amr, *Cleft Capitalism: The Social Origins of Failed Market Making in Egypt.* (Stanford, CA: Stanford University Press, 2020).

al-Anani, Khalil, 'Upended path: The rise and fall of Egypt's Muslim Brotherhood', *Middle East Journal*, 69:4 (2015): 527–43.

Kirkpatrick, David D., *Into the Hands of the Soldiers* (London: Bloomsbury, 2018).

Sayigh, Yezid, 'Owners of the republic: An anatomy of Egypt's military economy', Carnegie Middle East Center, 2019, https://carnegie-mec.org/2019/11/18/owners-of-republic-anatomy-of-egypt-s-military-economy-pub-80325 (accessed 20 June 2022).

Springborg, Robert, *Egypt* (London: John Wiley & Sons, 2017).

Wickham, Carrie Rosefsky, *The Muslim Brotherhood* (Princeton, NJ: Princeton University Press, 2015).

7 Lebanon

Arsan, Andrew, *Lebanon: A Country in Fragments* (London: Hurst, 2020).

Halawi, Ibrahim and Bassel Salloukh, 'Pessimism of the intellect, optimism of the will after the 17 October protests in Lebanon', *Middle East Law and Governance*, 12:3 (2020): 322–34.

Hirst, David, *Beware of Small States: Lebanon, Battleground of the Middle East.* (London: Bold Type Books, 2011).

Makdisi, Karim, 'Lebanon's October 2019 uprising: From solidarity to division and descent into the known unknown', *South Atlantic Quarterly* 120:2 (2021): 436–45.

Salloukh, Bassel, Rabie Barakat, Jinan S. Al-Habbal, Lara W. Khattab, and Shoghig Mikaelian (eds), *The Politics of Sectarianism in Postwar Lebanon* (London: Pluto Press, 2015).

Salloukh, Bassel, 'Taif and the Lebanese state: The political economy of a very sectarian public sector', *Nationalism and Ethnic Politics*, 25:1 (2019): 43–60.

8 Kurdistan

Allsopp, Harriet and Wladimir Van Wilgenburg, *The Kurds of Northern Syria: Governance, Diversity and Conflicts*, vol. 2 (London: Bloomsbury, 2019).

Gourlay, William, 'Kurdayetî: Pan-Kurdish solidarity and cross-border links in times of war and trauma', *Middle East Critique*, 27:1 (2018): 25–42.

Marcus, Aliza, *Blood and Belief: The PKK and the Kurdish Fight for Independence*. (London: NYU Press, 2009).

McDowall, David, *A Modern History of the Kurds* (London: Bloomsbury Publishing, 2021).

McGee, T., ' "Rojava": Evolving public discourse of Kurdish identity and governance in Syria', *Middle East Journal of Culture and Communication*, 15:4 (2022): 385–403.

Vali, Abbas, 'The Kurds and their Others: Fragmented identity and fragmented politics', *Comparative Studies of South Asia, Africa and the Middle East*, 18:2 (1998): 82–95.

9 The Gulf

Fulton, Jonathan, *China's Relations with the Gulf Monarchies* (London: Routledge, 2018).

Hanieh, Adam, *Money, Markets, and Monarchies: The Gulf Cooperation Council and the Political Economy of the Contemporary Middle East* (Cambridge: Cambridge University Press, 2018).

Jones, Marc Owen, *Digital Authoritarianism in the Middle East: Deception, Disinformation and Social Media* (London: Hurst, 2022).

Kamrava, Mehran, *Troubled Waters: Insecurity in the Persian Gulf* (Ithaca, NY: Cornell University Press, 2018).

Kinninmont, Jane, *The Gulf Divided: The Impact of the Qatar Crisis*, Research Paper (London: Chatham House, May 2019).

Ulrichsen, Kristian Coates, *Qatar and the Gulf Crisis: A Study of Resilience* (London; Hurst, 2020).

10 Horn of Africa

Bengessa Hirbe, Bekele, *Intrastate Conflict in the Horn of Africa: Implications for Regional Security (1990–2016)* (London: Lexington, 2021).

Clapham, Christopher, *The Horn of Africa: State Formation and Decay* (London: Hurst, 2023).

Darwish, May, 'Saudi-Iranian rivalry from the Gulf to the Horn of Africa: Changing geographies and infrastructures', *POMEPS*, 38 (March 2020), https://pomeps. org/saudi-iranian-rivalry-from-the-gulf-to-the-horn-of-africa-changing-geographies-and-infrastructures-1 (accessed 1 March 2023).

de Waal, Alex, *The Real Politics of the Horn of Africa: Money, War and the Business of Power* (London: Polity, 2015).

Melvin, Neil, 'The foreign military presence in the Horn of Africa', Sipri Background Papers, April 2019, https://www.sipri.org/publications/2019/sipri-background-papers/foreign-military-presence-horn-africa-region (accessed 1 March 2023).

Woldemariam, Michael, 'The Eritrea-Ethiopia thaw and its regional impact', *Current History*, 118: 808 (2019): 181–7.

INDEX

304

Egypt: British rule in, 144; Christian
community, 152, 160; coup (2013),
49–50; economic decline, 142;
foreign interventions, 154–9; history,
143–4; host to COP27, 163;
intervention in Yemen, 78; military
coup (2013), 152; military
dominance, 147–8; Muslim
Brotherhood, 149–52; Nasser's rule,
145–6; and Palestine, 94, 107, 108–9;
population, 141, 149, 163; and the
Qatar crisis, 233; Rabaa Square
massacre, 152; relations with
Ethiopia, 162–3; relations with
Turkey, 162; Salafist al-Nour party,
154–5; Sisi's rule in, 159–63;
Supreme Council of the Armed
Forces (SCAF), 150–2; threats to
invade Libya, 60; uprising (2011),
150–1
El-Sisi, Abdel Fattah, 55, 142, 152–3,
155–6, 158–65
Erbil, Iraqi Kurdistan, 208–9
Erdoğan, Recep Tayyip: consolidation
of control in Turkey, 275; and Israel's
blockade of Gaza, 108–9; and the
Kurds, 199–203, 205, 208; and Libya,
59; and Palestine, 113; and Syria,
25–6, 34–5, 38–9
Eritrea: and Iranian arms smuggling,
248; Middle East influence in,
258–60; religions in, 243; war of
independence, 244, 245; war with
Ethiopia (1998–2000), 246
Eritrean People's Liberation Front
(EPLF), 258
Ethiopia: Christianity in, 243;
dominance in the Horn of Africa,
242; Eritrean war (1998–2000), 246;
Eritrean war of independence
(1961–91), 244; famine (1984), 245;
involvement in Somalia, 247, 251,
252; Jews resettled in Israel during
1984 famine, 248; Marxist regime in,
244, 245; Middle East influence in,
256–8; never colonised, 243–4;
relations with Egypt, 162–3; relations
with US, 247; revolution (1974), 244;

Somali invasion (1977), 244–5;
Tigray insurgency (1991), 245;
Tigray war (2020–22), 257–8
European Union (EU): 'European
Neighbourhood Policy', 182; illegal
immigration to, 56; and Lebanon,
182–3; and Middle East conflict, 273;
mixed support in Libya, 56–7; and
Syrian refugees, 34

Faisal, King of Iraq, 120
Faisal, Prince Turki al, 230
Farmaajo (Mohamed Abdullah
Mohamed), 252, 253–4
Farouq, King of Egypt, 144
Fatimid empire, 143
FIFA Men's World Cup (2022),
217–18, 230
First World War, and Zionism, 91–2
football teams, owned by Gulf
states, 235
fossil fuels, and the Gulf states, 236
France: in Djibouti, 243, 245; interest
in Libya, 55, 57, 61; and Lebanon,
169–70, 183–4, 270; military base in
Abu Dhabi, 228; military base in
Djibouti, 242, 261; support for
Yemeni invasion, 82; and Syria, 270

Gadhafi, Muammar, 41, 43–6
Gaza, Palestine, 97, 101, 104, 106–9,
112–13
Gemayal, Bashir, 172
Global Climate Change Conference
(COP27), 163
Golan Heights, 19
Guelleh, Ismail Omar, 260–1, 262
Gulf Cooperation Council (GCC),
70–1, 75, 83, 219, 222–3, 226, 233–5
Gulf States: airlines, 236; and Al-Qaeda,
222–3; Arab Uprisings (2011), 223–6;
China's increasing role in, 228–31;
foreign investments, 235–6; foreign
military bases in, 228; geographical
importance, 226; position in Middle
Eastern geopolitics, 218–21; and
Russia–Ukraine war, 238; US
relations, 221–8